Managing Risk
in Alternative
Investment Strategies

Managing Risk in Alternative Investment Strategies

*Successful Investing in Hedge Funds
and Managed Futures*

DR LARS JAEGER

FT Prentice Hall

FINANCIAL TIMES

London ■ New York ■ Toronto ■ Sydney ■ Tokyo ■ Singapore
Hong Kong ■ Cape Town ■ New Delhi ■ Madrid
Paris ■ Amsterdam ■ Munich ■ Milan ■ Stockholm

PEARSON EDUCATION LIMITED

Head Office:
Edinburgh Gate
Harlow CM20 2JE
Tel: +44 (0)1279 623623
Fax: +44 (0)1279 431059

London Office:
128 Long Acre
London WC2E 9AN
Tel: +44 (0)20 7447 2000
Fax: +44 (0)20 7240 5771
Website: www.financialminds.com

First published in Great Britain 2002

© Pearson Education Limited 2002

The right of Dr Lars Jaeger to be identified as Author
of this Work has been asserted by him in accordance
with the Copyright, Designs and Patents Act 1988.

ISBN 0 273 656988

British Library Cataloguing in Publication Data
A CIP catalogue record for this book can be obtained from the British Library.

This publication is designed to provide accurate and authoritative information in regard to the subject matter covered. It is sold with the understanding that neither the author nor the publisher is engaged in rendering legal, investing, or any other professional service. If legal advice or other expert assistance is required, the service of a competent professional person should be sought.

The publisher and contributors make no representation, express or implied, with regard to the accuracy of the information contained in this book and cannot accept any responsibility or liability for any errors or omissions that it may contain.

10 9 8 7 6 5 4 3 2 1

Typeset by Pantek Arts Ltd, Maidstone, Kent
Printed and bound in Great Britain by Bookcraft Ltd, Midsomer Norton

The Publishers' policy is to use paper manufactured from sustainable forests.

To my wife Julie

About the author

Lars Jaeger is a Partner of Partners Group, one of the largest European alternative asset managers, based in Zug, Switzerland. He was a Managing Director and Co-founder of saisGroup, a Swiss-based specialist firm for multi-manager Alternative Investment Strategies (AIS) portfolios, which merged with Partners Group in late 2001. He is responsible for quantitative analysis and risk management for the Hedge fund portfolios managed at Partners Group.

Lars holds a PhD degree in theoretical physics from the Max-Planck Institute for Physics of Complex Systems in Dresden, Germany (1997). He studied physics and philosophy at the University of Bonn and Ecole Polytechnique in Paris. He worked as a researcher in different areas of theoretical physics (quantum field theory, atomic physics, and chaos theory).

Lars started his financial career at Olsen and Associates in Zurich as a quantitative researcher, where he designed econometric and mathematical models for financial markets (systematic trading models, portfolio and risk management).

He subsequently moved to Credit Suisse Asset Management, where he was responsible for risk management and quantitative analysis of Hedge fund and Managed Futures strategies.

Lars is author of numerous research publications in various leading scientific journals and has been a regular speaker at diverse seminars and workshops.

Contents

Preface

Alternative Investment Strategies (AIS) – Hedge funds and Managed Futures – have grown rapidly over the last few years and are on track to become a trillion-dollar industry in the next years. So it is not surprising that there is a surge in interest in AIS from a broad array of investors – institutional as well as private.

Until recently Hedge funds were considered the 'cowboys of financial markets' or 'courtesans of capitalism' (a title of a recent book by Peter Temple) and were of interest only to the superrich. But sophisticated investors now understand that, if properly included in a global portfolio, AIS can serve as a valuable diversifier. Approached carelessly, however, they can easily create an investment disaster. Current and potential AIS investors are thus demanding improved risk management so that the benefits of AIS can be realized while exposure to risk remains at acceptable levels.

Recent developments have given way to a new generation of AIS managers who are better and more professional risk managers and thus have more credibility in the eyes of a much broader class of investors. Yet few even in the professional investment community are prepared to meet the two key challenges of managing AIS risk: complexity and rapid change. Alternative investment strategies are much more complex and varied than traditional asset classes (equities and bonds). To add to the challenge, AIS strategies and overall risk management practices are changing even as investment professionals struggle to master them.

Despite its challenges, active AIS risk management adds tremendous value to the investment and asset allocation process of AIS investors and managers. This book will provide the reader with the knowledge needed to reap these rewards. It is not a 'cookbook' though, and does not provide fixed recipes for how to invest in Hedge funds or manage their risks. Proper AIS investment is both an art and a science. While the science refers to the increasingly quantitative approaches taken by many AIS managers, the 'art' of AIS investing is the understanding of the complexity of AIS and the experience necessary to appropriately allocate assets among different strategy sectors and managers. This book aims at giving the reader an understanding of this complexity and guides him in his assessment of AIS risks and the appropriate ways of managing those risks.

With the increasing popularity of Hedge funds, the literature about AIS has grown considerably during the last few years. The interested reader has a choice among many different views and approaches. But despite its immense importance to the AIS investment process, the topic of risk management has not yet been covered in sufficient detail. There is a variety of (in some cases excellent) articles – often collected in multi-authored books – that provide insight into particular facets of the topic. But the industry lacks coherent and comprehensive coverage of AIS risk management in one publication. This is what motivated me to write this book.

Acknowledgements

This book represents untold hours of effort by many people other than myself and I would like to thank everybody who helped me to complete this work. The first person I owe gratitude to is my dear wife, Julie, who provided love, understanding and support throughout many hours of writing. She also provided invaluable feedback and criticism while reading the manuscript and without her the book would not have taken its present form. I would also like to acknowledge Michael Jacquemai and Pietro Cittadini who were my partners and co-founders of saisGroup and are now my partners at Partners Group. They were the joint architects of many of the ideas presented in this book and who also provided valuable feedback on the manuscript. My thanks also go to Renato Amrein at Partners Group for valuable comments and proofreading of the manuscript. I also acknowledge the comments from the following individuals: Susanne Classen (Dr. Hehn Associates), Bill Feingold (Clinton Group), Michael Manning (Stratton Advisors), Patrik Säfvenblad (RPM), Jeffrey Pease (Business Objects), Peter Rice (Ecofin Investment Consulting), Daniel Rizzuto (Graham Capital Management), Adam Segal and Robert Rice (DLR Advisors), Anthony Todd (Aspect Capital), and David White (JE Matthew).

Last, but not least, I thank Financial Times Prentice Hall for their enthusiastic support of this book and for their assistance in editing and reviewing the manuscript. Despite the extensive support I received, there will be mistakes, misrepresentation and omissions in the book, for which I take full responsibility.

Lars Jaeger
April 2002

CHAPTER 1

Introduction

Investing in Alternative Investment Strategies (AIS), i.e. Hedge funds and Managed Futures, has become a multi-billion dollar industry and recent years have seen unparalleled capital inflows into AIS. The attractive risk–reward characteristics of AIS funds as well as their low correlation to traditional asset classes have led to widespread interest in AIS investing. It is estimated that there are currently more than half a trillion dollars invested with about 5,000 Hedge fund and Managed Futures programs worldwide, the largest part of which originates in the USA and Europe. The AIS industry is enjoying a 15–20% annual asset growth rate and it is expected that AIS investing will develop towards a trillion dollar industry in just a few years. Hedge funds and Managed Futures managers have become important players in world financial markets, accounting for a good part of the daily trading volume in numerous financial instruments.

Despite these very positive trends, in order for AIS to achieve its full potential, the industry must address growing investor concerns about the diverse risks of AIS investments as well as the lack of investment transparency, low liquidity and long redemption periods which are generally characteristic of Hedge fund and Managed Futures investments. The trend in investors' attitude from accepting ('trust me') to requesting ('show me') is clearly observable. While for years investors followed a 'black box' approach to AIS investing, a number of factors are leading to a shift away from this type of approach. Increased interest from

■ ■ ■ ■ ■ ■ ■ ■ ■ ■ ■ ■

Increased interest from institutional investors in AIS has led to new demands for disclosure due to the fiduciary responsibilities associated with investing clients' money

■ ■ ■ ■ ■ ■ ■ ■ ■ ■ ■ ■

institutional investors in AIS has led to new demands for disclosure due to the fiduciary responsibilities associated with investing clients' money. Further, several widely publicized Hedge fund failures during the market crisis of 1998 (e.g. LTCM) and periodic reports of other Hedge fund 'blow ups' and fraud (e.g. 'Manhattan Hedge Fund' in the spring of 2000) have added to the concerns of all AIS investors about the risks of such investments. Finally, rapid developments in the financial industry in the area of financial risk management have made risk analysis for even complex AIS portfolios feasible on a real-time basis and therefore have increased expectations with respect to the management of risk.

Discussion about how to address concerns regarding investment risk, low liquidity and insufficient transparency in AIS is in its early stages. In this book I will elaborate on what I refer to as the 'transparency paradigm' in which full disclosure by AIS managers, detailed understanding of sources of returns and risks on the part of AIS investors and active risk management by the AIS portfolio managers allow investors to reap the benefits of AIS investing while eliminating undesired risks. I will argue that such an approach is not only feasible but also essential for properly controlling the risks of AIS and satisfying investor expectations.

I will further provide the elements and tools necessary for effective risk management for AIS. An understanding of AIS risk issues necessitates thorough knowledge of the underlying investment strategies. Chapter 2 opens with a presentation of the evolution of Hedge funds and Managed Futures and gives a general characterization of AIS, before I provide, in Chapter 3, a more detailed description of the various AIS sectors. Here, my focus is on characteristics, sources of return and dominant risk factors of the individual strategies. It should be clear that I cannot claim complete knowledge about every single strategy, so my description is at risk of appearing incomplete or selective to some experts (e.g. Hedge fund managers), but it aims at providing the reader with a balanced view of all necessary aspects of the AIS sectors.

Chapter 4 contains a presentation of empirical properties of AIS strategies, including their diversification benefits, which are particularly important from the perspective of a portfolio manager. A description of the most important general AIS risk factors and a comparison and quantification of the specific risks of each strategy follows in Chapter 5. In Chapter 6, I outline the principles of risk analysis in financial markets, with the greatest focus on quantitative risk tools (Value-at-Risk, stress testing, scenario analysis, leverage control etc.). While the chapter is merely an overview, references to the literature are given for the reader interested in more details. Chapter 6 also discusses risk service providers and risk managing tools available to the AIS manager from third parties today. Finally, Chapter 7 describes the principles of managing risk in an AIS portfolio. It discusses how risk management can be integrated into the AIS asset allocation process, describes approaches to sector allocation and manager evaluation and outlines appropriate methods of portfolio monitoring and active risk control.

The book aims to provide a wide range of financial professionals, including Hedge fund and Managed Futures managers, fund of funds managers (AIS allocators), brokers, administrators, custodians and private and institutional investors with an understanding of AIS risks and risk management. But the book is also well suited for other types of professional involved with addressing the challenges of AIS risk such as regulatory agencies, consultants, legal authorities, financial journalists and students. Despite the broader view taken on the subject I hope even AIS experts will benefit from the discussion presented. As the book is addressed to a broad audience, I avoid the use of mathematical formulas. The knowledge necessary for this book is a basic understanding of equity, fixed income, foreign exchange and commodity markets (including plain vanilla derivatives such as options and futures) and the core principles of modern portfolio theory. The discussion of the quantitative risk analysis tools (Chapter 6) might require newcomers to the field of financial risk management to do some background reading (references are provided).

Changing investor demand

Traditionally, Hedge fund and Managed Futures investing has been dominated by high net worth investors who were willing to bear the disadvantages of illiquid and non-transparent investment strategies ('black box investing'). Their focus was

> **This new class of investor has put the issue of risk management at the top of their priority list**

often rather short term, they were less concerned about diversification and accepted high levels of volatility. Recently, institutional investors have become increasingly interested in AIS, drawn to their attractive risk–return characteristics and low correlations to traditional asset classes. However, this new class of investors has different demands to those of high net worth individuals. They have a comparably long-term view, show higher levels of risk aversion and emphasize the stability of investment returns. Institutional investors have put the issue of risk management at the top of their priority list.

Prerequisites of risk management are transparency and investment liquidity. Unfortunately, many of the investment vehicles for AIS available in the market today present investors with numerous liquidity and transparency issues and, therefore, risk management problems. Most managers supply too little information to investors. Monthly returns, standard deviations, maximal drawdowns and, in most cases, a monthly or quarterly letter to the investors, do not provide sufficient information about investment risk.

As a result of these recent developments (growing demand from institutional investors), the AIS industry is currently going through an institutionalization process in which Hedge fund and Futures managers are increasingly faced with demands for increased investment transparency, higher liquidity (i.e. shorter redemption periods) and greater clarity in terms of portfolio composition, strategy details, performance and fee attributions and leverage. Investors' views range from managing risk through diversification across many AIS managers such that a limited number of 'blow ups' have a minimal effect on the portfolio, to a fully transparent and actively risk controlled investment approach.

A note here on terminology: throughout the book, I will use the word 'manager(s)' to describe the individual(s) responsible for the development and execution of the Hedge fund or Managed Futures trading strategy (the word 'trading advisor' is also commonly used in the AIS industry). For a multi-strategy portfolio manager (AIS fund of funds manager), I will often use the term 'allocator'.

Due to the technical complexity of AIS, which include spread strategies, leverage, short selling and investments in a variety of different asset classes and instruments, risk management has become one of the most important elements (and most difficult challenges) of the AIS investment process. Risk management is key to achieving high future institutional asset inflows, for without effective risk control, pension funds, endowments and other institutional investors will resist increasing their allocations to AIS. Several recent surveys[1] indicate that Hedge fund managers themselves are growing more aware of the importance of risk management practices.

LTCM: What can go wrong for Hedge fund investors

Despite the ongoing changes in investors' expectations regarding transparency and sophisticated risk management mentioned earlier, the 'black box' investment paradigm remains surprisingly persistent within the AIS community. This includes the management of multi-strategy portfolios ('fund of funds'). Many investors and AIS allocators are excluded, or exclude themselves, from knowledge about the strategy details and the particular holdings in an AIS manager's portfolio. This can lead to severe risks for the investor, as illustrated by the story of LTCM.

In September 1998 the failure of the Hedge fund Long-Term Capital Management (LTCM) is said nearly to have brought down the world financial system. The losses LCTM incurred were so large that the Federal Reserve Bank took the unprecedented step of initiating the bailout of a private investment vehicle, as the fear spread that forced liquidation would cause global financial turmoil. Something very fundamental had gone wrong.[2]

During earlier years the fund had made very handsome returns with its core Fixed Income Arbitrage strategy, described as 'Convergence Arbitrage'. The managers at LTCM had placed a large amount of money in 'convergence spread trades' involving European interest rates within the European Monetary System. The most prominent example had been buying Italian Government Bond (BTP) futures and selling short German Bund contracts. Some other smaller trading positions involved yield curve Relative Value spreads and Japanese Government Bond swap spreads. Their strategy was clearly defined and paid off handsomely. By the end of 1997 the fund paid back a significant amount of money to investors (about one-third of its asset base of several billion US dollars). The original core strategy had clearly lost most of its edge; the yield spread between Italian and German 10-year government bonds had narrowed from about 550bp in early 1993 to only about 20bp by the end of 1997. The fund managers were looking for other opportunities and correspondingly found themselves engaged in a wider spectrum of strategies including Merger Arbitrage, Selling Short volatility, Mortgage-Backed Securities Arbitrage etc. Furthermore, in order to continue generating the attractive returns of the past, the fund increased its leverage substantially (from about 19 at the end of 1997 to about 30 in early 1998, and 42 in the summer of 1998).

Neither the style drifts nor the increase in leverage had ever been communicated to investors. By September 23, 1998 (the day of the bailout), the fund had lost 92% of its asset year to date and the leverage had gone up to about 120. The excessive leverage taken by the fund remained undetected until the fund had already lost most of its capital. The managers of LTCM had clearly shifted its investment practice in the course of the months before the disaster. Investors had no knowledge and understanding of the strategy LTCM was following.

Why effective risk management is crucial to realizing the benefits of AIS

For reasons of diversification, it is widely understood in today's investment community that, if properly included in a global portfolio, AIS can enhance the return and reduce the risk of a global investment portfolio. Improperly used, however, AIS can create an investment disaster. Evaluating the 'risk dimension' is critical for realizing the return and diversification benefits of AIS.

■ ■ ■ ■ ■ ■ ■ ■ ■ ■ ■ ■

Improperly used, AIS can create an investment disaster

■ ■ ■ ■ ■ ■ ■ ■ ■ ■ ■ ■

The challenges of AIS risk management are twofold: complexity and rapid change. AIS are much more complex and varied than traditional asset classes and AIS risk management requires a thorough understanding of many different underlying strategies. Yet these strategies are changing even as investment professionals and risk managers struggle to understand them. To make matters worse, the overall risk management practices of the investment community are also rapidly changing across all asset classes. The 'state of the art' in financial risk management has developed dramatically over past years, with new paradigms and ever more complex models continuing to emerge.

While confusing to some investors these new tools create new opportunities to monitor and 'fine tune' risks in AIS investments much more accurately than even a few years ago. Active risk management can add tremendous value to the investment and asset allocation process of AIS investors and managers. I believe that this book will provide readers and investors with the knowledge needed to reap these rewards.

A new investment paradigm

Much negative coverage has been dedicated to Hedge funds by the media. This is mainly due to a mixture of myth, misrepresentation and the large scale of a few Hedge fund failures and their global implications. The fact is that a detailed understanding of the various strategies, a thorough manager due diligence process *and* systematic third party monitoring and risk management will eliminate much of the risk that has led to past problems.

While the 'black box approach' still underlies much of AIS investing today, the 'transparency paradigm' that I will elaborate on throughout this book is, in contrast, characterized by:

■ A detailed understanding of individual managers' strategies and their risks.

■ Transparency in respect of the activities of each individual manager in the portfolio and frequent disclosure of the aggregated portfolio exposure to the end investor.

■ High investment liquidity. Most, but not all, AIS managers trade instruments that are traded on public exchanges that provide high (in many cases daily) liquidity.

■ Systematic and continuous monitoring of open positions and measurement of risk.

■ Active management of risk. Note the difference between *measuring* and *managing* risk: risk management entails using the results of risk analysis to allocate risk optimally among different assets/trading strategies.

A 'managed account' structure is the most effective means of achieving maximum investment transparency for AIS (the concept of managed account is explained in Chapter 7).

The AIS investment approach and integrated risk management for multi-manager portfolios ('fund of funds')

An increasing number of fund of funds managers have emerged who specialize in finding the most interesting and best performing managers and thus diversifying the traditional 'manager risks' of AIS investing. A fund of funds approach, if properly executed, can further provide the security created by continuous portfolio management and monitoring of managers. The added value of a fund of funds is realized provided the fund of funds manager fulfils some fundamental criteria in his investment approach regarding strategy allocation, manager due diligence and monitoring capabilities:

1 *Sector allocation (top down analysis): Allocation of capital to AIS sectors.* The goal is to invest in the right strategy sector at the right time and to achieve the appropriate level of diversification. This requires a sound understanding of the individual strategy sectors, their general risk factors and risk levels as well as their correlation features in various market environments. Chapter 3 looks at AIS sectors in depth and provides insight into their general sources of returns and most important risk factors.

2 *Manager evaluation (bottom up analysis): Detailed examination of the individual trading managers' strategies and a thorough manager due diligence process.* The investor should understand the strategic edge and competitive advantage of individual trading managers in great detail. He should also have a sound understanding of the firm's structure and evaluate the integrity of key personnel. Just looking at past returns of trading strategies is insufficient. One

must understand the general economic reason why and under what circumstances a strategy shows inherent returns to the investor. Chapter 7 provides a description of the manager due diligence process.

3 *Continuous monitoring/risk assessment: P&L, exposure and risk evaluation of the portfolio.* A prerequisite for continuous monitoring and risk assessment is transparency. This enables the allocator to identify potential style drifts quickly (i.e. the manager follows a different strategy than formerly indicated) including undesired market bets that do not match the desired risk profile of a strategy. Leverage controls and risk limits can be implemented and enforced efficiently (e.g. VaR, stress test and leverage limits) and undesired risks can thus be eliminated in time. Ongoing analysis allows the investor better to understand the core strategy's behaviour in different market circumstances. The fund of funds manager's performance expectations for the strategy can be compared to its actual P&L and risk profile at different times and action can be taken quickly if necessary. The anticipation of market conditions that would cause the manager's edge to disappear allows the allocator to exit the strategy in time. Chapter 6 provides an overview of risk analysis tools available today and Chapter 7 describes the process of active AIS risk management in detail.

The first two elements represent 'pre-investment risk management', while the third element represents 'post-investment risk management'. I refer to these three elements as the 'three dimensions of active and integrated risk management for AIS investments'. It is important to note that all three, sector allocation (point 1), manager due diligence (point 2) *and* transparency (point 3) are essential to AIS risk management; one cannot replace the other.

Is transparency achievable in AIS investments?

Despite growing investor awareness of the importance of transparency, there remains a surprising degree of resistance to such transparency in the AIS industry. Three main arguments are frequently used against transparency and frequent disclosure of trading positions. AIS managers often bring up the first two arguments and many allocators (fund of funds managers) raise the third point:

1 Confidential position information will reach the market place, potentially causing the manager to: (a) lose his edge if more players adopt the same approach; and (b) be actively traded against by certain market players.

2 Investors lack the skill to evaluate the massive amount of information associated with disclosure of positions. This could lead to investors being overwhelmed by information and/or feeling a false sense of comfort.

3 Requiring transparency will eliminate the opportunity to work with the best managers within the universe of Hedge funds. It is argued that for a variety of reasons, including point 1, the best managers will not disclose their positions.

With respect to the first argument, one must consider who actually poses a threat to AIS managers. This threat comes mainly from the dealer community and proprietary trading desks within large investment banks rather than from fund of funds managers or individual investors. The prime brokers, most of whom have large proprietary trading facilities in house, do request and receive full disclosure of all positions (and 'Chinese walls' are sometimes less secure than is desirable). There is thus no reason why investors should be excluded from the same level of information. Once Hedge fund and Managed Futures managers know who their investors are and what their intention with the disclosed information is, they can set up confidentiality agreements related to such information. Thus the positions can be kept confidential while still providing the necessary transparency to the multi-manager fund or the investor directly.

The second argument neglects the increasing expertise and capabilities of AIS fund of funds managers. If the allocator has a sufficient understanding of the underlying strategies, downloads with positions and transactions can be evaluated very efficiently. With the advent of information technology, the compilation of large quantities of data has become quite feasible for sophisticated investors and professional portfolio managers. A wide variety of tools and software packages for sophisticated risk management is now available. Risk management experts within the team of the multi-strategy fund of funds manager can deal with the complex job of interpreting the disclosed information and therefore tremendously increase the benefits of transparency.

Multi-strategy fund managers frequently raise the third argument, claiming that the best Hedge fund managers (which are, in the view of many, the largest) will not provide transparency or insight into their trading. It is therefore argued that fund of funds managers requiring transparency (i.e. frequent disclosure of positions) are left with lower performing trading advisors. This statement bears little truth. For the large majority of strategies, good performance has nothing to do with lack of transparency. In fact, many high-quality 'first tier' managers are today willing to offer transparency if asked or required (for an investment) to do so. Contrariwise, AIS managers with strong past performance but refusing to provide transparency do not necessarily present a better investment to the investor. Often, a non-transparent strategy corresponds to a manager who is unable to illustrate his edge and therefore hides behind a 'black box' approach. In other words, a manager who refuses to explain his edge may not have one!

■■■■■■■■■■■

AIS managers with strong past performance but refusing to provide transparency do not necessarily present a better investment

■■■■■■■■■■

Many investors regard AIS as an industry in which returns are generated by mysterious means and judge successful Hedge fund managers only by their stellar past returns. The incorrect belief that better performing managers must operate in secret is linked to this persistent misperception about AIS. In fact, most managers follow systematic investment strategies that are understandable if studied sufficiently and that, not surprisingly, perform better in certain market environments than in others. Past performance is an insufficient indicator of the future potential of a strategy (or as the statement on most disclaimers for publicly offered funds puts it: 'Past returns are not indicative of future results'). Rather, transparency is needed in order to allow for an adequate and ongoing assessment of risks and rewards. Considering the additional risks of AIS investing when transparency and investor control are absent, one must question whether institutional investors fulfil their fiduciary responsibility when they invest in a 'black box'.

Examples of non-transparent and, for certain periods of time, very successful strategies are LTCM, Quantum Fund (G. Soros), Tiger (J. Robertson) and Niederhoffer, all of which failed spectacularly in the end. Even the most brilliant investors in the past are not protected against losses and drawdowns, as many investors in Hedge funds have learned, to their detriment, in the past. Investors must learn to look beyond past return and instead look at how the returns have been achieved. Conditions for success are constantly changing. Recent studies have shown that there is little convincing evidence that winning funds repeat in a way that can be exploited,[3] and have also shown that small and young programs show their best performance in the first two years.[4]

The appropriate level of disclosure to investors and institutional asset managers (fund of funds) is the subject of ongoing discussion within the industry. A working session of the Investor Risk Committee (IRC) was held on the topic, 'What is the right level of disclosure for alternative asset managers?'.[5] One of the conclusions was that risk monitoring and style drift monitoring were among the most important objectives of disclosure (see Chapter 7 for a more detailed discussion of the IRC report).

Transparency can take a number of different forms, from regular conversations with managers about their strategies (the weakest form) to obtaining a daily download of all positions from a manager's prime broker (the strongest form). There is much discussion around the question of whether aggregated 'risk information' is sufficient for risk management purposes versus requesting disclosure of all positions. The belief that AIS risk can be adequately monitored without obtaining underlying positions is widespread. I disagree with this view. Chapter 7 will provide a more detailed discussion of this issue. One may argue that for some strategies disclosure of individual positions may not be absolutely necessary.[6] But in most circumstances detailed position information is the only way to provide the information necessary for the risk-monitoring task.

The level of information that should be provided to the investor or fund of funds manager also depends on the investment style of the individual manager as well as the strategy sector in which he is operating. There are different degrees of usefulness of transparency for the various strategy sectors. Model-based Systematic strategies and Arbitrage strategies are easier to monitor and understand on a daily basis than discretionary Long/Short Equity, Macro and Short Selling strategies, where positions are more difficult to comprehend without further manager-provided information. For Relative Value strategies (Fixed Income Arbitrage, Convertible Arbitrage, Equity Market Neutral) and Event-Driven strategies (Merger Arbitrage, Distressed Securities, Convertible Debenture Arbitrage) transparency can be very useful, as leverage, instrument liquidity and potential style drift are important issues for these strategies.

Liquidity of AIS investments

Transparency is of most value when combined with the appropriate level of liquidity. Risk management has to be proactive and the risk manager should be in a position to take steps to remedy critical situations in timely fashion. Often, when a crisis has arrived, it is too late to make adjustments. If, for his investment with a single manager, the AIS allocator faces a redemption period that does not correspond to the level of provided transparency, he is prevented from responding to time-sensitive information as he cannot mandate immediate adjustments to investment positions.

Some AIS investors prefer high liquidity, i.e. short redemption periods, while others are willing to assume liquidity risks, i.e. accept extended redemption periods, in pursuit of attractive returns. As the AIS industry grows, and the spectrum of investors becomes more heterogeneous, requests for liquid multi-manager products are increasing. Currently, the industry offers three types of multi-manager AIS products to investors: open-ended funds with redemption periods ranging from one month to six months are the most numerous. Second, structured notes are increasingly offered, especially in Europe, for the purpose of circumventing the regulatory requirements of listed funds. They are usually traded in a secondary market provided by the issuer. Finally, a number of closed-end investment vehicles wrapped as investment companies and listed on exchanges have been set up.

All these structures result in liquidity problems for investors. Besides the long redemption periods for open-ended funds and structures notes, additional factors can lead to a significant increase in the time span between redemption and the receipt of monies. Settlement problems do not exist for an exchange-traded investment company (as the instrument can be traded on an exchange on a daily basis), however, other problems render these products unsuitable for most investors. Due to the lack of a broad market, these instruments are not traded very actively, i.e. their liquidity is extremely low. Larger sizes cannot be sold without a severe negative price impact. This usually leads to a significant discount in the trading value compared to the NAV. Since most AIS managers invest in highly liquid instruments, one must ask why there cannot be an AIS investment fund with daily liquidity based on NAV which is as easy to buy and sell as any traditional mutual (equity) fund.[7]

The challenges of AIS risk management

There is not, as yet, a 'risk management standard' in the AIS industry, but generally, the management of AIS risks goes beyond quantitative methods and includes essential qualitative assessments. The 'art and science' of AIS risk management is developing as this book is being written and the discussion about proper tools and approaches is ongoing. Some types of risk (e.g. market risk, credit risk) are today easier to quantify and manage than others (e.g. operational risk, model risk),[8] but available tools and models for risk management are subject to constant change. The AIS industry itself has started to become an important target for risk management tools as well as a pioneer in the development of new risk analysis standards.

> *AIS risk management can only be successfully performed if the risk manager has a thorough understanding of trading strategies*

Compared to traditional investments (bonds, equities), the risk factors of Hedge funds and Managed Futures strategies are quite complex. The spectrum of AIS is very broad and stretches along a wide universe of investment strategies and asset classes. Strategies earn their returns in a variety of ways and are exposed to different types and degrees of risk. AIS risk management can only be successfully performed if the risk manager has a thorough understanding of trading strategies on the strategy sector level as well as on the level of the individual manager. I will provide the reader with the building blocks necessary to understand and assess sources of risk and return of the various strategies. I will further demonstrate why it is essential to move beyond risk monitoring to active risk control and will show how to integrate risk management into the asset allocation process itself.

Risk technology has become computationally fast, efficient and considerably less expensive than a decade ago. Similar to the current development towards 'institutionalization' of the investment process in the AIS industry, one can anticipate a trend towards standardization of AIS risk management tools. Next to a detailed knowledge of the strategy sectors and careful manager evaluation, active risk management will become an essential element of AIS investing.

Notes

1. Capital Market Risk Advisors (www.cmra.com/html/hedge_fund.html) also published in the *AIMA Newsletter*, Feb 2002. HedgeMar (Dec. 2000), the Investor Risk Committee and the Hennessee Hedge Fund Advisory Group ('Transparency In Any Form Is In Demand', by S. L. Barreto, HedgeWorld.com News on Nov. 27, 2000, under http://www.hedgeworld.com/news). Recent publications of industry surveys include the Barra Strategic Consulting Group FOHF market survey (2001) and the Goldmann Sachs and Frank Russell Alternative Investment survey (2001). Furthermore, a group of five Hedge fund managers including Soros Management LLC issued the report 'Sound Practices for Hedge Fund Managers' in February 2000 as a response to the President's Working Group report on financial markets after the collapse of Long-Term Capital Markets ('LCTM') (see Chapter 6).

2. For a detailed discussion of the LTCM bankruptcy, see Ph. Jorion, 'Risk Management Lessons from Long-Term Capital Management', downloadable from http://www.gsm.uci.edu/~jorion/research.htm; also 'Hedge Funds, Leverage, and the Lessons of Long-Term Capital Management', report of the President's Working Group on Financial Markets, April 1999, on http://risk.ifci.ch/146530.htm.

3. See, for example, the following articles: M. Peskin, M. Urias, S. Anjilvel and B. Boudreau, 'Why Hedge Funds Make Sense', *Quantitative Strategies,* Morgan Stanley Dean Witter, November 2000; and 'The Young Ones' by Crossborder Capital, Absolute Return Fund Research, April 2001.

4. See reference in footnote 3. A more general audience is addressed in the following article: 'The Big, the Bold, and the Nimble', *The Economist*, Feb. 24, 2001, p.87.

5. 'Hedge Fund Disclosure for Institutional Investors', available on the IAFE web page http://www.iafe.org. The IRC report from October 2000 was updated in July 2001.

6. The IRC members state that full disclosure does not necessarily allow the portfolio managers to fulfil their monitoring objectives. Reporting of summary risk, return and position information can be sufficient, the report states.

7. Currently, I am aware of only one such fund, which started in October 2001 (Bank Hofmann/saisGroup – now Partners Group).

8. The current discussion concerning the amendment to the BIS rules for capital charges reflects the dynamics of the risk management discussions in the financial industry very illustratively.

CHAPTER 2

The Universe of Alternative Investment Strategies (AIS)

The spectrum of AIS is very broad, as it stretches along an extended and heterogeneous universe of investment strategies, asset classes and instruments. It is essential for an AIS risk manager to have a detailed understanding of this wide range of strategies and investment styles. In this chapter, I define the AIS universe and provide an overview of the characteristics and the historical development of AIS as an asset class. I also introduce the fund of funds concept for AIS. Chapter 3 then discusses in detail each AIS sector in terms of its investment and risk characteristics. Chapter 5 presents a general description of AIS risks, a quantification of the various risks and the most important risk management guidelines for each strategy sector.

Definition of the AIS Universe

Due to the complexity and heterogeneity within the industry there is an ongoing debate about how to define the AIS Universe.[1] Nonetheless, a certain general classification scheme has emerged, which I present in Figure 2.1.[2] 'Alternative Investment Strategies' (on the left-hand side of Figure 2.1) form a subset of the global 'Alternative Investment' Universe, which consists of all investments beyond traditional bond and equity investments. AIS are commonly referred to as 'skill-based' or 'absolute return strategies'. In contrast to traditional stock and bond investments, returns are often unrelated to developments in the broader financial market (this does not apply for all strategies by far, however).

I have excluded Private Equity from the 'absolute return' (AIS) universe on the grounds that its investment, liquidity and correlation characteristics set it apart from the AIS Universe discussed here. Some do consider Private Equity as part of the AIS Universe,[3] and then distinguish Hedge funds and Managed Futures from Private Equity by categorizing them as 'liquid AIS'. I do not follow this classification, as the degree of liquidity varies extremely even between the different Hedge fund and Managed Futures strategies. Further, liquidity (or the time horizon of investment) is not the only factor that sets Private Equity apart from Hedge funds and Managed Futures. Another factor is the smaller degree of strategic flexibility for Private Equity investments (there is no short selling and only little derivatives trading involved; it is basically a 'buy and hold' strategy). Another interesting distinctive feature is also the degree of 'efficiency' of the markets that Private Equity and Hedge fund managers operate in. Private Equity markets (similarly to real estate) are not information efficient, i.e. research and informational advantages lead to above average returns. Most Hedge fund strategies, in contrast, operate in markets with a generally higher degree of efficiency (equity, FX, fixed income, commodities, see later discussion). The sources of AIS return are thus much more diverse.

AIS can be further divided into two main categories: Hedge funds and Managed Futures. *Hedge funds* invest in a variety of different asset classes (including equity, fixed income and foreign exchange) on both a directional and a non-directional basis. Hedge funds take advantage of their great flexibility regarding asset classes, trading styles, markets, leverage, short selling and liquidity. They may hold long and short positions and many strategies employ leverage through borrowing, the level of which varies greatly among different strategy sectors. *Managed Futures* programs are investment entities that assume long and short positions in exchange-traded derivatives, in particular Futures and Options on commodities and 'financials' (equity, fixed income and foreign exchange). Most Futures strategy managers are registered with the National Futures Association (NFA) and the Commodity Futures Trading Commission (CFTC) as 'Commodity Trading Advisors' (CTA) and/or 'Commodity Pool Operators' (CPO).

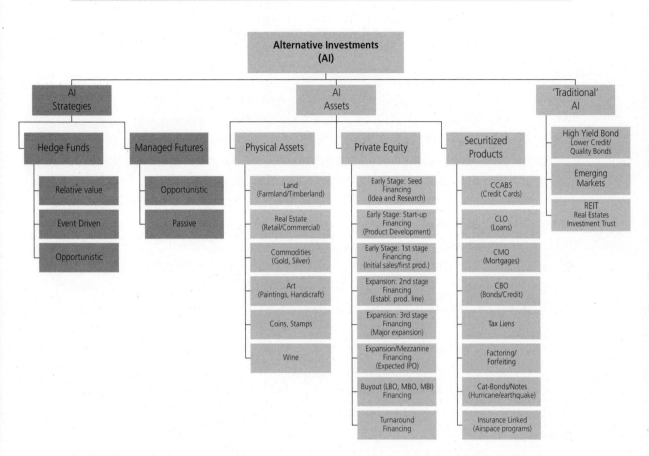

FIGURE 2.1 ■ Alternative Investment Strategies in the global universe of Alternative Investments

AIS funds are typically organized as limited partnerships or limited liability companies and are often domiciled offshore for tax and regulatory reasons.[4] Another characteristic of AIS is the way the investment manager is compensated, which mostly occurs on two levels: an annual management fee, plus an additional performance-based fee. This serves the purpose of aligning the manager's interest with that of investors'. It is worthy of note that many managers allocate a significant amount of their personal net worth to their own funds in an attempt to demonstrate commitment both in the pursuit of returns and exposure to risk.

Development of AIS

The origins of some strategies within the AIS Universe date from well before the terms 'Hedge funds' and 'Managed Futures' entered into the investment vocabulary. The large consolidation wave in the railway, oil and financial industries in the late 19th century created an attractive environment for speculation and arbitrage on mergers. Convertible Arbitrage strategies were particularly attractive and performed well in the years 1929–32 during the stock market crash. Short Selling and Distressed Securities investing have existed since the late 19th century. However, these investment activities were largely pursued as isolated trading activities by individuals.[5] The systematic application of these strategies within an investment vehicle offered to third party investors is a relatively modern phenomenon and emerged in the early 1950s.

Unfortunately, the name 'Hedge fund' is somewhat misleading. In fact, most Hedge funds are leveraged rather than hedged. Further, most 'Hedge funds' are technically not 'funds' but Limited Partnerships. The original understanding of a Hedge fund was an equity investment strategy where managers reduced their exposure to adverse downward movements in the broad market by combining long and short positions in stocks. The investment manager bought stocks he believed to be undervalued and then sold short other stocks he considered overvalued. Today this strategy goes by the name 'Long/Short Equity'. It was A. W. Jones who created the first Hedge fund of this kind in 1949 when he combined the purchase of stocks with Short Selling and leverage, two main elements of Hedge fund strategies today (derivates, a third element, was not yet widely available). Furthermore, he charged a performance fee to his investors, which enabled him to benefit directly from his investment success. This became another common feature of AIS.

The first large Hedge fund boom started with an article about the Jones' strategy in *Fortune* magazine in the mid-1960s.[6] While this boom died off quickly in the bust years of the late 1960s and early 1970s, another Hedge fund strategy emerged in the late 1960s, 'Global Macro'. This strategy entails 'taking sophisticated bets' on probable future price moves of specific instruments based on particular macroeconomic views. The Global Macro strategy is connected with two names that for many years were the symbols of Hedge fund investing: Julian Robertson and George Soros. Both showed high returns over almost three decades and gained wide public attention through an article about Julian Robertson's fund in *Institutional Investors* magazine in the mid-1980s[7] and through the British pound opting out of the European Currency System in 1992, which, it is widely believed, was caused by George Soros' 'Quantum' Hedge fund (and which created large profits for 'Quantum').[8]

Futures predated equity markets, but it was not until the late 1960s that the use of Futures and other derivatives emerged within diversified trading strategies. Managed Futures strategies were born around the same time as Hedge funds. Richard Donchian created the first Futures-based investment program in the same year (1949) as A. W. Jones launched his first Hedge fund. Today the distinction between the two is somewhat blurred and some actually no longer distinguish Futures from Hedge funds. In 1965, Dunn and Hagitt started trading commodity Futures using technical trading systems (they also offered the first offshore commodity pool in 1973). A first boom in Managed Futures investment programs occurred with the introduction of financial Futures in 1972 and the increasing availability of computing power in the 1970s. Most of the investment programs were based on technical trading and charting systems. Managed Futures quickly came to be viewed as an interesting alternative investment class with attractive returns uncorrelated to returns in equities (which were rather modest in the 1970s). Traditionally, Commodity Trading Advisor ('CTA') funds are distinguished from Hedge funds on the simple notion that they are limited to trading primarily Futures contracts and that they are registered with the CFTC and comply with its regulatory rules. But nowadays, many CTAs also trade in OTC securities markets, while Hedge funds also use Futures as essential risk management tools (some Hedge funds are or used to be registered with the CFTC, e.g. Long-Term Capital Management – LTCM).

The AIS industry recovered strongly from problems related to the rapid increase of interest rates in early 1994 and the crisis following the Russian Bond default and the liquidation of LTCM in 1998. The time period after 1998 can be referred to as the 'institutionalization phase'. The AIS industry's growth in 1999–2002 was enormously supported by falling equity markets and the 'NASDAQ crash'. The AIS industry is now so far developed that many investors consider it as an asset class itself. On the demand side, due to the attractive risk–reward characteristic as well as their low correlation to traditional investments, institutional investors have increasingly expressed interest in AIS.[9] On the supply side, the AIS industry has been and will continue to be a lure for the most intelligent talents in finance. The smartest finance professionals and most promising investment ideas are attracted to an industry that offers greatest flexibilities for the implementation of investment and hedging strategies together with a very high level of monetary compensation. Most banks and other large finance institutions have begun to offer a diverse range of AIS investment structures,[10] as they come to view AIS as a new and increasingly profitable business segment.

The question, whether AIS constitutes an asset class in itself or whether Hedge funds and Managed Futures only extend the range of investment strategies within certain existing asset classes, is subject to debate and is mostly a matter of perspective. Investors increasingly consider AIS as a separate class in their asset allocation process (sometimes together with Private Equity investments). On the other hand, Hedge fund and Managed Futures programs do not trade any particular new assets or instruments but rather execute certain investment strategies within a set of existing instruments and asset classes. They can be seen as the active counter-party to passive (i.e. index-linked) investment strategies in a 'core–satellite' portfolio set-up.

Sceptical market participants and investors have recently compared the development of Hedge funds with the technology bubble in the 1990s and predict that the current AIS euphoria will similarly end in tears.[11] In the most simple sense, a investment bubble is a phenomenon that builds up when expectations skyrocket and everyone does the same thing at the same time.[12] The heterogeneity of AIS clearly contrasts with historical bubbles such as the Dutch tulip mania in the 17th century, the US equity markets in the late 1920s, the Japanese stock market in the late 1980s or the internet hype in the late 1990s. The AIS industry covers a very broad range of asset classes and favourable and unfavourable market environments deviate strongly across strategy sectors. Economic developments, political events and changes in the market environment create and destroy different profit opportunities for different strategies. The AIS industry in its entirety is sufficiently well diversified to deal with extreme market circumstances.

The opposite view is that Hedge funds are a new asset class that has a legitimate place in every investment portfolio. The main argument underlying this view is that AIS have strong absolute returns and low correlations to traditional asset classes. But this might turn out to be new wine in old wineskins. A few years ago investing in emerging markets was marketed as a new way of decreasing overall portfolio risk. But experiences in the 1990s (Mexico, Thailand, Russia) have aligned the hype with reality. The diversification benefits of AIS might also be overestimated, as the AIS industry has had a long equity bias in recent (equity bull market) years and it is debatable whether the AIS industry can decouple completely from global economic trends. Further, given the strong inflows into Hedge funds, one has seriously to ask whether return expectations are decoupling from reality. Lower absolute Hedge fund performance achieved in 2000 and 2001 may help gradually to align expectations with reality. AIS investing will increasingly require strong skills on the side of the allocator (fund of funds manager, direct investor) in order to realize the benefits of Hedge funds and Managed Futures while avoiding excessive risk.

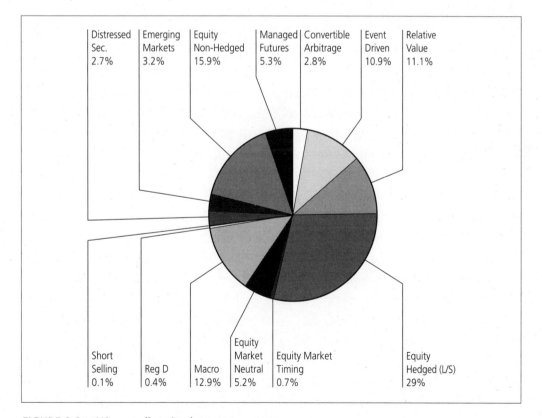

FIGURE 2.2 ∎ AIS asset allocation by strategy sector

Source: Hedge Fund Research

Figure 2.2 displays the distribution of how assets are approximately invested in the different sectors (as of October 2001). Long/Short Equity is the dominant sector with more than 40% of all AIS assets invested in this strategy sector (Equity Hedged 29% plus Equity Non-Hedged 16%), followed in roughly equal size (11–13%) by Event Driven, Relative Value and Global Macro strategies. Futures strategies and Equity Market Neutral each take about 5%, Convertible Arbitrage, Distressed Securities and Emerging Markets about 3% each. Convertible Arbitrage and Equity Market Neutral are Relative Value strategies, but they are counted separately here. Other strategies like Short Selling, Regulation D and Equity Market Timing fall below the 1% range. Note that these numbers depend on the classification scheme chosen (in this case by Hedge Fund Research).

Understanding the sources of AIS returns

It is widely understood among investment professionals that Hedge funds and Managed Futures generate investment returns that are significantly more attractive than average equity and bond investments measured on a risk-adjusted basis using commonly available quantitative risk assessment tools. This creates some confusion and scepticism, as most investors believe that financial markets provide no 'free lunch' to investors. It is important to realize that Hedge funds and Managed Futures are in fact exposed to a variety of different risk factors and thus possess a corresponding number of return sources. In many cases the main part of the answer lies in the inability of conventional risk measures and theories to measure the diverse risks of AIS and to describe the corresponding sources of return properly.

Conventional finance theory as described by the Capital Asset Pricing Model (CAPM) and similar asset pricing models states that expected investment returns are directly related to the amount of market risk taken (e.g. the risk of the broad equity market falling). The excess return over a risk free investment is linked to the 'beta' of the investment. Any excess return above and beyond the return for taking risk is considered the result of particular manager skills (or pure luck), e.g. detecting mispriced securities, having superior and price relevant information, or correctly timing the market. This return is called 'alpha'. Consistent alpha generation appears to contradict a well-established paradigm in financial market theory, which is the 'efficiency market hypothesis' (EMH). The EMH comes in various forms related to different types of information available to investors: a weak form, a semi-strong form, and strong form.[13] The EMH (in its strongest form) states that there is no price relevant information available to any investor that is not yet reflected in market prices. This implies that investment managers will not consistently generate alpha. Most investment and academic professionals do not hold the EMH in its strong form for true, but its weak and semi-strong form has more numerous supporters. The market efficiency battle between proponents of standard finance and their counter-parties (e.g. advocates of behavioural finance) is waged over the interpretation of price anomalies and consistent alpha generation in the main equity, foreign exchange and fixed income markets.[14] But it is rather undisputed that the overall global spectrum of financial markets presents varying degrees of efficiency. The major foreign exchange markets, G7 Government Bond markets as well as the large capitalization segment of the major international equity markets are generally considered to be quite efficient, while real estate and private equity markets generally display a much lower degree of efficiency, i.e. superior information or skill in these markets pays off in above average returns. Hedge fund managers operate in security markets with various efficiencies and are thus in some middle position between public equity and bond portfolio managers on the one side and private equity or real estate experts on the other side.

For a further understanding of the 'battle of alpha', it is important to assess the basic assumptions of common asset pricing models. The CAPM is based on the following (and some other) important assumptions:[15]

▪ Investors choose investments according to a mean variance framework (i.e. they measure reward by the mean return and risk by the variance – or standard deviation – of returns). Investors are generally risk averse and have a quadratic utility function with respect to risk.

▪ All investors have the same forecast of expected return variances and correlations. This leads all investors to hold the same risky market portfolio (with varying weights relative to the risk-free part of their portfolios, depending on their risk profiles). Consequently, there is only one source of risk for which investors are rewarded, which is the 'broad market risk' (as measured, for example, by an equity index).

- Trading is frictionless, i.e. there are not transaction costs, taxes, etc. Investors can (and will) sell short securities without any restrictions.

The first assumption becomes questionable when the probability distribution of investment outcomes is skewed (i.e. non-symmetric) or leptohurtic (i.e. exhibits 'fat tails'). In this case, the conventional measure of risk, namely the standard deviation, provides an imprecise basis for risk measurement. Some AIS – comparable to option strategies – have non-symmetric return distributions. The fact that investors have a preference for positively skewed outcomes and an aversion against negatively skewed outcomes is not captured by a risk measure that weighs each part of the distribution identically. For many AI strategies, the right amount of return for the given exposure to risk cannot be unambiguously determined in the framework of CAPM.

The second point is plainly false, as investments, particularly those in AIS, are subject to numerous other risks beyond broad market risk. The 'Arbitrage Pricing Theory' (APT) provides a more general framework,[16] which allows the inclusion of more factors to explain asset returns. The crucial question of which particular factors to include remains a matter of dispute.[17] The numerous extensions of the one-factor CAPM usually include additional fundamental factors such as firm size or value factors (price-earnings ratio, price-book value, etc.) or macroeconomic factors (such as unexpected inflation or credit spreads).

Considering only market risk leads to the incorrect conclusion that superior returns are always the result of unique manager skills or superior access to information. But the reality is that investors who are willing to assume risks beyond market risk (e.g. liquidity risk, credit risk, event risk) can earn additional returns unconditional on superior information or skill. The investor might incur losses from bearing one of these risks during some periods, but over time the returns should be sufficient to make the investment profitable. These returns are called 'risk premiums'. Multi-factor models (like APT) allow capturing these other dimensions of risk besides overall market risk and they include the corresponding 'factor risk premiums' in the modelling of asset prices.

The third restriction is at best only partly true. Transaction costs are indeed an important factor for investors to consider. Further, many investors are constrained in selling short securities. This can create inefficiencies in financial markets that

Hedge funds try to take advantage of (see the discussion of 'Long/Short Equity' and 'Short Selling' in the next chapter).

Effective AIS risk management requires a sound understanding of how returns are generated and what risks come with these return sources. The limitations of quantitative measures of risk-adjusted returns have to be considered (e.g. as in the case of skewed return distributions). As already mentioned, it is generally useful to distinguish the following two (real) sources of returns (besides 'luck'): risk premiums and manager skill. These two sources are by no means mutually exclusive. It takes skill to capture a premium effectively and to manage the related risk. By the same token, some strategies are based largely on a manager's skill in forecasting price moves or detecting relative mispricings, which is often performed with the help of quantitative valuation models. One can argue that these strategies earn a 'complexity' (risk) premium. Further, price anomalies and apparent Arbitrage opportunities are often related to different risk premiums.[18] Despite certain overlaps and ambiguities that come with this classification scheme, distinguishing 'risk premium strategies' from 'pure skill strategies' nevertheless provides a good framework for an analysis of the AIS Universe.

Economic functions and Risk premiums

Investors in financial markets fulfil different economic functions and assume certain risks in expectation of a return that is higher than (risk free) money market interest rates. One should understand these economic functions and their role in the AIS return generation process. The most broadly known economic functions are:

- *Capital formation*, providing companies with access to capital.
- *Risk transfer,* providing commercial hedgers with the possibility of transferring unwanted risk in futures markets.
- *Price transparency and efficiency*, making financial markets more efficient.
- *Providing liquidity*, creating a market for less liquid investments.

I believe that many AIS earn their returns by assuming risk in a risk averse financial world, rather than from the identification of market inefficiencies. By taking these risks the investor is compensated with an expected return, the risk premium. I therefore refer to these strategies as 'risk premium strategies'. Analogously to the earnings of an insurance company, which is rewarded with a premium for insuring its clients that is higher than the expected average claim per insurance contract, premiums in financial markets are positive expected returns that exceed the 'risk free interest rate'[19] in exchange for accepting the possibility of a financial loss. Over time, risk premiums provide an inherent and permanent positive expected return, the source of which does not disappear if spotted by other investors (although it can fluctuate over time). The nature of its underlying risk premium is directly related to a strategy's risk profile. The risks and premiums vary among different strategies. It is important to understand the economic rationales for the premiums of each individual strategy sector. They are discussed in detail in Chapter 3. For 'risk premium strategies', manager skill primarily expresses itself through premium identification, proper timing and the appropriate risk management.

The existence of premiums as inherent sources of returns is most apparent for Relative Value and Arbitrage strategies (Fixed Income Arbitrage, Risk Arbitrage and Convertible Arbitrage). Note that the word 'Arbitrage' does not refer here to the strictest meaning of the word (which is 'generating a profit without risk'). In this context, by 'Arbitrage', I mean 'buying relatively undervalued securities and selling overvalued securities'. There is a risk involved here, specifically the risk that the undervalued securities become even cheaper and the overvalued ones more expensive. 'Arbitrage' strategies earn spreads (i.e. premiums) between market prices of two or more strongly related instruments as compensation for taking very particular risks such as company specific risk, FX risk, commodity price risk, credit risk, duration risk, liquidity risk and deal risk. Risk (Merger) Arbitrage returns, for example, are directly linked to the spread between the market price of the target company and the price offered by the acquiring company and are earned in return for taking the risk that the deal does not go through. The following list summarizes different risk premiums and identifies for each one of them the particular strategies attempting to capture it:

- equity Market risk premiums (Equity Market Timing, Long/Short Equity, Convertible Arbitrage)

- corporate event risk premiums (Risk Arbitrage, Long/Short Equity, Distressed Securities, Regulation D)

- risk transfer premiums (Futures strategies)

- complexity premiums or 'efficiency' premiums (Equity Market Neutral, Statistical Arbitrage, Fixed Income Arbitrage)
- liquidity premiums (Distressed Securities, Regulation D)
- duration risk premiums (Fixed Income Arbitrage)
- credit risk premiums (Fixed Income Arbitrage, Regulation D, Distressed Securities, Convertible Arbitrage)
- FX risk premiums (FX strategies, some Global Macro strategies).

Equity risk premiums are compensation for the 'capital formation' function that investors fulfil through buying companies' stocks and thereby giving companies access to working capital. Investors take the risk of financial loss, for example, due to an economic downturn, less favourable earnings developments or bankruptcy. According to the Capital Asset Pricing Model (CAPM) and related models, equity risk is twofold. First, broad market risk is related to the volatility of the broad market or industry sector. Second, corporate specific risk is the idiosyncratic risk of loss due to an adverse development, which affects the stock of a particular company (note that, according to the CAPM, idiosyncratic risk does not earn a risk premium).

Many Futures strategies, especially trendfollowing strategies, are related to an economic function that is very different from equity investments. Investors in Futures are willing to expose themselves to the natural risks of commercial hedgers, thereby providing those hedgers with the possibility to transfer their undesired price risks. By fulfilling this function of *risk transfer* speculators in Futures markets earn a corresponding premium, which could alternatively be called 'commodity hedging demand premium'. More details are provided in Chapter 3 in the sections on Futures strategies.

Many Arbitrage strategies earn premiums for *providing market efficiency and price transparency*. Their aim is to detect pricing inefficiencies through the application of (mostly proprietary) valuation models to complex financial instruments. It can be argued that their returns are based on a 'complexity' (or, alternatively, an 'efficiency') premium for taking the risk of mismodelling the underlying financial instrument and its complexity and thus suffering a loss. Further, investors who are willing to *accept lower liquidity* in their investments earn a liquidity premium. Such liquidity risk often goes together with credit risk. Credit and duration risk premiums are connected to investing in fixed income instruments with lower credit quality and longer maturity respectively.

What are the sources of returns for FX strategies? Currency markets (at least for the major currencies) are considered the most liquid financial markets in the world, and the inter-bank FX market is often seen as the market that operates closest to complete efficiency. This high liquidity has to be generated by somebody with monetary incentives, which means the speculators. It can be argued that the (very strong) liquidity request of commercial participants in FX markets generates a return source for FX traders, as supply and demand from commercial players alone barely ever balance each other exactly. This argument is similar to the risk transfer premium in commodity markets. The return of FX strategies is thus a premium paid by commercial market players for the generation of liquidity and price continuity (see the discussion on currency strategies in Chapter 3 for more details). Another premium earned by certain FX strategies is related to the risk of a (stronger than expected) currency devaluation and expresses itself as a positive (interest rate) carry (i.e. the differential in interest rates) between two currencies. The corresponding strategy consists of buying a high yield currency and selling one with a low yield.

One problem for the evaluation of risk premium-based strategies is that, while they earn returns due to the assumptions of certain risks, empirical measures of these risks might be calculated for a time period that does not include a relevant 'risk event'. This can lead to a severe underestimation of a particular strategy's risk.

Risk premiums as a source of return are less (if at all) obvious for some opportunistic strategies like Global Macro, Short Selling and many Long/Short Equity strategies. The returns of these strategies are rooted in the manager's skill in forecasting price developments, detecting pricing anomalies and acting quickly on anticipated market moves. The underlying opportunities and market inefficiencies are usually temporary and quickly disappear when spotted by other investors. The greatest potential for these 'pure skill-based' strategies is where information is not freely available. As I mentioned before, the distinction between manager skill and risk premium as sources of return is not always absolutely clear. Manager forecasting skill and a 'complexity premium' can both be argued to be sources of returns for some opportunistic strategies.

Ideally, financial economists would prefer to develop a universe of fundamental risk factors that can explain the time series behaviour of AIS returns. For traditional investments much work has been dedicated to examining the components of active equity and bond manager performance and numerous studies have directly assessed their sources of return.[20] Similarly, more recent research indicates that certain factors (return drivers) help to explain AIS performance patterns.[21] Some go even further and argue that 'generic' systematic trading programs (with no discretionary or skill-based input) can replicate most strategies' returns (and subsequently say that the high fees for AIS managers are not justified).[22] The current academic thinking on how to evaluate AIS returns is to include 'style factors' (e.g. option-like payoffs) in the set of performance factors rather than just explain AIS return based on other asset returns.[23]

The detection of specific performance drivers for AIS strategies with the help of quantitative tools such as factor models has been subject to intense discussion and research in the academic and the financial community in recent years. Hedge funds are now often classified as either 'long biased', i.e. primarily influenced by the direction of international bond and equity markets ('return enhancers'), or non-directional attempting to be less affected by the direction of the major financial markets ('diversifiers'). But the statistical significance of AIS factors models has to date been rather low. This is partly due to the short time series available for research. Empirical measures for some AIS risk factors may not yet sufficiently describe the significant losses after 'big events' which are part of many strategies' risk profiles. Most AIS professionals agree that qualitative reasoning has to supplement such quantitative analysis. Schneeweiss et al. in a recent publication provide a good summary of the discussion on sources of AIS return.[24]

The structure of AIS multi-manager funds

Along with the rapid growth and expanded complexity of AIS in multi-manager portfolios has come the increasing prevalence of pooling Hedge funds in multi-manager portfolios managed by a specialist 'fund of funds' manager. This way investors are relieved of the complex task of strategy sector allocation, manager due diligence and investment monitoring. A 'fund of funds' is an investment vehicle that mixes and matches Hedge funds and Managed Futures, spreading investments across strategies, thus diversifying AIS sectors and managers. Selecting the appropriate managers requires an experienced portfolio manager with the necessary knowledge, infrastructure and relationships in the industry.

A fund of funds can also be a more liquid investment than direct investments with single Hedge funds or Managed Futures. Furthermore, if properly managed, it can provide the security created by continuous monitoring of managers and portfolio and risk management. Therefore, investing in a fund of funds is the preferable route for new investors, institutional as well as private.[25] But the added value of a fund of funds is only realized if certain conditions are met. The fund of funds manager must have a complete understanding of the individual strategy sectors and their risks and correlation features, perform thorough due diligence on all managers and their respective 'edges', implement a system for continuous monitoring of open positions, and actively manage risk (see Chapter 7 for a more detailed discussion).

The structure of AIS investment products such as funds of funds can be quite complex and innovations change the industry continuously. Managing a multi-manager product requires expertise not only on the level of instruments and markets, but also in respect of legal and regulatory issues. The set-up of a multi-manager AIS investment vehicle involves a variety of different parties (see the discussion in Chapter 7 for more details):

1 *Management company or fund of funds investment manager:* The investment manager selects and monitors the individual trading managers and determines the legal and administrative structure of the investment vehicle. He usually receives a management as well as a performance fee.

2 *Investment advisors/managers:* The managers are hired by the investment manager and are responsible for the actual investments, either in his own fund or through a managed account.

3 *Administrator:* The administrator is responsible for registration and issuance of the shares, performing the necessary legal and tax tasks, calculation of NAV and performance fees, account administration, handling of subscriptions and redemption and the organization of audits.

4 *Prime broker:* Prime brokers provide for the global settlement, clearing and execution of trades done by the managers. They also provide credit lines for financing leverage and Short Selling capabilities. Furthermore, prime brokers often give the investment manager access to value added services like research reports and risk management tools.

5 *Execution brokers:* The execution broker arranges the execution of trades, either over the counter or on an exchange. Most managers use several executing brokers in order to get best prices. A good part of the trades is usually executed through the prime broker.

6 *Custodian:* The custodian is the connecting piece between the broker and the administrator. He tracks the receipts and payment obligations for subscriptions and redemptions, monitors the brokers and records the different transactions.

The number and variety of multi-manager AIS investment products is growing rapidly.[26] They come in a variety of structures, the details of which depend on the chosen domicile, promotional issues (sales restrictions), required investment flexibility and tax issues. Many funds of funds are set up offshore, as offshore centres provide investors with tax benefits and relieve the managers of regulations on the use of derivatives, short sales and leverage. US fund managers primarily choose the nearby Caribbean islands (Bahamas, BVI, Cayman Islands, Bermuda, Netherlands Antilles), while Europeans select Luxembourg, Ireland, the Channel Islands (Jersey, Guernsey) and Switzerland (where regulations are usually stricter than in Caribbean countries).[27] The actual location of the AIS portfolio manager usually differs from the fund domicile and is usually in the proximity of main financial centres (New York, London, Geneva, Zurich, Hong Kong, Tokyo, Frankfurt etc.). Today four general structures of AIS fund of funds investment vehicles can be distinguished: open-ended funds, closed-end funds, structured notes and managed accounts (see also Chapter 7 for a discussion of the different redemption policies of these fund of funds products).

Open-ended funds of funds with redemption periods ranging from one to six months are usually structured as limited liability companies in the USA and the Caribbean offshore centres, trust structures in the UK (including the Channel Islands) or some form of collective investment contract scheme in continental Europe (e.g. SICAV in France and Luxembourg). Low liquidity (long redemption period) and limited investment transparency are the main disadvantages of this structure.

Structured notes are designed to fulfil specific investor needs such as capital protection, regulatory specifications, legal constraints and tax protection.[28] They have become a common structure for multi-manager AIS products in Europe, often offered by investment banks in cooperation with fund of funds specialists. In Germany, for example, index-linked bonds, so called 'Zertifikate', are currently the most common AIS investment structures for tax and regulatory reasons (most AIS vehicles offered to German investors are based on some self-created 'index' made up of the selected managers). The customization to specific needs is the advantage of structured notes, but their disadvantage is that they often come with higher fees. A common form is a principal protected note which guarantees the 100% payback of the investment at maturity. Capital guaranteed notes are usually structured with a zero coupon bond or an option.[29] For most structured notes the issuer provides for some liquidity in a secondary market.

Other AIS products take the form of a closed-end investment vehicle, which often enjoys more regulatory flexibility than an open-ended fund. These products are wrapped as investment companies, which issue non-redeemable shares. After an initial offering period the investment company is closed for subscription and redemption and the shares are traded on an exchange. The problem of these investment structures is that trading is often extremely low in volume and liquidity. This can lead to significant discounts of the market price to the net asset value (NAV).

Investors and allocators can structure their investments with individual managers through managed accounts, where the money is held in an account with an independent custodian or broker. Managed accounts structures offer the most flexible and transparent investment structure. But they require a significant minimum investment with each manager ranging from around $2 million to about $25 million. In a multi-manager investment set-up, a 'fund of managed accounts' requires a special legal framework to ensure that the individual managed accounts carry no liability from the other accounts.

Notes

1. A good discussion of the characteristics of AIS strategies (including their historical return properties) and an AIS classification scheme is presented by A. Ineichen in 'In Search for Alpha', October 2000 (updated and extended version 'The Search for Alpha Continues', September 2001).

2. Some authors present classification schemes which deviate in certain nuances. I will try to indicate other schemes, wherever it is appropriate.

3.   For example, A. Ineichen in 'In Search for Alpha', October 2000 and 'The Search for Alpha Continues', September 2001.

4.   See the article 'A Primer on Hedge Funds' by S. Fung and D. Hsieh for more details of AIS legal and regulatory issues.

5.   See the book by Edwin Lefevre, *Reminiscences of a Stock Operator* (1923) for more details.

6.   C. Loomis, 'The Jones Nobody Keeps Up With', *Fortune*, April 1966, p.237.

7.   J. Rohrer, 'The Red Hot World of Julian Robertson', *Institutional Investors*, May 1986, p.86.

8.   An interesting history of Hedge funds is presented in T. Caldwell, 'Introduction: The Model for Superior Performance', in J. Lederman and R. Klein, *Hedge Funds: Investment and Portfolio Strategies for the Institutional Investor*, Irwin Professional Publishing, New York, 1995.

9.   Three surveys by Watson Wyatt/INDOCAM illustrate the increasing institutional demand for AIS products: 'Alternative Investment Review Relating to the Continental European (respectively United States and United Kingdom) Marketplace', Fall 2000. See also report by Golin/Harris Ludgate, 'The Future Role of Hedge Funds in European Institutional Asset Management 2001'. PricewaterhouseCoopers performed a survey among private banks in European with respect to the status quo and their expectations of AIS and their importance, 'European Private Banking / Wealth Management Survey 2000/2001'. Other surveys with similar results were performed by Goldman Sachs/Frank Russell (2001 Alternative Investing Survey), Deutsche Bank's equity prime services unit (see http://www.hedgeworld.com/news/read_news. cgi?story=peop606.html&section=peop), and the Barra Strategic Consulting Group FOHF (market survey, 2001).

10.   An illustration of Hedge fund activities in the USA and Europe is presented in 'The Hedge Fund "Industry" and Absolute Return Funds', Goldmann, Sachs & Co. and Financial Risk Management Ltd., *The Journal of Alternative Investments*, Spring 1999 and in 'Starting a Hedge Fund – a US Perspective' and 'Starting a Hedge Fund – a European Perspective', both published by ISI publications.

11.   See, for example, 'Hedge Funds – The Latest Bubble?', *The Economist*, September 1, 2001, 'The $500 billion Hedge Fund Folly', *Forbes Magazine*, August 6, 2001, 'The Hedge Fund Bubble', *Financial Times*, July 9, 2001.

12. For a more detailed discussion on bubbles in the financial world, see the paper by R. Shiller, 'Human Behavior and the Efficiency of the Financial System', and the book by H. Shefren, *Beyond Greed and Fear: Understanding Behavioural Finance*, Harvard Press, Boston (1999).

13. These are discussed in detail by E. Fama in a seminal paper: 'Efficient Capital Markets: II', published in the *Journal of Finance*, December 1991.

14. Standard finance proponents argue that market efficiency is not testable because such tests must be jointly accompanied by a test of an asset pricing model.

15. Most finance books cover the CAPM including its fundamental assumptions in great detail, e.g. F. Reilly and K. Brown, *Investment Analysis and Portfolio Management*, The Dryden Press, 1997.

16. The APT was introduced by S. Ross in the early 1970s and first published in 1976: 'The Arbitrage Theory of Capital Asset Pricing' in *Journal of Economic Theory*, December 1976.

17. See Chapter 10 of *Investment Analysis and Portfolio Management* by F. Reilly and K. Brown for a good discussion of recent research results.

18. One example is the fact that stocks with high book to price value (BV/PV) have outperformed other stocks significantly in past years. It is still disputed whether this is a pricing anomaly or a risk premium. An argument raised by E. Fama and K. French in their papers 'The Cross-Section of Expected Stock Returns' and 'Size and Book-to-Market Factors in Earnings and Returns' is that investors pursuing a strategy of buying high BV/PV stocks provide 'recession insurance' for other investors.

19. The risk free rate of return has nothing to do with a risk premium. In economic terms, the risk free rate of return is the compensation to the investor for not persuing current consumption in exchange for higher future consumption.

20. See the seminal paper by W. Sharpe, 'Asset Allocation: Management Style and Performance Measurement' and the paper by E. Fama and K. French 'Multifactor Explanations of Asset Pricing Anomalies'.

21. See the following articles for a further discussion: T. Schneeweiss and R. Spurgin, 'Multifactor Analysis of Hedge Funds, Managed Futures, and Mutual Fund Returns and Risk Characteristics'; B. Liang, 'On the Performance of Hedge Funds'; W. Fung and D. Hsieh, 'Empirical Characteristics of Dynamic Trading Strategies: The Case of Hedge Funds'; W. Fung and D. Hsieh, 'Benchmarks of Hedge Fund Performance: Information Content and Measurement Biases'; W. Fung and D. Hsieh, 'The Risk in

Hedge Fund Strategies: Theory and Evidence from Trend-Followers'; V. Agarwal and N. Naik, 'Performance Evaluation of Hedge Funds with Option-based and Buy-and-Hold Strategies'; F. Edwards and M. Caglayan, 'Hedge Fund Performance and Manager Skill'; See also the summary discussion of different articles on this subject by A. Ineichen in 'The Search for Alpha Continues', pp.93–95. An interesting study on return profiles of Hedge funds is also the following: G. Amin and H. Kat, 'Hedge Fund Performance: 1990–2000: Do the Money Machines Really Add Value?'

22.   See the article 'Hedge Funds Placed Under the Microscope' by G. Polyn in *Risk Magazine*, August 2001, and references therein (especially the study by the International Security Market Association). Academic research has also focused on the direct replication of the AIS with generic trading models, see e.g. the discussions by T. Schneeweiss and R. Spurgin in 'Trading Factors and Location Factors in Hedge Fund Return Estimation', T. Schneeweiss and H. Kazemi, in 'The Creation of Alternative Tracking Portfolios for Hedge Fund Strategies', as well as the paper by W. Fung and D. Hsieh, 'The Risk in Hedge Fund Strategies: Theory and Evidence from Trend-Followers'.

23.   A promising approach of a 'style factor model' is presented by A. Weismann and J. Abernathy in the article 'The Dangers of Historical Hedge Fund Data', in *Risk Bucketing: A New Approach to Investing*, 2000.

24.   'Understanding Hedge Fund Performance: Research Results and Rules of Thumb for the Institutional Investor', Lehman Brothers Publication, Dec. 2001.

25.   For a detailed discussion of the characteristics and value added of fund of funds, see also the contribution by A. Ineichen, 'The Search for Alpha Continues – Do Fund of Hedge Fund Managers Add Value?'

26.   A good (but somewhat outdated) overview of the different structures is presented in *Hedge Funds and Managed Futures* by P. Cottier, p.55.

27.   A discussion of the different legislations for Hedge funds is presented in 'The Capital Guide to Alternative Investments', ISI publications, 2001.

28.   See the following articles for more details: P. Astleford, W. Yonge and R. Edwards et al. and I. Cullen in 'The Capital Guide to Alternative Investments', ISI Publications, 2001; P. Watterson, 'Offering Private Investment Funds in the Capital Markets', *Alternative Investment Quarterly*, October 2001, p.43.

29.   For an interesting discussion of structured AIS products, see the article 'French Fight over Hedge Fund Products' by N. Dunbar in *Risk Magazine*, February 2001.

CHAPTER 3

Alternative Investment Strategies: Hedge funds and Managed Futures

In this chapter each AIS sector is discussed in terms of its investment strategy, sources of return and risk characteristics. In order to acquaint the reader better with the strategies, realistic examples are provided.

Hedge fund strategies

Figure 3.1 expands on Figure 2.1 and displays an overview of today's Hedge fund and Managed Futures strategies. For Hedge funds, I distinguish the sub-categories Relative Value, Event Driven and Opportunistic.[1] The most important differentiating factor between these three categories is the degree of sensitivity to the direction of financial markets. While the returns of Opportunistic strategies often depend on the (equity) market direction, Relative Value strategies earn returns that are largely independent from it. Event-Driven strategies fall in some medium range in terms of their directional market sensitivity.

Most of the strategies in the array of Hedge fund styles emerged in the last 15 to 20 years. Relative Value strategies (Convertible Arbitrage, Fixed Income Arbitrage, Equity Market Neutral) seek out different specific risk premiums and arbitrage opportunities in equity and fixed income markets. Event-Driven strategies (Distressed Securities, Merger Arbitrage and Convertible Debenture Arbitrage) in contrast capitalize on the occurrence of special events that impact the value of certain securities. Opportunistic strategies cover a heterogonous third sector.

Relative Value strategies usually have very little net exposure to broad equity and bond market, while Event-Driven strategies have some exposure to specific equity and fixed income risk factors. Opportunistic strategies (Long/Short Equity,[2] Macro, Short Sellers, Equity Market Timing) are broadly influenced by the returns in broad equity, fixed income and foreign exchange markets.

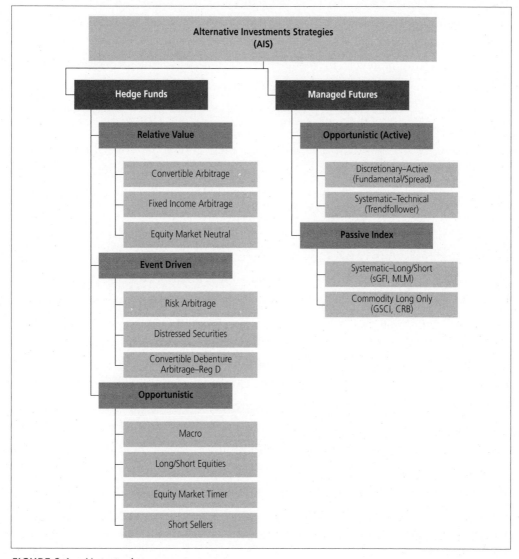

FIGURE 3.1 ■ AI strategies

Source: Partners Group

Relative Value – Convertible Arbitrage

The strategy

Convertible securities are equivalent to holding both a bond and an option on the stock of the issuer.[3] The pricing relationship between the convertible bond and the stock can be complex and market pricing is often not completely efficient for this combination (especially if, as is often the case, the bond is in addition callable and/or putable). Because the option part(s) of the bond is (are) not traded separately, pricing anomalies occur regularly, particularly in volatile periods. With the help of quantitative valuation models accounting for the bond's specific characteristics, Convertible Arbitrage managers pursue Arbitrage opportunities by identifying these pricing disparities. The strategy consists of taking long positions in 'cheap' convertible securities and hedge their equity part by selling short the corresponding stock. Long positions in convertible securities include convertible bonds, convertible preferred stock and warrants. When the convertible ultimately achieves its 'fair value' relative to the stock price, the position is sold and profits are realized. Besides equity risk, managers often hedge other risk factors such as credit and interest rate risk using a variety of hedging techniques.

Convertible Arbitrage managers usually start with a universe of convertible securities and screen candidates with a bottom-up valuation analysis. In order to identify 'cheap' securities managers compare the convertible's market price with its calculated expected value based on interest rate levels, the market price and volatility of the underlying equity, the bond floor, the expected equity premium, the conversion price and ratio, the conversion premium and other variables related to the issue (credit quality, call schedule etc.).[4] While most Convertible Arbitrage managers target a market (beta) neutral position, some take a fundamental view on the issuer and build this opinion into a net short or net long position. The equity hedge ratio (delta) generally ranges from 0.3 to 1.0. Most Convertible Arbitrage managers employ leverage ranging from 1:1 to 6:1. The relatively high risk-adjusted returns of Convertible Arbitrage strategies in the past are partly attributable to positive beta positions in the bull equity markets of the 1980s and 1990s.

Different variations of Convertible Arbitrage strategies are:

- buying convertible bonds and selling short the underlying stock/stock option
- buying convertible bonds and shorting index Futures/index options
- searching for price inefficiencies in complicated convertibles with numerous conversion characteristics and callable and put-able schemes
- focusing on low credit quality or distressed convertibles in combination with the stock.

The concept of Convertible Arbitrage strategies is threefold:

1 earning static returns

2 being long stock price volatility

3 exploiting price inefficiencies.

Profits can be generated in all the following ways:

Static return:

    (a)   Convertibles pay interest or preferred dividends (current yield).

    (b)   The short equity portion generates positive cash flow (interest income from short rebate minus dividends).

The highest level of static return is earned with in-the-money convertibles with low credit ratings. These pay high coupons and require a high equity hedge, i.e. they earn high short rebates (assuming a constant bond floor and, in particular, constant credit rating).

Volatility trading:

The strategy is typically long volatility. As the stock price volatility changes, the convertible's value will change due to the commensurate change in the inherent option value (conversion premium). The higher the volatility of the underlying stock, the more opportunity for the manager to realize trading profits. The optimal trade involves healthy companies (from a credit perspective) with overvalued stocks. Being delta hedged and long gamma, the strategy benefits from an increase in stock price volatility or a decrease in stock price.

Fair value:

> Utilizing quantitative pricing models, the manager identifies mispriced securities. These 'cheap' positions are acquired and hedged. When 'fair value' is ultimately reached, these positions are sold and profits are realized.

Figure 3.2 illustrates the way in which Convertible Arbitrage returns are achieved.

An important distinction between different Convertible Arbitrage managers is their varied focus on the 'moneyness' of the convertible, i.e. how much the option is in or out of the money. Some managers focus on deep-in-the-money convertibles, while others trade mainly out-of-the-money issues (or even 'busted convertibles', i.e. deeply out-of-the-money issues). Depending on the moneyness of the option, credit quality of the convertible securities can be an important factor to consider. Together with prevailing interest rates, the credit quality determines the bond floor of the convertible security. The average grade of the bonds in a typical Convertible Arbitrage portfolio is BB to BBB with individual ratings ranging from AAA to CCC. However, as the default risk of the company is somewhat hedged by shorting the underlying common stock, especially for in-the-money

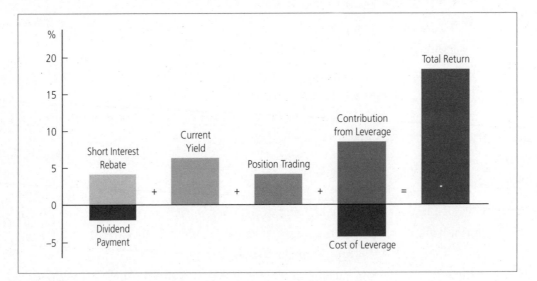

FIGURE 3.2 ■ Return sources of Convertible Arbitrage

Source: Discussion with Clinton Group

convertibles, the overall risk of the combined position is considerably better than the agency rating of the non-hedged bond indicates. Typically, lower credit rating implies the necessity for a higher equity hedge.

Convertible Arbitrage is more than solely identifying 'cheap volatility'. The management of tail risk is a key component of a successful strategy implementation. In addition to hedges for protection against movements in stock prices, most managers also seek to hedge interest rate exposure. Furthermore, as a somewhat liquid credit derivatives market is developing, credit risk swaps are becoming an important hedging tool for Convertible Arbitrage managers.[5] The level of sophistication in hedging techniques for Convertible Arbitrage Strategies is developing rapidly.

EXAMPLE

The US XYZ Co. issues a 5-year, 7% convertible bond due December 1, 2002 and the manager buys $1.5m face value of the bond. The bond sells at a price of $120 1/2 with a current yield of 5.81% and a conversion premium of approximately 17.5%. The holding period of this position is assumed to be 21 days. At the same time, 87,500 shares of XYZ Co. common stock are sold short at $14 per share creating additional interest income from the rebate of 5%. The static returns and assumed trading returns on this position are listed below.

The following shows the different parts of the trade and the returns:

Activity	Security	1/1/2001	1/21/2001	Gain
Buy	Bond	($1,807,500)		
Sell	Bond		1,812,495	
				$ 4,995
Short	Stock	$1,225,000		
Repurchase	Stock		(1,214,062)	$10,938

$$\text{Coupon interest at } 7\% \left(\text{accrual basis: } \frac{\text{number of days}}{360} \right) \qquad \$\,6,125$$

Short stock interest rebate at 5%	$ 3,573
Total gain	$25,631
Annualized rate of return	24.6%

Sources of return

Convertible Arbitrage strategies have a variety of return sources. An important economic source of return of Convertible Arbitrage strategies is the risk premium related to taking 'long volatility' positions. Being able to take a position cheaper than 'fair value' is rewarding this risk of being long volatility. Furthermore, depending on their specific implementation, Convertible Arbitrage strategies earn various premiums for taking credit, duration, liquidity and negative convexity risk (if the bond is callable). The relationship between convertible bonds and their underlying stock is rather complex and the market of this combination is often not completely efficient. The ability to detect mispriced securities is a function of the manager's skill in valuing convertible bonds correctly when the market does not. Most pricing inefficiencies of convertibles are due to 'volatility mispricings'. Convertible Arbitrage is the search for underpriced volatility. It can be argued that the model risk, i.e. the risk of modelling complex securities incorrectly, corresponds to a premium the manager earns. Besides capturing cheap volatility, a further important source of returns is identifying undervalued credits and benefiting as the market recognizes the undervaluation and corrects it.

Risk factors

Although the strategy might appear conceptually rather simple at first sight, Convertible Arbitrage is actually quite complex and a variety of risk factors are involved. The successful implementation requires experience and skill in managing these risks. The value of convertible securities depends on different characteristics, mostly the bond floor, the credit rating, the premium over conversion value (i.e. the 'moneyness' of the option component) and the stock volatility.

There are different focuses within Convertible Arbitrage strategies with respect to moneyness and credit quality of the convertible security. These differences induce various profiles with respect to credit, equity and interest rate risk. Equity risk is highest for at-the-money Convertible Arbitrage positions (they have the highest gamma), while in-the-money and out-of-the-money convertibles have lower gamma exposure, i.e. their delta hedges are less sensitive to changing equity prices. Note that this lower sensitivity to the stock price refers to the combination of the long convertible/short stock position (the convertible security by itself, of course, has highest equity risk when it is far in the money). Convertibles trading close to their bond floor (i.e. the option component is far out of the money) are most sensitive to changes in interest rates. Among these 'busted' convertibles, given an equal credit quality, the bonds trading above par are more interest rate sensitive than bonds trading below par (due to positive bond convexity). Convertibles trading at discounts below 65% of par value face significant credit risk in the form of high default probability (i.e. their 'bond floor falling through'). In this case it is unclear whether the strategy actually benefits from an increase in volatility, as mostly credit issues determine the value of the convertible security.

An important input for the determination of the option's fair value is the estimate for the underlying stock's volatility. Correspondingly, one of the key risk factors for Convertible Arbitrage strategies is *vega risk*, which denotes the risk that the volatility will decrease, rendering the option value of the convertible (conversion premium) lower. In addition, the strategy is long gamma, i.e. the delta of the long option position increases with a rising and decreases with a falling stock price. *Gamma risk* is not as significant as vega risk, but both risks are difficult to hedge, as maturity and strike price are in most cases not known. An incomplete delta hedge (e.g. after a move in the stock price) exposes the strategy to *delta risk*, i.e. being over- or under-hedged with respect to future moves in the stock price (*equity risk*). Related to this is the risk of an increase in the dividend of the stock sold short, which reduces the static returns and decreases the value of the option. It is finally very important to consider any callable features of the bond (i.e. the risk of the bond being called by the issuer) when evaluating the appropriate hedging strategy.

A long convertible bond position is (like any regular bond) a long duration and long convexity position. The bond price moves inversely with interest rates.

Therefore, Convertible Arbitrage strategies face *interest rate risk* or *duration risk* (plus negative convexity risk, if the bond is callable). With rising interest rates, the straight debt value (the 'bond floor') decreases. Although stock returns tend to be negatively correlated to interest rates, losses on the bond part are usually only partly offset by the short equity position held against it. Another partial hedge is given by the positive rho of long convertible position. The option value increases with rising interest rates. Many managers use interest rate derivatives such as interest rate Futures and options on interest rate Futures, interest rate swaps and high yield total return swaps to hedge against duration risk. Option adjusted spread (OAS) is a concept widely used in valuing bonds with embedded options.[6]

Convertible Arbitrage strategies are exposed to *corporate event risk*. While some corporate event risk is hedged through the combination of long convertible and short stock, particular events can still influence the overall position negatively, e.g. through a credit event or a merger transaction involving the company. Generally, stock takeovers often involve simultaneously a credit upgrade and a reduction in volatility, so it is difficult to say a priori whether they will help or hurt a given issue. Cash takeovers in contrast are generally punitive for convertible arbitrageurs, as the underlying goes from a highly volatile asset (equity) to cash (that by nature has no volatility). As for any non-G7 government bond, a long convertible bond position is subject to *credit risk*, i.e. the risk of credit downgrade, spread widening or straight default (bankruptcy). Changes in credit quality affect the security's bond floor. Part of the credit risk is hedged with the short equity position. Degrading credit quality of the bonds usually comes along with a decrease in the market value of the stock. This correlation is not always exact, however. With very sharp drops in the equity value of the issuing company, the value of the convertible bond becomes a pure function of the bond floor, which might behave differently than the stock (and can fall faster than the stock in some scenarios, indicating the presence of negative gamma/vega). The technology market downturn in 2000/2001 provides numerous examples of busted convertibles with degraded credit quality. Credit risk generally becomes most dominant for convertible securities trading below 65 to 70% of par value. Credit swaps and other credit derivatives can be used to 'strip out' the credit risk.

The market for convertible securities has its own valuation cycles driven by supply and demand for convertibles that are more or less independent from stock market valuations. The performance of Convertible Arbitrage strategies is largely uncorrelated to equity market directions in periods of average volatility. Due to the increasing option values, periods of higher volatility are usually favourable to the strategy. Extreme stock market volatility often gives rise to 'flight to quality' situations, however, in which convertible security prices fall rapidly, liquidity dries up and bid–ask spreads widen abnormally (as e.g. in the summer/fall 1998). This exposes Convertible Arbitrage strategies to *liquidity risk* through:

- Higher bid–ask spreads for the convertible bond.[7] Most convertible bonds are traded OTC with less regular price updates than exchange-traded instruments.

- 'Short squeezes', a situation where there is insufficient supply of stocks to deliver on the short position (the fact that the convertible can be converted into stock makes the loss from this marginally less pronounced; conversion to cover a short stock involves losing all conversion premium, which causes major losses on all converts except busted converts on good credits and deep-in-the-money issues with little or no call protection).

- Higher margin haircuts.

An important factor in a manager's 'edge' is the valuation model underlying the pricing of the convertible securities. But every valuation model is exposed to *model risk*, i.e. the risk that the model is mis-specified. Even a 'correct' model can lead to problems in the hands of a manager who blindly follows it, because models can, by their very nature, only capture parts of the market dynamics. Models should be combined with experience.

To the degree Convertible Arbitrage managers are dealing with foreign issues, their investments are exposed to *foreign exchange risk*, i.e. the risk of adverse moves in the bond's currency against the manager's home currency. FX risk can be hedged with Forwards, Futures and options. Other types of risks include *legal risks* and *regulatory risk*. Details of the convertible's prospectus can be important, e.g. the treatment of special dividends or the treatment of merger situations. As Convertible Arbitrage strategies involve stock shorting, the strategy is exposed to the specific risks of Short Selling (*shorting risk*) connected to the fact that the short seller has to borrow stock (e.g. short squeezes, execution risk). (These risks will be discussed in detail in the section about Short Selling strategies.)

Generally, markets with high and rising volatility combined with decreasing interest rates are the most favourable for Convertible Arbitrage strategies. In these circumstances being long volatility and long gamma pays off. In cases where the manager keeps a positive overall delta, rising equity markets produce better returns, while falling equity markets lead to losses. Generally, rising interest rates and decreasing volatility create a negative environment for the strategy. Extreme volatility combined with a flight to quality environment and a liquidity crisis can be very damaging for the strategy.

Relative Value – Fixed Income Arbitrage

The strategy

Fixed Income Arbitrage is a generic description for a variety of arbitrage strategies involving different fixed income instruments. The strategy generally seeks profits by exploiting pricing inefficiencies between related securities and their derivatives. Investment instruments include US government and agency debt, G-7 government debt, sovereign emerging market debt, corporate debt, municipal debt and mortage-backed securities. By investing in one or more securities and simultaneously taking an opposite position in another related instrument (e.g. T-bill versus Eurodollar), the Fixed Income Arbitrage manager neutralizes exposure to interest rate risk factors such as yield curve changes. These positions are referred to as 'spread positions'. Different types of Fixed Income Arbitrage trades are yield curve trades (spread positions including bonds with different maturities), corporate versus treasury yield spreads, municipal versus treasury yield spreads, cash versus Futures and on-the-run versus off-the-run bonds. The Fixed Income Arbitrage Universe also includes a variety of strategies involving Asset-Backed Securities (ABS). Managers differ quite substantially in terms of how and to what degree interest rate risks, credit risks, foreign exchange risks and inter-market spread risks are hedged. Some managers even take 'directional bets' with respect to yield curve or credit spread changes, others employ spread trades only.

Different forms of pure, i.e. market neutral, Fixed Income Arbitrage are as follows:

■ Arbitrage between similar bonds (e.g. long underpriced 7-year duration US T-bond and short overpriced 7.1 Y duration US T-bond). This often involves cheapest-to-deliver bonds underlying a Futures contract on the bond or on-the-run vs. off-the-run issues.

■ Butterflies (e.g. long cheap 7 year and 9 year, short expensive 8 year). Relative mispricings along the yield curve often occur due to high institutional demand for certain benchmark bonds. The strategy is also referred to as 'yield curve arbitrage'. Figure 3.3 displays an example of a profitable yield curve arbitrage situation.

■ Basis trading is an arbitrage between physical securities and their Futures (e.g. short overpriced US 10-year note Future, long underpriced US 10-year note). Bond Futures have a delivery option and a wild card option, which can lead to pricing inefficiencies and provides for arbitrage opportunities.

■ TED spread, i.e. spread between Treasury bill Futures and Eurodollar Futures (this can be seen as a credit spread trade: government debt versus AA rated inter-bank debt).

■ Arbitrage between on-the-run and off-the-run bonds (e.g. short the latest government issue of a 10-year note and long the second most recent issue).

Other, non-market neutral, strategies include the following:

■ Yield curve spread trading based on a forecast of the directional change of the yield curve. An example could be going long the short end of the curve (up to 3-year maturities) and going short the long end (i.e. 10–15 years) anticipating a steeper yield curve in the future.

■ Credit arbitrage or credit spread trading capturing a credit-pricing anomaly and profiting from yield curve differentials for papers with different (but generally closely related) credit qualities (e.g. short an AAA rated bond with a spread to T-bonds of 50bp and long an AA rated bond with a spread of 80bp). Sometimes a 'credit barbell' strategy is employed, a technique whereby managers assume credit risk in short and intermediate maturities and use safe government issues with long maturities.

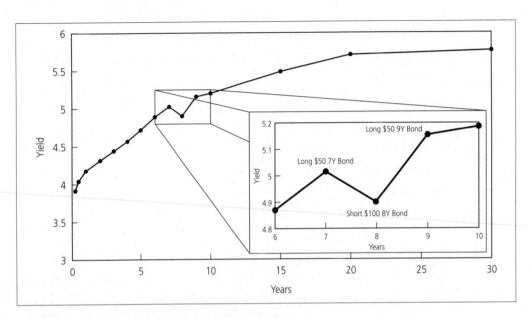

FIGURE 3.3 ■ Profitable Fixed Income Arbitrage situation

- Asset-Backed Securities (ABS), e.g. credit card receivables, auto loans or mortgage debt, offer enhanced returns for investors, which assume exposure to the embedded option features (prepayment, call option) and accept lower liquidity and possible credit risk of the ABS. Examples for ABS arbitrage strategies are:
  - Spread position ABS against T-bonds (e.g. long government secured Fannie Mae or Freddie mortgage-backed securities (MBS) and short US Treasuries with similar duration).
  - Spread position of MBS against collateral mortgage obligations (CMO). An example is selling certain tranches of a CMO and buying a plain pass-through MBS.
  - Arbitraging between different CMO classes. Two examples are: going long interest-only tranches (IOs) and shorting principle-only tranches (POs); shorting a Principal Amortization Class (PAC) tranche and going long a support tranche.

The hedging of prepayment risk is rather complex but nevertheless commonly employed within ABS Arbitrage strategies.

The spreads available for Arbitrage strategies in fixed income markets tend to be small. In order to earn attractive returns, most Fixed Income Arbitrage strategies must employ a high level of leverage, which may range from 10 to 25 (in some cases even higher) times the asset base and is created through borrowing, repo (repurchase) transactions or the use of options, Futures or swaps. A creditworthy investor with good dealing relationships might be able to transact $100 million notional value while putting up less than $1 million collateral. The simpler strategies (e.g. basis trades) are generally more highly leveraged than trades that are systematically exposed to more risk and specific risk factors (e.g. ABS strategies).

Sources of return

Pricing inefficiencies and arbitrage opportunities in fixed income markets occur for a variety of reasons including sudden market events, exogenous shocks to supply or demand, investors having maturity preferences or restrictions in certain fixed income investments (e.g. lower credit ratings), recent downgrade in credit ratings, complex options/callable features connected to a bond, deliverable characteristics for a Futures contract and complex cash flow properties. Most of these 'pricing anomalies' are related to certain risk premiums due to liquidity or credit risk. Fixed Income Arbitrage managers are often long and short equal amounts of securities with similar but not equal credit quality and liquidity. Thus the strategy earns a premium (the 'spread') for holding less liquid or lower credit quality instruments and hedges other risks (e.g. interest rates, duration) by selling short securities with higher liquidity and credit ratings. In an abstract sense, the strategy sells economic disaster insurance. Managers take positions that correspond to 'short put positions' on financial market turmoil.

The successful implementation of a Fixed Income Arbitrage strategy requires a very high degree of sophistication as prices of fixed income instruments depend on a large variety of factors with complex interactions: yield (spot, forward) curves, volatility curves, (credit) spread curves, expected cash flows, prepayment features (for ABS) and option characteristics (e.g. call, put and prepayments schedules). A 'complexity premium' can be determined as one source of the return of Fixed Income Arbitrage strategies, as they are paid to understand complex pricing relationships that others do not follow and take the risks of mismodelling this complexity.

Risk factors

Fixed Income Arbitrage strategies are 'short volatility' strategies. Conceptually, they sell financial crisis insurances and subject themselves to 'sudden event risk'. The risks of the strategy become apparent in market stress situations. For many years LTCM successfully executed a highly quantitative Fixed Income Arbitrage strategy, until it failed spectacularly in the weeks after the Russian default in August 1998. Fixed Income Arbitrage is exposed to *correlation breakdown risk*, which is related to the *event risk* of 'flight to quality'. Correlation breakdown is the sudden change of historical co-movement patterns between corresponding instruments which occurs due to changes in government policy, sovereign default (e.g. Russia in August 1998) or other economic shocks or dramatic events (e.g. the terrorist attacks on September 11, 2001), when interest rates move rapidly, credit spreads widen and liquidity dries up ('flight to quality' scenario). These 'flight to quality' events usually happen when many market participants want to liquidate positions at the same time ('everybody running for the door'). They occur relatively infrequently, but when they do occur the value of Fixed Income Arbitrage portfolios can drop significantly on a mark to market basis resulting in losses of several standard deviations (*tail risk*).

In volatile markets the strategy can easily become a captive of the extreme leverage, where a single margin call on a position can destroy an entire portfolio. Often fixed income arbitrageurs are short liquidity, i.e. they hold a long position in a comparably illiquid security and an offsetting short position in a relatively liquid asset, thereby earning a *'liquidity premium'*. Liquidity risk comes in two forms: the inability to meet margin calls (*funding risk*) and the (temporary) inability to unwind a position at normal bid/ask spreads (*liquidation risk*). Prime brokers may withdraw financing at particularly difficult times, which might necessitate the liquidation of the portfolio. This phenomenon should be taken into consideration when examining liquidity risk. Again, the failure of LTCM is an illustrative example of the liquidity problems a Fixed Income Arbitrage strategy faces in situations of market distress.

The strategy is exposed to *credit risk* (spread risk, risk of change in rating, default risk) of the underlying bonds, which is sometimes hedged with credit derivatives. Fixed Income Arbitrage managers often hedge interest rate risk, but some managers (e.g. yield curve arbitrage) execute a particular view on the future shape of the yield curve. In such an approach the manager is therefore exposed to *yield curve risk*, the risk of change in level, slope and curvature of the yield curve. Yield curve risk mainly stems from *duration risk* and *convexity risk*. Some strategies are contingent on low financing costs and are therefore affected by higher financing costs due to rising interest rates. Strategies that involve ABS are particularly exposed to *prepayment risk* (risk of not receiving cash flows at foreseen times). Prepayment risk is directly linked to the level and direction of interest rates and interest volatility.

Operational risks include model risk, execution risk and legal/tax risks. As many trading managers employ very complex quantitative models to find pricing discrepancies in different markets, they are exposed to *model risk*, i.e. the risk of mis-specification of the valuation method or risk models employed. Certain strategies take a large number of different positions simultaneously, which leads to *execution risk* (bad fills, slippage, clumsy order execution by the broker). Changes in tax laws or a financial or political change (*tax or legal risk*) can cause a stable relationship between two instruments to break up.

Fixed Income Arbitrage strategies perform well during times when there is a low likelihood of financial distress and in markets with constant or slowly changing volatility and correlation between different fixed income instruments. In times of severe financial disorder (e.g. sovereign default, rapid increase of interest rates, political change), the strategy is exposed to potentially large losses.

Relative Value – Equity Market Neutral
The strategy

Equity Market Neutral strategies usually involve being simultaneously long and short matched stock positions taking advantage of relatively underpriced and overpriced stocks. The strategy strives to generate positive returns in both bull and bear markets by selecting a large number of long and short positions with a total portfolio net exposure of zero, which can be established in terms of size ($ neutral), beta (beta neutral), country (country neutral), currency (currency neutral), industry (sector neutral), market capitalization (size neutral), style (value/growth stock neutral) or a combination thereof. An interesting feature of Equity Market Neutral strategies is the doubling of alpha. The manager targets returns on the long side as well as on the short side. The strategy sector is seen as 'alpha generator' par excellence. Obviously, however, there is a double amount of risk involved. Equity Market Neutral strategies can be classified into Statistical Arbitrage trading and Neutral Long/Short Equity (also called 'Fundamental Arbitrage'). Statistical Arbitrage usually involves model-based short-term trading, while Neutral Long/Short Equity strategies have longer holding periods, realizing profit when inefficiencies disappear and prices return to 'fair value'. A rather straightforward Arbitrage opportunity an Equity Market Neutral manager would exploit is a situation where a company's stock is traded with different prices on two exchanges.

Statistical Arbitrage strategies utilize quantitative and technical analysis to detect profit opportunities in under- and overvalued stocks of related companies, often operating in the same sector. Normally, a particular type of arbitrage opportunity is hypothesized, formalized into a set of trading rules and then back-tested with historical data. This way the manager expects to identify a persistent and statistically significant scheme to detect profit opportunities. Critics refer to this strategy as 'black box investing', as characteristics of the model are often not made transparent to investors. One example is 'mean reversion' of price differences between two companies. This describes the tendency of the price difference of two stocks to revert to some 'normal' level after they have developed apart from each other, often following an extreme move by one or both stocks. Figure 3.4 gives a graphical illustration of the corresponding 'buy the dips, sell the rally' strategy: the price difference of two stocks is expected to develop around a certain mean.

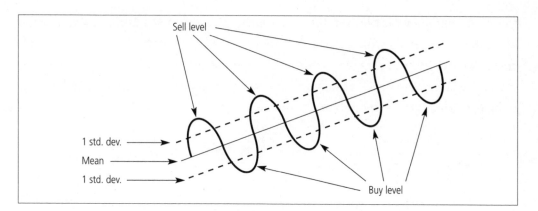

FIGURE 3.4 ■ Equity Market Neutral: buy low, sell high

There are generally three steps in Statistical Arbitrage strategies: initial screening and ranking, stock specific selection and portfolio construction. Technical models are used to rank a universe of stocks according to return expectations and risk in order to determine attractive long positions in undervalued stocks and short positions in overvalued stocks, thereby neutralizing the exposure to general market risk. The underlying quantitative models are often linear multi-factor models that result from a regression analysis on past data and establish a predicting formula linking the chosen factors to subsequent stock returns. The trading decisions usually result from relative ranking systems. For the portfolio construction, many managers utilize sophisticated computer algorithms.[8] Powerful optimizers are commercially available (e.g. by BARRA), while some managers construct their own proprietary tool set. Trading for a Statistical Arbitrage strategy is often short-term oriented and portfolio turnover is typically high. Often, significant leverage is used to enhance returns.

The neutral Long/Short Equity strategy mainly consists of building portfolios of long positions in certain industries' strongest companies and short positions in those companies that show signs of weakness. Analysis here is mostly of a fundamental nature and less quantitative than Statistical Arbitrage strategies. Some managers use technical and price momentum indicators including moving averages, relative strength and trading volumes as supporting decision tools. Fundamental factors used in the analysis include earnings ratios (price/earnings, price/book value, price/cash flow), discounted cash flows, return on equity, operating margins, earnings growth and other performance indicators. Portfolio turnover is comparably low and, typically, modest levels leverage is employed. The size of the universe the individual stocks are selected from is usually more limited, as more discretionary analysis has to be performed on the individual companies.

EXAMPLE

Consider the following pair trade: Based on a valuation model, Company A in an industry sector is determined to have a fair value of $50 a share, while it is trading at $48 at the moment and is expected to pay $1.32 dividend next quarter. Company B, in the same sector with similar distribution channels, suppliers and financial performance, is determined to have a fair value of $60 a share but trades at $63 and is expected to pay $1.70 within the next three months. The manager buys 13,125 shares of A for $48 and sells short 10,000 shares of Company B for $63 (the short sale might require additional margin which is included under financing costs). Three months later he reverses the trade paying and receiving fair values.

Today

Buy Company A	(630,000)	(13,125*48)
Sell Company B	630,000	(10,000*63)
Transaction costs	(1,200)	

Three months later

Sell Company A	656,250	(13,125*50)
Sell Company B	(600,000)	(10,000*60)
Bank A dividend (long)	17,325	(13,125*1.32)
Bank B dividend (short)	(17,000)	(10,000*1.7)
Financing costs	(4,725) (margin requirements for short: 50%	
	of 630,000 at 6% annualized rate)	

Transaction costs   (1,200)

$ 49,450

Annualized return is $$\frac{\$\ 49,450}{\$\ 630,000} \times \frac{365}{90} = 31.83\%$$

Sources of return

Equity Market Neutral managers employ their skill to detect market inefficiencies. The basic assumption is that anomalies in relative stock valuations may occur in the short term but, in the long term, these anomalies correct themselves as the market processes information. As Equity Market Neutral strategies often employ complex models to detect pricing inefficiencies, it can be argued that they earn a 'complexity premium'. This is particularly true for Statistical Arbitrage strategies, less so for Long/Short Equity Market Neutral ('Fundamental Arbitrage') strategies. The inefficiency is determined as the difference between market price and a theoretical 'fair value' price determined by a model. Good models earn consistent returns as long as others cannot replicate them in the market. However, the strategy bears the risk of using inappropriate or incorrect models or the markets moving further against 'fair value' (as seen with internet company valuations in 1999 and early 2000).

According to the CAPM, specific (or idiosyncratic) risk is not rewarded by extra return. The generation of alpha by Equity Market Neutral managers appears to be a contradiction to the efficient market hypothesis. It has indeed been shown by several studies that the semi-strong form of the EMH must at least partially be reconsidered.[9] Studies of market anomalies focusing on firm size (smaller companies outperforming larger ones), book to market value (investing in companies with high book to price value yields significantly higher returns than those given by the CAPM), and price to earnings ratios (low P/E ratio companies tend to outperform companies with high P/E values) have called the EMH into question.[10] However, an interesting argument raised by Fama and French is that investors following investment strategies based on these statistical effects, e.g. a value versus growth strategy or a focus on small to mid-cap companies, earn risk premiums related to particular risks not covered by the CAPM rather than contradicting the EMH.[11] Examples of these additional risks are small firm risk, recession risk and company leverage risk. Small firms have a higher probability of bankruptcy. They also tend to be followed by fewer analysts which causes the reliability of information to be lower and the stock to be less liquid. Low book to value stocks tend to be cyclical, i.e. they are particularly hurt by a recession. Rather than saying that a strategy provides a positive alpha one might include additional risk factors in the pricing models and note that Equity Market Neutral strategies' returns result at least partially from exposure to these risks.

Risk factors

Statistical Arbitrage strategies are 'short volatility strategies' and can, in some sense, be seen as the 'equity market comparable' to Fixed Income Arbitrage strategies. With the help of statistical models managers detect relative mispricings in different stocks, which in 'normal' periods should align themselves to fair value. The event risk of the strategy is similar to a 'short option position', which makes money in most circumstances, but in rare cases takes a significant hit (some Equity Market Neutral manager actually do write options). This happens when simultaneous event and volatility shocks lead to extreme deviations from fair value models. This risk is referred to as *tail risk*.

Many Neutral Long/Short Equity strategies take particular equity pair positions hoping that the market value of the mispriced securities moves back to fair value levels based on fundamental analysis. Ultimately, the success of Equity Market Neutral strategies comes down to stock selection and the principal risk factor of the strategy is *specific stock risk* or *sector risk*. Stock/sector risk includes *event risk* and any risk that affects the value of a company or sector in an unforeseen way, e.g. a surprise announcement such as earnings revision, merger or changes of management.

Equity Market Neutral strategies aim to generate returns which are statistically uncorrelated to the overall equity market and therefore usually insulate their portfolios from market risk factors such as beta, sector, country, style, size and sometimes even interest rates and commodity prices. Most managers do not hedge against all these risk factors and are therefore exposed to *residual risk*. Even if the manager targets neutrality against market risk, this does not mean that the strategy bears no risk related to the broad market. The strategy sector is generally exposed to *volatility risk*. Extreme volatility can lead to significant losses. Most dangerous for the strategy is non-reverting volatility.

Model risk is the risk that valuation methods used by the manager are inappropriate for the basket of stocks traded. Changes in market structure, e.g. the emergence of new industries such as the internet, can expose the strategy to the risk that certain valuation paradigms become inapplicable. In the late 1990s the market value of internet stocks exceeded the outcome of most model calculations and looked largely overpriced. Managers who shorted these stocks based on their valuation models suffered huge losses. The use of multi-factor models, which are based on regressions on past data, introduces the risk of 'over-fitting'. Over-fitted models have high predictive value on past data but little forecasting ability for future returns. Managers have to be in a constant process of model review and must refine models dynamically in order to keep them accurate.

Equity Market Neutral strategies, in particular Statistical Arbitrage strategies, usually make hundreds of complex offsetting trades and have a wide web of positions in many different instruments open at any moment. Thus, the strategy bears *operational risk* in the form of *execution risk* (slippage, clumsy order execution by the broker). A large number of positions have to be monitored and many trades executed. This normally happens either through humans or automatically through computer systems, both of which are prone to errors. As Equity Market Neutral strategies involve short selling of stock, the strategy is exposed to the specific risks of Short Selling (*short risk*) connected to the fact that the short seller has to borrow stock (e.g. short squeezes, execution risk). These risks will be discussed in detail in the section about Short Selling strategies.

Markets with extended trends and valuations moving out of line with historical patterns create an environment where Equity Market Neutral strategies face problems. Periods where for an extended period of time valuations are extreme render the valuation models inappropriate and therefore cause problems to the strategy. Inversely, volatile and choppy markets with erratic price moves but generally showing 'normal' valuation levels create positive environments for Equity Market Neutral strategies.

Event Driven – Risk Arbitrage

The strategy

Risk Arbitrage (also called Merger Arbitrage) involves investing in securities of companies which are the subject of some form of extraordinary corporate transaction, such as acquisition or merger proposals, exchange offers, cash tender offers and leveraged buyouts. A merger generally involves the exchange of securities for cash, other securities or a combination of cash and other securities. Typically, Risk Arbitrage managers purchase the stock of a company being acquired or merging with another company and, if feasible, sell short the stock of the acquiring company. Tender offers for a merger are usually made at a significant premium to the pre-announcement share price. During the negotiations of a merger the target company's stock typically trades at a discount to the announced value of the merger transaction, as there remains a residual risk that the merger will fail and the stock price will drop back to the original pre-announcement level. Figure 3.5 illustrates the evolution of the two companies' stock prices in a successful merger situation. A profit is derived on realizing the differential (the 'spread') between the price paid on entering the positions and the value ultimately received when the deal is consummated. In mergers and acquisitions and other corporate transactions the market is generally not completely information efficient. As information is very specific and difficult to obtain (and correspondingly high in value), the situations offer opportunities to investors knowledgeable about the specific features of a deal. The experienced manager usually translates the spread into an annualized return, estimates the probability that the deal will be completed and then gauges the risks of the particular deal against its return. He invests in deals that offer sufficient compensation for the estimated risk of the transaction failing.

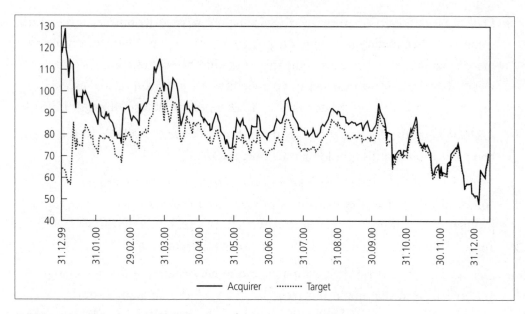

FIGURE 3.5 ■ Spread convergence in successful merger deals (illustration)

A successful Risk Arbitrage strategy relies strongly on fundamental research of the involved companies and the issues surrounding the deal, such as legal and regulatory (e.g. anti-trust) matters. The deals are often highly complex and the task of the manager is more related to risk management than to stock picking.[12] Important elements of the analysis include the following:

■ *Analysis of publicly available information* on the companies involved in the transaction. This includes the competitive environment in which they operate, their financial position, assessment of the quality of management and anti-trust concerns.

■ *Assessment of the buyer's motivation for the merger* or acquisition as well as the impact of the contemplated transaction on his reputation, competitive position and financial performance. A review of the buyer's past acquisition history might provide interesting insights.

- *Evaluation of potential information* regarding business developments at the target company which might undermine the proposed transaction. Many uncompleted mergers fail because the target company's situation deteriorates unexpectedly. Detailed analysis of the business and competitive environment as well as the financial situation of the target company is essential for an assessment of this risk.

- *Assessment of the efficiency of any anti-takeover devices* available to the target company (poison pills, golden parachutes etc.).

- *Assessment of the strategic rationale of the transaction.* The merging companies should realize valuable strategic opportunities, such as geographic, product or distribution expansion, new technological integration or applications, significant cost savings or other synergies.

- *Financial analysis* (cash flow estimates, ratio analysis etc.) *of the post-merger outlooks* (pro-forma financial forecasts). This includes an analysis of the amount of funding available for the merger and in what form funding is available (e.g. stock, cash, LBO). Detailed financial analysis provides important insights for assessing the probability that the merger will be completed.

- *Consideration of the background of the merger.* The operational and financial history of the companies have to be examined. The manager should know about the merger history of the involved companies, who initiated merger talks and whether there have been discussions about a merger with other companies before. It is also important to examine whether key management interests have been addressed. Some mergers fail because of disagreement over the future roles of senior management (often CEOs).

- *Review of valuation parameters.* The valuation analysis should determine whether the price being paid for the target company is excessive relative to the buyer's business strategy, the market valuation of comparable companies in the particular industry and the target company's competitive position and financial performance.

- *Calculation of the spread on the deal.* The spread is the difference between the price offered for the acquired company and the current market price. Based on the spread, the manager calculates the return expected on closure of the deal.

■ *Examination of merger conditions.* The terms of the transaction can contain conditions which may significantly impact the likelihood of the transaction completing and which therefore must be carefully assessed. Such conditions may include walk-away clauses, price provisions related to the acquirer's stock, financing contingencies, earnings tests, pending completion of due diligence, minimum shares to vote in favour of the merger, revenue or profit hurdles or possible debt covenants.

■ *Estimate of the likelihood of regulatory interference with the deal* and the likely outcome of such. The constant monitoring of applications for regulatory clearances is vital for Risk Arbitrage strategies. Different regulatory agencies have to be considered (from the perspective of a US merger): Federal Trade Commission (FTC)/Justice Department, SEC (must approve merger proxies), individual states, specific industry (banks: Federal Reserve, utilities: Federal Energy Regulatory Commission, communication: Federal Communications Commission) and foreign regulatory agencies (e.g. EU, specific countries).

All this information is necessary for making an informed assessment of the risk of a proposed transaction failing. A transaction can fail for a wide range of reasons due to anything from failure to achieve the required shareholder approval, to negative earnings news from the target company and a significant drop in the stock price of the acquiring company. Along with the assessment of the probability of a transaction failing, one must estimate the financial impact of such an event. The stock price before the deal announcement can serve as a general guide as to where stock prices might go in case the deal does not go through. However, in many cases applying a discount to the target company's pre-announcement stock price is appropriate. The failure of a merger is often caused by fundamental issues (e.g. earning revisions of target company) and the market will probably value the target company lower than before.

Information sources for this last analysis are stock market valuation, trade data sources, past enforcement policies of justice department (DOJ), Federal Trade Commission (FTC) and anti-trust agencies, discussions with management, investment bankers and legal advisors, court hearings and press publications.

Risk Arbitrage managers differ in the amount of deal risk they are willing to take as well as the level of leverage and diversification employed. Most managers only invest in announced transactions and some even invest only in deals that are sufficiently progressed towards completion. Others enter in positions with higher deal risk (and therefore wider spreads) and a few base their investment decisions on rumours or speculation about possible transactions. Managers also distinguish themselves with respect to sectors and geographical location.

The two basic types of merger offers are a cash tender offer, where a fixed amount of cash is offered for the acquired company's stock, and a stock swap, where stock of the acquiring company are being offered at a fixed ratio in exchange for the stock of the acquired company. More complex features of a merger transaction are cases in which the exchange ratio is based on the price of the acquiring company's stock when the deal is closed or those in which the target firm can call off the merger if the acquirer's stock falls below a certain value. In these situations, the manager has to adjust its hedges constantly and unwind positions if the price falls below the floor value. The chosen merger procedure can affect the balance sheet of the combined company drastically. While cash offers have to be accounted for by the 'purchase method' in the USA, in mergers processed through an exchange of stock, the companies can under some circumstances employ the 'pooling method'.[13]

EXAMPLES

The following two examples illustrate the way returns can be achieved for a stock swap transaction and a cash tender offers.[14]

Stock swap
Assume Bank A and Bank B announce a merger structured as a stock swap in which each holder of one share of Bank B is entitled to receive 0.84 shares of Bank A. The merger is to be completed in 90 days. Bank A and Bank B pay dividends of 39 cents and 37 cents respectively during this period. Assume a manager buys 10,000 shares of Bank B at 28½ per share for a total cost of $285,000 and sells short 8,400 shares of Bank A at 35½

per share for a total credit of $298,200. Because of the leverage (2:1), the manager will be required to post 50% of the value of the long position ($142,500) and 50% of the value of the short position ($149,100) with the prime broker, thus resulting in a total cash outlay of $291,600. Assume the manager finances the balance of the long position ($142,500) at an annualized rate of $6^{3}/4$ % for 90 days for a total cost of ($2,371.75). Further assume that the manager receives a short stock rebate of 5.1% annualized on $298,200 for the period of 90 days, which is $3,749.97 and that the manager's transaction costs equal ($184) or one cent per share. The net profit on this transaction upon completion of the merger is as follows:

Bank A / Bank B spread	$ 13,200.00
Transaction costs	(184.00)
Bank A dividend (short)	(3,276.00)
Bank B dividend (long)	3,700.00
Financing costs	(2,371.75)
Short stock rebate	3,749.97
Profit	$ 14,818.22

Annualized return is

$$\frac{\$ 14,818.22}{\$ 291,600.00} \times \frac{365}{90} = 20.61\%$$

Cash tender offer

Assume X Corp. receives a $17.50 cash tender offer from Y Corp. on February 1 and that the tender offer expires on March 5 . Further assume that the price of X Corp. was 17.25 on February 1 and that the manager purchases 500,000 shares at that price. The cash outlay for a manager will be 50% (leverage 2:1) of the purchase price of the stock ($4,312,500). Assume the manager can finance the remaining balance of $4,312,500 for 34 days at a rate of $6^{3}/4\%$ per annum for a cost of $27,115.58 and that the manager's transaction cost is one cent per share ($5,000).

The net profit therefore is:

Net cash proceeds	$ 125,000.00
Financing costs	(27,115.58)
Transaction costs	(5,000.00)
Profit	$ 92,884.42

Annualized return is
$$\frac{\$\,92{,}884.42}{\$\,4{,}312{,}500} \times \frac{365\ \text{days}}{34\ \text{days}} = 23.12\%$$

Sources of return

The inherent return of Risk Arbitrage strategies is the risk premium for taking exposure in deals with uncertain closing. This is referred to as the 'deal risk premium'. The Merger Arbitrage manager assumes the risk that the deal could fail in which case the manager assumes large losses. The strategy is thus similar to a short option on the close of the deal.

Risk factors

The downside risk of a Risk Arbitrage position is large compared to the expected return if the merger succeeds. The premium paid by the acquirer in a merger deal, which is the difference between the acquired company's market price right before the merger announcement and the offer made by the acquirer, is usually large compared to the remaining spread between offer price and market price after the announcement of the deal. The risk profile of a typical Risk Arbitrage position is thus comparable to a short position in an option. The manager receives a (more or less predetermined) risk premium for entering the position in return for accepting the risk of significant losses if the merger fails.

Risk Arbitrage positions are a 'bet on the merger completion'. The strategy's principal risk factor is thus *deal risk*. Deal risk includes everything that affects the completion of the merger or the timing of it, e.g. the risk of the acquirer getting out of the deal, the risk of lack of shareholder support, or the risk of (federal or state) regulators not approving the deal. These risks are influenced by a number of different factors:

■ *Financial position of the acquirer*. Certain market factors (interest rates rise, stock market downturn) can worsen the financial status of the acquirer leaving him unable to finance and complete the transaction.

■ *Earnings*. A sudden decline in the target's earnings may make a deal fail. Different market factors can cause earnings to deteriorate.

■ *Size of the premium*. The higher the premium (difference between offer price and market price before the merger announcement) paid in the transaction the higher the downside risk.

■ *Market sentiment*. A general downturn in broad equity markets can increase insecurity about mergers going through.

■ *Regulatory concerns*. Regulators influence the deal uncertainty spreads as they affect directly the likelihood of deal completion. An example of regulatory disapproval causing a deal to fail is the General Electric/Honeywell merger in June 2001. When the European Commission announced that it was unwilling to approve the merger for anti-trust reasons, the spread widened from 5 to 36% within two days (see Figure 3.6).

■ *Consideration*. The form of the proposed transaction (stock swap, cash or any combination) can influence the deal probability.

■ *Time to completion*. A delay in the completion of the deal can significantly reduce the expected return.

Cash deals are not completely market neutral, because the manager cannot hedge market risk with short position in the acquirer's stock. In case the merger is not completed the position is additionally exposed to the risk of market declines. Other risk factors of the strategy are *liquidity risk* and *deal flow risk*. Lack of sufficient market depth and liquidity can become a problem for small cap positions. The returns of Risk Arbitrage managers depend on the number and the 'quality' of merger transactions. In times when merger activity is high (as in 1999) Merger

Arbitrage is very profitable compared to environments where deal flow is declining and deal quality deteriorating (as in early 2001). The returns earned by Risk Arbitrage strategies are not independent of general equity valuation levels. Deal flow and quality are usually higher in equity bull markets. Companies are more likely to initiate mergers in times of rising equity markets, when the economic outlook provides the necessary comfort and high stock prices provide ready currency for mergers. Sharp equity declines can widen spreads and increase deal risk. Consequently, Risk Arbitrage strategies face *market risk* in forms of extreme volatility and deteriorating deal flow. The strategy is also exposed to *interest rate risk*, as significant and unexpected rises in interest rate increase borrowing costs and make it more difficult for the acquirer to finance the deal. Furthermore, higher interest rates might negatively affect the acquired company's earnings.

As Merger Arbitrage strategies involve short selling of stock, the strategy is exposed to the specific risks of Short Selling (*shorting risk*) connected to the fact that the short seller has to borrow stock (e.g. short squeezes, risk of dividend increase, execution risk). These risks will be discussed in detail in the section on

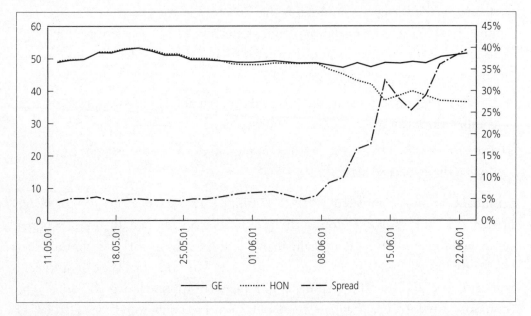

FIGURE 3.6 ■ Price and spread development for the GE–Honeywell deal (rejected by the European Commission on 15 June 2001)

Short Selling. *Operational risk* factors include unfavourable trade executions (bad fills, slippage, clumsy order execution by the broker) and wrong information (this includes *fraud risk* due to manipulated financial statements).

Highly volatile markets combined with increasing interest rates create an environment where Risk Arbitrage strategies are the most vulnerable. Insecurity about earnings, stock prices and future economic outlook usually decrease the number of announced deals dramatically and mergers are more likely to break up. An example for an unfavourable period for Risk Arbitrage strategies was the first half of 2001, when Risk Arbitrage managers suffered significant losses. Generally, periods of falling interest rates and normal to low market volatility are positive for the strategy. It is interesting to note that positive and negative market environments for Risk Arbitrage strategies are somewhat the opposite to those for Convertible Arbitrage strategies. A combination of these two strategies provides good diversification benefits in a multi-strategy AIS portfolio.

Event Driven – Distressed Securities

The strategy

Distressed Security strategies invest in or sell short securities of companies that have been or are expected to be affected by financial difficulties. 'Distress' can be caused by any number of the following: liquidity problems; excess debt; operational or strategic shortcomings; changes in the competitive marketplace; legal or regulatory difficulties. Distressed Securities managers invest in bank debt, bonds, subordinated debt, trade claims, letters of credit, common stock, preferred stock or warrants. There may also be opportunities to buy specific assets being spun off by distressed companies that need to raise cash.

While the level of interest in Distressed Securities has increased over the years, the market remains relatively illiquid. Many private and institutional investors are not willing to hold Distressed Securities in their books. For years distressed investing was seen as a 'dirty' business because investors attempt to profit from other's misfortune. Now, however, distressed or 'vulture' investors have begun to lose their 'bad guy' image, as many institutions have come see the benefits of an active secondary market for distressed debt. This has increased the overall amount of debt available for purchase and improved liquidity in primary markets.

Investing in Distressed Securities requires specialist expertise and extensive pre-investment analysis in order to allow for an accurate assessment of the impact of restructuring negotiations and/or bankruptcy proceedings on the value of a company and its underlying securities.

Managers generally take a core position in a distressed company's securities and hold it throughout the restructuring or bankruptcy process. The industry distinguishes between managers who participate actively in creditor committees and assist the recovery or reorganization process and 'passive managers' who buy and hold Distressed Securities until they appreciate to the desired level. Some strategies are particularly focused on short-term trading in anticipation of specific events, such as the outcome of a court rule or important negotiations. Managers may use some leverage, but generally the level of leverage is fairly low. Another form of a Distressed Securities strategy is 'Capital Structure Arbitrage', where the manager purchases undervalued securities and sells overpriced securities of the same firm, e.g. long mezzanine debt and short common stock. Fund managers may run a market hedge using S&P put options or put options spreads. Distressed managers can benefit substantially from creative financial engineering.

Examples of investment opportunities in distressed investments include the following:

- *Anticipated Restructuring*. A corporate restructuring event caused by financial problems is pending. This can be the announcement of a restructuring plan, a change in management or the board, a refinancing or even a merger/acquisition. Often the restructuring event will lead to a significant change in the management of assets and allocation of capital. Careful analysis may identify value post-restructuring that is not yet reflected in the price of the company's securities.

- *Chapter 11 Reorganizations*. The final stages of bankruptcy reorganizations may create attractive investment opportunities. The securities of companies undergoing Chapter 11 Reorganizations are often underfollowed by Wall Street analysts and may trade at depressed valuations versus the firm's fundamental value.

▪ *Legal/Regulatory Overhang*. Legal or regulatory issues which are not fully understood may depress the valuation of the securities to values below their fundamental fair value.

▪ *Corporate Restructurings/Spin-offs*. An investor may provide buyout capital in the form of equity or debt for privatizations (leveraged buyouts from management), spin-offs, acquisitions or takeovers. Significant changes in the management of assets and allocation of capital can amplify and accelerate positive financial trends.

EXAMPLE

Company ABC is unable to meet its debt amortization and is negotiating a debt restructuring with a consortium of banks. The long-term debt of ABC with an 11% annually paid coupon is trading at 55% of par value due to the firm's liquidity problems and fear of bankruptcy. The manager buys the company's debt for 55% of par value after determining that the company is likely to reach an agreement with its banks to stretch out debt repayments and therefore avoid bankruptcy, and that the longer term prospects of the firm are good. After 12 months, due to a restructuring of the firm's debt and first signs of financial recovery, the long-term debt can be sold for 70% of par value and the firm is able to meet interest payments on its debt. The annualized return of the investment (capital gain of 27.3% plus interest income of 20%) equals 47.3%.

Sources of return

Distressed Securities strategies earn a risk premium for being exposed to credit and other company specific event risks. Further, the investment is usually locked in for an extended period of time, as the market for the investment is likely to be very limited. This lack of liquidity corresponds to a liquidity premium earned by the investor. Returns of Distressed Securities strategies strongly depend on the skill and experience of the manager. There are many un- or under-researched and attractive investment opportunities, as there are generally very few analysts looking at such situations. Managers have thus the opportunity to capitalize on restricted availability of information and other market inefficiencies.

Risk factors

Investments in Distressed Securities strategies are generally very illiquid. Extended redemption periods are the norm for Distressed Securities investments and most managers seek a long-term commitment of the investors' capital. Bankruptcy proceedings are, by nature, very time consuming, as are restructuring negotiations outside bankruptcy, and their outcome is very uncertain. Distressed Securities investments have characteristics that are similar to private equity investments.

The principal risk of Distressed Securities is *corporate and situation-specific risk*. The strategy requires correct valuation of the underlying business and its individual securities using a 'bottom up' analysis. The release of adverse information or the occurrence of certain events can be extremely damaging to the value of the investment (*event risk*). Any investment in distressed debt involves significant *credit risk* in the form of bankruptcy risk.

Investments in Distressed Securities bear high *liquidity risk*. Often there is no regular market for the security, and the positions are extremely difficult to value (*mark to market risk*). As with private equity investments, the investor has to commit invested capital for a longer period of time and might suffer significant losses if he redeems prematurely. The termination date of the investment is not known in advance (*timing risk*). Further, for distressed bank debt, the manager is exposed to *settlement risk*, as the trade documentation process can be rather complex and takes a significant amount of time.

Distressed Security strategies are heavily exposed to *legal risks*. Legal questions become particularly important once insolvency procedures or litigation are initiated. Chapter 11 of the US bankruptcy law provides relief from creditor claims for companies in financial distress in order to allow for an orderly restructuring process. The objective is to save distressed companies from liquidation. In Europe and most other countries, however, bankruptcy laws are less debtor friendly, so the chances of a company surviving as a going concern are reduced. Important issues in the restructuring process are debt-restructuring practices and laws, ranking of creditor claims (particularly in relationship with employee and tax claims), disclosure policies, voting rights of creditors, debt terms and the treatment of secured claims. Further, distressed companies may face lawsuits or legal threats that could significantly impact the company's financial position. The 'workout' process requires legal expertise and the navigation of legal pitfalls.

Besides bearing large exposure to firm-specific risks, Distressed Security strategies are also exposed to general *market risk* factors. Especially in environments of falling equity markets and rising interest rates, the performance of distressed securities investment is highly correlated to the broader market. A generally negative equity market perception worsens the outlook for distressed companies significantly and rising interest rates make it more difficult for companies to refinance themselves. Furthermore, long duration debt positions are exposed to *duration* or *interest rate risk*. For non-publicly traded instruments such as bank debt and trade claims, the investor is exposed to *settlement risk* as trades are complex to document and can take months to settle. Besides *foreign currency risk* as part of the operational risk of the company, the investor faces foreign exchange risk if the company goes bankrupt and its claims are all converted into the applicable currency in the jurisdiction of the bankruptcy.

A market environment favourable to Distressed Securities strategies is generally characterized by economic growth, rising equity prices and low interest rates. The strategy is very vulnerable in environments of rapidly falling equity markets and deteriorating economic conditions. An example was the second half of 2000/first quarter of 2001, when Distressed Securities strategies had significant losses.

Event Driven – Convertible Debenture Arbitrage ('Regulation D')

The strategy

Convertible Debenture Arbitrage (or 'Reg D') strategies involve investing in publicly listed companies of micro and small capitalization through privately structured investments. The investment is usually negotiated directly with the company and takes the form of stocks, convertibles or other derivatives (options, warrants) in return for an injection of capital. Investments are usually structured in the form of privately placed unregistered high coupon convertible securities or debentures with maturities ranging from 18 to 60 months which can, upon registration with the SEC, partially (e.g. 1/18th every month in case of an 18-month debenture) or entirely be converted into ordinary shares of the issuer. Conversion usually happens at a predefined discounted price. Investments are made pursuant to an exemption from registration as provided by Regulation D of the US SEC Act of 1933. Normally after 75 to 90 days, the SEC declares the registration of the convertible securities effective. The Regulation D manager can then sell the fully tradable and registered shares in the public markets and realize the spread between the market price and the discounted price of the stock he converts into (usually about 15–20%) as a return. The Convertible Debenture Arbitrage strategy can be seen as Convertible Arbitrage with privately structured debentures.

Unlike standard convertible bonds or preferred equity, the exercise price can be floating at a predefined discount or subject to a look-back provision. Convertible debentures can also have a fixed price and it sometimes is at the investor's discretion to choose the fixed or floating price on conversion. A floating price has the effect of insulating the investor from a decline in the price of the underlying stock. Investments are therefore fully price hedged. In some cases the manager also receives warrants on top of the debenture.

The process of Regulation D investments requires extensive bottom up analytical work. Pre-investment due diligence usually consists of:

1 thorough analysis of the firm's financial position (earnings, cash flow, assets and liabilities, ratio analysis)

2 examination of the company's stock liquidity (volume, volatility, market capitalization, number of market makers, diversity of shareholder, short interest)

3 assessment of the business and the quality management (interviewing management, examination of competitive environment, firm's strategy, product and market structure, country and sector analysis).

On the sale of the convertible security to the investors, the company begins the process of filing for registration of the privately placed shares, typically an S-3. Pursuant to the terms of the offering negotiated between the company and the investor, there is a time period by which the company must submit the registration to the SEC and cause it to be declared effective (i.e. 'the common shares are registered and freely tradable'). The term is generally between 60 and 120 days. The debenture agreement can be structured such that, if the registration is delayed beyond a certain time, the company has to pay a penalty to the investor. On approval of the registration, the investors may sell the newly registered common stock at any time after a specified holding period. The holding period is negotiated such that the stock is not immediately 'dumped' on the market, but rather sold in an orderly fashion. As a general rule, once the shares are registered and converted, it will take a month or more to sell the shares in the open market. Experience shows that most Regulation D transactions, all in all, take 18 months to five years from the day of closing until the conversion and sale of all shares is completed.

The most critical decision to be made during the negotiation process is the price at which the investor will be able to convert his position into common stock. In this regard, the investors must decide whether to fix a 'price' of the stock (which is 'higher risk – higher reward'), or the less risky approach of protecting a fixed 'discount' to the market price.

EXAMPLE

Company ABC's stock currently sells for $10.00 per share and on average 130,000 shares are traded per day. The company negotiates with an investor (Hedge fund manager) for a private placement of a debenture convertible into its common stock. ABC and its investors agree to a 15% discount to the share price at the time of conversion with registration to be completed in 90 days. The share price is defined as the average of closing bids for the five days prior to conversion. On completion of registration the investors can exercise their conversion right and begin selling the shares in the open as described in the offering memorandum. In this example, assuming that the share price remains at $10 and the investment is $10 mio, the discounted price would be $8.50 and the number of shares the investor receives equals 1,176,470 shares ($10,000,000/$8.50). The investor trades out of the position and receives a total sale price (assumed to be $10 per share) of $11,765,000 or a non-annualized 17.65% profit. If the stock drops to $8.00 before the investor can convert his shares, under the agreement ABC would now have to issue enough additional shares at the new discounted price of $6.80, i.e. 1,470,588 shares. Alternatively, the investor could have chosen to 'lock in' the share price of $8.50 and assumed the price fluctuation risk. However, in most cases, managers choose the 'protected discount' structure as opposed to the 'protected price' alternative.

Sources of return

When public companies need to raise capital, e.g. in order to make an acquisition that has to close quickly, they have three alternatives:

1 debt issuance

2 secondary offerings

3 private equity placements pursuant to Regulation D.

Each of the first two alternatives has certain requirements which make access to the capital very difficult and time consuming and, in some instances, impossible. These encumbrances include limited borrowing capacity, high expenses in the case of a secondary offering and time constraints. These factors, along with other more subjective issues, cause many companies to pursue the third option, which allows smaller companies to raise equity capital more quickly, cheaply and conveniently.

Similar to the returns of Distressed Securities strategies, Convertible Debenture Arbitrage strategies' returns are mostly related to credit and liquidity premiums earned for taking positions with lower credit quality that cannot be easily liquidated. Large parts of the returns of the investments arise from smaller companies conceding an advantageous price to investors willing to hold an illiquid investment for a certain period (until registration with the SEC occurs). Manager skill and expertise in evaluating potential investment targets are essential for Convertible Debenture Arbitrage investments.

Risk factors

A Regulation D investment is a debenture from a company in need of capital whose debt is non-rated. The strategy faces a similar risk profile as private equity investments. The most significant risk factor of the strategy is *credit risk*, in the form of *default risk*, on the principal amount or on the coupon payments. A debenture with a floating conversion price provides some marginal protection from default risk (if the default comes after registration) through the possibility of converting into the company's equity. However, tradability and liquidity of the stock may be very low. In cases where the market capitalization of the company drops to levels close to where the entire company's equity is insufficient to cover the debenture, the conversion right no longer protects from the company's default. In some cases default risk is decreased by the issuance of a letter of credit from a bank for part of the debenture.

Important risk factors of the strategy are the *registration risk* and the related (*pre-registration*) *liquidity risk*. While the usual process of registration with the SEC takes about 90 to 120 days, significant delays in the process can occur if the company is not providing necessary information or is facing deteriorating financial conditions. The length of registration can then increase significantly with an uncertain outcome. Before registration with the SEC there is no market for investors to liquidate their position.

In many instances, the need to protect their investment during the registration or the 'non-conversion' period leads investors to hedge their investment through shorting the firm's stock. The credit risk related to the financial condition of the company might mandate these hedging activities. This can result in a dramatic reduction of the company's market price. The consequence is a dilution of the stock once the debenture is converted, i.e. the debenture will be converted to more stock. The industry refers to this as the 'death spiral' of Regulation D deals (and often refers to Regulation D deals themselves as 'death spiral convertibles').

Most Regulation D transactions involve companies with micro or small capitalization. The necessary trading volume equals a significant percentage of the firm's capitalization (especially after a significant stock price decline, when more shares have to be issued against the Convertible Debenture). Trading out of the converted stock can become rather difficult, despite an SEC registration. The strategy faces a great deal of (*post-registration*) *liquidity risk*.

Due to the private nature of the transaction, Convertible Debenture Arbitrage strategies are exposed to *legal risk* and also to *fraud risk*; for example, the company may misinform or use manipulated earnings statements.

Besides bearing large firm specific risks, the Convertible Debenture Arbitrage strategy is exposed to general *market risk* factors. The strategy is vulnerable in environments of rapidly declining equity markets, as falling stock prices increase the number of shares received from conversion which make liquidation of the position more difficult. The company itself might also face less favourable business conditions in such environments. The *duration risk* of the debenture depends on its time to maturity, but is usually rather low.

As for Distressed Securities strategies, a market environment that is favourable to Convertible Debenture Arbitrage strategies is generally characterized by rising equity prices and low interest rates. During the boom years of equity markets in the second half of the 1990s, Convertible Debenture Arbitrage strategies were among the most outstanding performers of all Hedge fund strategies. With falling equity prices in 2000/2001, however, Convertible Debenture Arbitrage strategies suffered significant losses.

Opportunistic – Global Macro

The strategy

Global Macro strategies are characterized by making (generally leveraged) bets on anticipated movements of equity, interest rates, foreign exchange rates and commodity prices. Global Macro managers employ a fundamental and/or systematic 'top down' approach and may invest in any market or instrument in order to profit from expected market moves. These moves may result from forecasted shifts in world economies, political developments or changes of global supply and demand for physical and financial resources. Managers typically earn returns by having access to better information or by their ability to analyze existing information more accurately than others.

Global Macro strategies assume that prices are determined by fundamental economic factors that affect the supply and demand of a financial asset. They consider investors to be rational in the long term and believe that prices will sooner or later converge to levels consistent with investor rationality as determined by fundamental economic factors. In the short run, however, prices can deviate substantially from their true economic equilibrium in which all available information is correctly and fully discounted. This occurs because information is not a free good. Investors must spend time and resources to acquire and properly interpret new data. New information is incorporated gradually rather than instantaneously into market prices. Furthermore, price volatility may cause investors to react emotionally in ways not consistent with a dispassionate analysis of economic factors. Finally, trade restriction (e.g. currency regimes) can prohibit prices from moving to their real economic value. The goal of Global Macro strategies is to identify long-term macroeconomic trends in times when prices deviate substantially from the price that corresponds to their true fair value. The Macro strategy does not necessarily try to make money from market inefficiencies, but rather by anticipating price changes (reversals) early.

Global Macro managers employ macroeconomic forecasting models, which can be divided into technical and fundamental models. Technical analysis predicts market returns by looking for trends and patterns in historical prices. Fundamental approaches use different micro- and macroeconomic indicators to predict expected returns. Often a combination of the two is used.

Global Macro managers usually have one of two backgrounds: Long/Short Equity or derivatives (mostly Futures) trading.[15] The first sort of manager operates in liquid equity markets, mostly large cap stocks in the USA, Asia and Europe. The second class of manager invests in liquid derivatives markets such as fixed income, foreign exchange and equity index Futures. Both use exchange-traded and over-the-counter derivatives to magnify returns. Some currency and Futures managers declare themselves Global Macro traders, as they trade based on a fundamental analysis of underlying economies. Currency and Futures managers are examined in the Futures strategy section that follows later in the chapter.

An example of a famous Global Macro trade was the short position on the British pound sterling against continental European currencies (mainly the Deutsche Mark) Global Macro managers held in 1992. Despite increasing pressure for a devaluation of the British pound, the British central bank and other European central banks continued to intervene in order to support the currency and keep it within the 3% boundaries defined by the European Monetary System. Eventually it became clear that the British currency had to be devalued. When the central banks decided to let the currency float freely, the currency dropped about 20% in value and pound short positions became extremely profitable. Soros' Quantum fund is said to have earned more than $1 billion in the course of the devaluation.[16]

Sources of return

Global Macro managers consider themselves acting in markets which are not completely efficient and claim to earn a return by exploiting temporary price anomalies. Their goal is to anticipate long-term macroeconomic trends in times when prices deviate substantially from the price that corresponds to their true fair value, which can happen for a variety of reasons (slow information flow, emotions, regulatory constraints). They try to anticipate the economic developments in the coming months and to exploit the predictability of economic cycles (it is disputed among economists, though, that there is such predictability). For most opportunistic strategies it is difficult to identify specific risk premiums earned. Global Macro managers move between a variety of different strategies and capitalize on mispricings and price moves depending on available opportunities. Their strategies rely heavily on the manager's skill, which is the most important source of returns generated, but also most difficult to assess properly.

Risk factors

Global Macro strategies involve leveraged directional bets on market moves. Managers move 'from opportunity to opportunity, from trend to trend, from strategy to strategy'.[17] There is therefore no homogeneous risk profile of Global Macro strategies. Global Macro strategies are exposed to most of the typical Hedge fund risk factors (market risk, credit risk,[18] liquidity risk, event risk, corporate risk, foreign exchange, operational risk, fraud risk, regulation risk, legal risk).

Ultimately, the success of the strategy comes down to a manager's ability to predict market moves. The strategy is especially exposed to *market risk*, i.e. the market moving against the directional positions. Market risk often comes in the form of *event risk*, i.e. the risk of macroeconomic and market developments coming out differently than expected by the manager. This includes political developments, sudden currency moves that are often related to regime changes (fixed to floating), sudden earnings revisions by key companies, important merger announcements or key firms' changes of management.

In March 2000, Julian Robertson announced the closure of the Tiger Funds blaming 'irrational markets' for the funds' poor performance. His statement read: 'Earnings and price considerations take a back seat to mouse clicks and momentum.' At the same time George Soros cut back his $8.5 billion Quantum Fund after having faced double-digit losses. Evidently the two largest long-term Macro players were unable to cope with 'irrational markets' during the second half of 1999 and first quarter of 2000.[19]

Global Macro strategies act worldwide. Investments in foreign securities bear *foreign exchange risk*. Some managers invest specifically in foreign exchange markets predicting depreciation or appreciation of specific currencies. Others invest in foreign equities and bonds bearing the implicit risk of the underlying currency moving against the position.

Global Macro strategies also bear *model risk*, which is the risk that the quantitative method or the fundamental model is inappropriate for the instruments or market invested in. *Execution risk* in the form of slippage or clumsy order execution by the broker is a further operational risk factor. Global Macro funds have been among the largest Hedge funds in size, a fact that magnifies execution risk and exposes the investments to *liquidity risk*. Some Global Macro strategies involve short selling of stock causing the strategy to be exposed to the specific risks of Short Selling, i.e. *short risk* (see section on Short Selling strategies).

Many investors believe that the closure of the Tiger Funds and the downsizing of George Soros' Quantum Fund provide evidence that the days of successful Global Macro investing are over. Global Macro strategies are most successful in inefficient markets. One can observe increased market efficiency (mainly through modern communication and information distribution tools like the internet) throughout global financial system, a development that clearly works against the Global Macro strategy. The year 2001 has seen a revival of Global Macro managers, however, which have been among the best performing during the equity bear market in 2000/2001. New immature markets with a lower degree of efficiency (such as financial products related to electricity or weather) have emerged. Investors' money has flown back to the strategy sector and only time will tell whether Global Macro managers can continue to perform in increasingly efficient markets.

Opportunistic – Long/Short Equity

The strategy

Long/Short Equity (also called 'Equity Hedged') is by far the most prevalent strategy in the AIS industry. New investors in AIS tend to think of Long/Short Equity strategies as synonymous with Hedge funds. The Long/Short strategy consists of investing in a core holding of equities and then partially hedging the long equity position with short sales of other stocks and/or stock index derivatives (this corresponds in principle to the 'Jones strategy' of 1949). In contrast to the Equity Market Neutral strategies, opportunistic Long/Short Equity strategies generally have a long bias, i.e. their long market exposure is not completely offset by short positions.[20] The focus of the strategy is stock selection with regional, sector-specific or particular style emphasis (e.g. US equity, European equities, high tech focus, value versus growth) rather than market timing or prediction of the broad stock market direction. Ideally, the return profile of a Long/Short Equity manager resembles a call option with full or partial participation (and possibly out-performance) of the broad market in bull markets and protection against losses (and ideally net gains from the short positions) in bear markets.

The Long/Short Equity sector is far from homogeneous.[21] The amount of net exposure to the broad equity markets varies widely among different managers as do concentration levels in specific industry sectors. Conservative managers mitigate market risk by maintaining net market exposure ranging from 0 to 100% while aggressive funds may magnify market risk by employing leverage exceeding 100% market exposure, e.g. 160% long and 50% short. In some rare instances, managers maintain a short net exposure.

The Long/Short Equity community distinguishes between 'bottom up' strategies and 'top down' approaches. The former follow individual companies and invest on the basis of fundamental analysis. The net equity exposure of a manager following a bottom up approach is based on his views regarding the extent to which the stocks of individual companies are over- or undervalued rather than being a function of expected broad market developments. The latter try to identify economic trends and upcoming 'investment themes' in certain asset classes and industry sectors (e.g. technology, biotech, growth companies) and change their allocation and net long exposure based on expected trends. Fundamental analysis, nevertheless, is an important element of top down investing. Some Long/Short Equity managers possess detailed knowledge and experience in specific industries and therefore focus their efforts on single sectors such as technology, healthcare, energy or financial companies, while others invest across various industries. Some managers have a particular focus on micro and small capitalization stocks, where potential inefficiencies are most prevalent.

Compared to Long Only strategies, Long/Short Equity strategies have significant flexibility regarding the use of leverage and short positions. The manager targets returns on the long side as well as on the short side, which ideally results in the doubling of alpha. Short positions have three different purposes and managers differ by the varying degrees they emphasize each one of these. First, the short positions are intended to generate 'alpha'; second, the short positions serve the purpose of hedging market risk; and third, the manager earns interest on the shorts, as he collects the short rebate. Some managers use Futures and/or puts on the S&P500 index for hedging purposes.

Fundamental analysis refers to the examination of the different factors that affect a company's stock price. Sources of information are research reports from banks, journals and newspapers, trade shows and industry contacts, company visits and personal interviews with management, conference calls and press conferences, as well as discussions with competitors, suppliers and distributors. Managers examine the individual company in terms of earnings, cash flow, balance sheet quality, assets and liabilities, ratio analysis etc. This goes along with an analysis of the industry sector with focus on the industry's competitive environment, the demand and supply situation, industry profitability and foreign influences. Qualitative analysis involves a detailed due diligent process and analysis of management, the product and the market.

As most managers have limited capacity to conduct fundamental research, they often focus on a limited universe of stocks, which can be defined through a screening process involving market capitalization, industry sectors, value versus growth or particular investment themes. Long/Short Equity managers diversify their portfolio by holding a larger number of different positions and many managers diversify through different industries and sectors. The construction of a well-diversified portfolio requires careful attention to the relationship between the different holdings of the portfolio.

EXAMPLES

Typical examples of Long/Short Equity trades are the following:

■ Long undervalued countries/sectors/individual stocks, short overvalued countries/ sectors/individual stocks.
■ Core long positions with a partial hedge overlay with short index Futures positions, long out-of-the-money puts or short covered call positions.
■ Short-term trading of initial public offering stocks ('hot issues').

Sources of return

Long/Short Equity strategies participate in the economic function of capital formation and distribution. The managers are normally net long and are therefore exposed to broad market risk. A part of Long/Short Equity returns is therefore market risk premium, i.e. 'beta return' (depending on the net long position). Beta has arguably been a major source of the high absolute returns for Long/Short Equity strategies in the equity bull market of the 1990s. But Long/Short Equity managers claim to return significant alpha, too. The discussion about the managers' alpha generation can follow the same lines as earlier for Equity Market Neutral strategies. 'Alpha' is partly a consequence of particular risks taken such as small firm risk, recession risk and company leverage risk. Certainly, the specific manager's stock-picking skills and trading talents are a meaningful source of generated returns, but the precise contribution of manager skill versus risk premiums to Long/Short Equity returns remains an open question. Market inefficiencies (and the possibility of generating alpha by detecting and exploiting them) are most prevalent for stocks of companies with small capitalizations, as those are often not well covered by analysts. ('Wall Street is quite lazy', I once heard a manager saying with respect to small and micro cap stocks.)

One important feature of Long/Short Equity strategies is that managers are not limited in generating 'alpha' by the constraint of having to 'hug a benchmark'.

They do not carry 'dead weight' portfolio position in which they have no insight or conviction for the sole reason of controlling idiosyncratic risk (i.e. the risk of underperformance relative to an index). Only positions for which the manager has performed his research and has a strong conviction about are held. The art of the manager is to control non-market residual risk through other less capital-intensive techniques than holding 'dead weight' positions.

The ability to sell short creates unique profit opportunities. Many investors face psychological or regulatory barriers to engaging in Short Selling. Regulatory authorities or internal compliance rules prohibit many financial institutions and asset managers from Short Selling. This creates market inefficiencies and price anomalies which Long/Short managers benefit from. When Short Selling is restricted, market prices might not be entirely efficient, as without complete freedom to sell short, the pessimism of some investors is not fully represented by security prices and some stocks will be overpriced relative to others. Bankruptcy proceedings or restructuring can create unique profit opportunities for Short Selling.

Risk factors

Long/Short Equity strategies usually have a net long exposure. The resulting correlation to the broad equity market or particular sectors causes the strategy to be exposed to *market risk*. The determination of what level of net exposure to the market to hold requires the trading manager to perform some assessment of the future direction of the market. Declining equity markets usually lead to losses for the strategy, although less so than Long Only Equity strategies because of the partial hedge with short positions. For the evaluation of a Long/Short Equity manager, it is important to understand the source of a strategy's alpha in order to distinguish the managers who benefit mostly from beta from those which are 'real alpha generators'.

Depending on the manager, Long/Short Equity strategies have specific exposures to certain industry sectors (*sector risk*), countries (*country risk*) and currencies (*FX risk*), company sizes (*market capitalization*) and styles (*value/growth*). Ultimately, the success of the Long/Short Equity strategies comes down to stock selection. The strategy is exposed to (corporate or sector) *event risk* in its individual holdings or the corresponding sectors invested in. Specific-company or sector risk is anything that affects the values of the company or the sector in an unforeseen way, e.g. the risk of surprise announcements like earnings revision, merger announcement or changes of management. An unbalanced and non-diversified portfolio enhances the risk of significant losses from individual stock events.

As Long/Short Equity strategies involve short selling of stock, the strategy is exposed to the specific risks of Short Selling (*short risk*) connected to the fact that the short seller has to borrow stock (e.g. short squeezes, execution risk). It is important to note that the process of shorting stocks requires a unique set of skills and experiences, which are different from buying stock on the long side only. A pure fundamental approach to picking short candidates is much less appropriate than the equivalent strategy for long only strategies. The internet excitement in 1999 and early 2000 provides a good example of a situation in which managers who sold stocks short because of fundamental overvaluation got badly hurt and, in many cases, went out of business. Experienced short sellers look for a catalyst that will expose the poor fundamentals of the corresponding company. Many Hedge fund managers coming from Long Only asset management have gone through painful learning experiences in handling the short side. An investor has to be aware of the 'shorting learning curve' and should avoid letting a Hedge fund manager gather his first experience with Short Selling at his expense.

If the strategy trades small cap stocks (on the long or the short side), *liquidity risk* becomes a considerable risk factor. Some Long/Short Equity managers hold a significant number of positions simultaneously, so their strategy can bear significant *operational risk*.

Long/Short Equity strategies tend to perform very well in periods of rising equity markets benefiting from a net long exposure, while during periods of falling equity markets the same net long exposure usually leads to losses. Nevertheless, even in falling equity markets, Long/Short Equity managers are able to generate alpha, i.e. outperform an equity market index (but as an 'absolute return strategy' it does not have a benchmark).

Opportunistic – Equity Market Timing

The strategy

Equity Market Timing strategies (also referred to as 'Mutual Fund Timing') utilize a variety of statistically based technical trading models which screen the global equity markets to identify temporal short-term opportunities (trends, momentum) in individual industry sectors (e.g. financial, pharmaceutical, biotechnology, telecommunication etc.). The managers opportunistically switch between long equity exposure and money market instruments or short-term bond investments. Long equity positions are taken in favourable moments, i.e. an established upward trend market and the position is neutralized in less favourable moments, i.e. the start of a downward trend. Trading mutual funds offers the most price efficient method for the implementation of an Equity Market Timing strategy. Capital allocation to different sectors is based on relative opportunity and level of volatility. In rare cases, managers hedge using stock index Futures. This may occur in times of suddenly perceived downside risk.

Typically, managers employ technical trendfollowing models based on short- and mid-term momentum indicators to determine the direction of a sector and to identify buy and sell signals. On an 'upward move buy signal', money is transferred from a money market fund into a specific equity sector mutual fund in an attempt to capture a short-term capital gain. After a downward move the positions in the mutual fund are sold and the assets moved back into a money market fund for safe keeping until the next potential upward move occurs. Typically, the manager is invested in money market funds about 50% of the time and invests only if the odds are highly in favour of an upward move on the following day.

Two types of Market Timing strategies can be distinguished:

■ *Sector Timing*: This momentum strategy aims at profiting from micro upward trends in single industry sectors. These trends occur as good news (e.g. an earnings surprise) about a particular company within a sector affects the stock price of other companies in the same sector. The information is not processed immediately, but over a time period of one to several days. Particularly, small capitalization stocks, which are infrequently traded, tend to lack the immediate price action of the broad market, a phenomenon referred to as 'stale prices'.[22] This leads to Time Arbitrage opportunities that can be exploited by shifting into a corresponding mutual fund on a rise in the sector.

■ *Time Zone Arbitrage*: This strategy exploits an inefficiency in the pricing of US mutual funds that is based on the conditional price correlation between different time zones. US-based mutual European and Asian equity funds can be purchased right around US market close at European/Asian closing prices. Particularly after weak European or Asian markets and a late US rally there is a high probability that these funds trade higher on the next day. Typically, the manager is invested in the equity market only 10–20% of the time and remains in safe money market funds otherwise.

Trading highly liquid US mutual funds (such as Kemper, Franklin Templeton, Pimco etc.) allows the manager to buy and sell market exposure without a price spread (trading at mid-market price) or other transaction costs (no-load mutual funds). This enables the trading advisor to earn a return even on micro moves, as the margins are not taken away by trading costs.

EXAMPLE

A real example of a typical trade is illustrated in Figure 3.7. After a few days of weak equity market performance, the US stock market, based on incoming good news, rallies strongly one hour before market closes. The manager invests in US-based international mutual funds shortly before the market closes assuming that, on the next day, Asian and European markets will perform similarly well. As the international funds are priced at the local closing prices (e.g. evening European time, i.e. noon US time), there is a high probability a profit can be taken, once these funds are sold at the end of the following day.

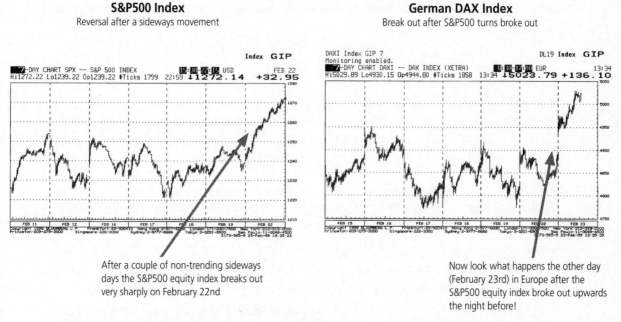

S&P500 Index
Reversal after a sideways movement

German DAX Index
Break out after S&P500 turns broke out

After a couple of non-trending sideways
days the S&P500 equity index breaks out
very sharply on February 22nd

Now look what happens the other day
(February 23rd) in Europe after the
S&P500 equity index broke out upwards
the night before!

FIGURE 3.7 ■ Typical Time Zone Arbitrage trade by Equity Market Timing strategy (Copyright 2002
Bloomberg LP. Reprinted with permission. All rights reserved.)

Sources of return

For Equity Market Timing, manager skill does not play as dominant a role as with
other opportunistic Hedge fund strategies. The strategy is reactive rather than
predictive. Equity Market Timing strategies participate in the economic function
of capital formation and distribution. Part of their return is the risk premium for
being exposed to the broad equity market, which in the terminology of the CAPM
is beta. But a significant part of the return is based on exploiting particular inefficiencies of equity markets generally, and the pricing of US mutual funds in
particular, which are expressed by certain statistical relationships involving different geographical regions, sectors and firm sizes:

■ Individual equity sectors show trending behaviour.[23]

■ Small cap securities (and funds or baskets thereof) tend to lag the price action
of large capitalization securities by one to two days.[24]

■ Regional equity markets have different market opening hours (time zone
difference).

Note that it is likely that these inefficiencies will disappear or be reduced over time.

Risk factors

Equity Market Timing strategies enter and exit equity positions very opportunistically. The strategy is mainly exposed to *market risk* or *sector risk*, whenever positions are taken up on a signal. Note that the strategy is not exposed to general market risk, e.g. the risk of a bear market, but rather to *conditional market risk*, e.g. a sudden reversal of an up trend.

Mutual Fund Timing strategies are not very popular among mutual fund companies. An important challenge for the manager is to find the right funds for the implementation of the strategy. Frequently, mutual fund companies try to make it unattractive for Equity Market Timing managers to invest in their funds by imposing front-load fees, switching costs or redemption penalties. Recent developments in the mutual fund industry are very unfavourable to the strategy. Mutual fund companies are increasingly resistant to Mutual Fund Timing. The SEC recently issued a recommendation to mutual funds to perform fair pricing which will stop market timers using their funds for Time Zone Arbitrage. The strategy is exposed to the *operational risk* of suddenly not being able to trade in specifically attractive mutual funds any longer. Further, operational risk is present due to the daily switching within different mutual funds. This leads to significant *execution risk* in the form of wrong or missed trades.

Unfavourable environments for Equity Market Timing strategies are choppy market conditions with a high tendency for trend reversal on a time scale of one day, i.e. strong upward trend followed by a strong downward move the next day. Examples for such market behaviour are the months of February and March 2001, when Timing strategies suffered unusual losses. Favourable markets are continuously upward-trending markets, as seen in 1999 and early 2000. In extended bear markets, which are not interrupted by short-term rallies, the strategy's performance is largely determined by prevailing risk free interest rates, since managers remain invested in money market funds. The strategy will, however, generate significant alpha (outperformance compared to the broad equity market) in bear markets that display periods of short-term rallies (i.e. a few days or weeks).

Opportunistic – Short Selling

The strategy

Short Selling strategies involve the sale of stocks not currently owned by the seller in order to take advantage of their anticipated price decline. To initiate a short sale, the seller has to borrow the securities from a third party (the securities lending department of a broker) in order to make delivery to the purchaser. From the proceeds of that sale he receives cash, which earns interest called the short rebate interest. At a later time, the seller returns the borrowed securities to the lender by purchasing back the securities in the open market. If the short seller can buy the stock back at a lower price, a profit results. If the price of the stock has risen, a loss will occur. Theoretically, the short sale (just like a Futures contract) does not require any initial capital, but in practice, the stock lending brokerage firm requires substantial collateral. On top of the cash received from the sale, a short seller usually must pledge cash or cash-like securities to the lender in an amount equal to 30 to 50% of the stock's market value.[25] Some managers use derivatives (forwards, futures, options on indices and stocks) to execute a Short Selling strategy. Others partially hedge the short sale with long positions or out-of-the-money call options, which makes the strategy similar to a Long/Short Equity strategy with a short bias.

The income on short positions has two components: profit from buying back stock at a lower price than it was sold at and the short rebate interest. Similar to Long/Short Equity strategies, the investment process requires much analytical work. Many managers follow a bottom up approach, where an individual company's financial standings and business prospects are examined (earnings, cash flow, assets and liabilities, ratio analysis, products, costs etc.), followed by an analysis of the industry sector (competitive environment, demand and supply, profitability, foreign influences). A common theme of Short Selling strategies is the identification of companies using aggressive accounting techniques. But a pure fundamental approach to picking short candidates is much less appropriate than the equivalent strategy for long strategies. Most short sellers look for an additional catalyst that will expose the poor fundamentals of the company, e.g. an earnings revision.

Short Selling requires a good relationship with an established prime broker. Potential problems related to borrowing stocks are share availability, stability of the borrowing (since the broker can always call back the stock), the level of the short rebate interest earned and protection against short squeezes (the temporary sudden demand for the stock forcing short sellers to cover their positions at unfavourable prices).[26] With respect to short squeezes, the important issue is the broker's buy-in policy, which determines how quickly a short seller has to cover his positions.

EXAMPLE

An example of a successful short trade in 1998 was Pediatrix Medical Group Inc.,[27] a provider of physician management services to hospital-based neonatal intensive care units. The valuation of the company was based on a projected growth rate that far exceeded the expected birth rate of new babies. The research performed by Short Selling managers showed further aggressive accounting practices and inappropriate charges to insurance carriers. The stock price between September 1998 and March 1999 is displayed in Figure 3.8. Short Selling managers started shorting the stock in late 1998/early 1999. On February 12, the company announced it would miss earning expectations, after the company's auditor expressed the opinion that the accounting for acquisition costs in 1998 was going to be rejected by the SEC. The stock dropped more than 50% following the announcement.

Sources of return

The unlimited risk of loss to which Short Selling is exposed creates psychological barriers for many investors. As a result, most investors never consider Short Selling. Further, analysts are hesitant to give a detailed analysis of a potential 'Short Sell Candidate' and only a few give explicit 'sell' recommendations. Additionally, many financial institutions and asset managers are prohibited by regulatory authorities or by internal compliance rules from Short Selling. All this can lead to market inefficiencies and good opportunities for Short Selling managers. When Short Selling is restricted, market prices might no longer be efficient. Without the freedom to sell short, the pessimism of some investors will not be fully represented in security prices and some stocks can become overpriced. Short sellers also contribute to the efficient capital allocation process within an economy and thereby take corresponding risks. They can be seen as earning market risk premiums analogously as long equity investments. Comparable to Long/Short Equity strategies, the key performance driver of Short Selling strategies is security selection. The manager's stock-picking and portfolio management skills remain the most important sources of generated returns.

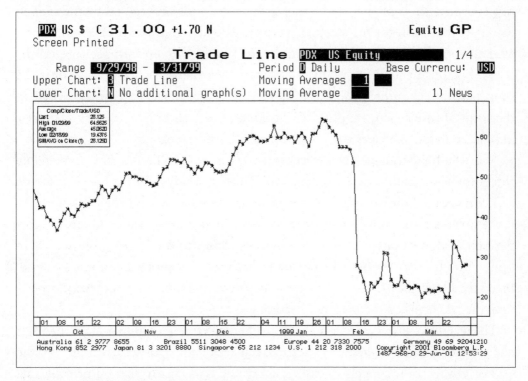

FIGURE 3.8 ■ Profitable Short Trade: Pediatrix Medical Group Inc., 1998 (Copyright 2002 Bloomberg LP. Reprinted with permission. All rights reserved.)

Risk factors

Short Selling strategies are exposed to the same risk factors as long equity investment strategies: general *market risk*, specific *stock risk* and *corporate event risk* (unexpected good news, takeovers, split-ups), *execution risk* (bad fills) and *liquidity risk*.

On top of these risks, Short Selling strategies are subject to specific risks related to the fact that the securities have to be borrowed before they can be sold. The extra steps of borrowing stock, maintaining the corresponding liability and then buying back the shorted stock creates a set of unique risks which I call the *borrowing risks* (or *short risks*). Certain stocks that a manager would like to short might be unavailable, which limits the execution of good investment ideas (*availability risk*). Second, short sellers can be subject to '*short squeezes*' caused by the sudden increase of demand for the stock. This can create a vicious cycle. One short seller after the other has to cover his position, creating further upward pressure on the stock. Finally, a short sale requires collateral. As the market moves against the short position, additional collateral is required. The manager faces *liquidity risk* in the form of insufficient funding. The degree of overall borrowing risk is greatly influenced by the manager's relationship with his prime broker.

Short Selling strategies face specific *portfolio risks*. The number of available stocks for Short Selling is usually limited. This can lead to difficulties in reaching sufficient portfolio diversification. A particular feature of Short Selling strategies is the inverse relationship between performance and exposure. A loss in a short position leads to a larger overall portfolio exposure to the losing position. There is an unlimited risk of loss when a stock that has been shorted continues to rise. Inversely, many short positions face the problem that the more successful a position, the less invested the manager becomes.

The usual *execution risks* apply to Short Selling strategies, in particular bad fills due to poor liquidity (slippage), fast markets and clumsy order execution by the broker. On top of these general risks a short sale is subject to the 'up-tick rule' set by market regulators. A short sale can only be executed on a plus or zero-plus tick. Because of this rule some of the short sale ideas with great profit potential might never get executed.

The short sale of stock generates cash which is usually held as collateral. Most of the interest earned on this cash goes to the short seller and forms an income stream for the strategy, but a portion is retained by the broker. When a stock is in limited supply, the broker can retain a higher portion of the interest and the short interest rebate to the short seller is reduced. Short rebate income is also reduced by stock dividends that the short position has to pay. Failing to properly negotiate short interest rebates or an unforeseen dividend increase creates a significant income risk to the strategy (*short rebate risk*).

Inverse to Long Equity investing, Short Selling strategies perform the most poorly in rising equity markets and the most favourably in bear markets. The strong equity bull market of the 1990s caused this strategy to be consistently the worst performing Hedge fund sector of that decade and extinguished most Short Selling managers. The correction in the stock market that started in March 2000 revived the Short Selling industry and made it among the best performing sectors during 2000/2001. Nevertheless, Short Sellers displayed rather disappointing performance in 2001 (negative returns according to the CSFB/Tremont index) when global equity markets lost broadly.

Managed Futures and Currency strategies

Managed Futures strategies seek to generate returns through long and short positions in various Futures contracts. This includes Futures on commodities (metals, grains, etc.) and financial securities (fixed income, foreign exchange and equity indices). The strategies are in most cases executed by 'Commodity Trading Advisors' (CTA) and 'Commodity Pool Operators' (CPO) who have to be registered with the National Futures Association (NFA) and the Commodity Futures Trading Commission (CFTC) in the USA or the Securities and Futures Authority (SFA) in the UK. Within the set of Futures strategies, I distinguish between Opportunistic (or Active) strategies on the one side and Passive strategies on the other side (see Figures 2.1 and 3.1). Opportunistic Futures strategies are characterized by either discretionary trading based on long-term fundamentals and short-term information or proprietary model-based techniques such as trend following, countertrend trading, spread trading and a variety of others. Passive strategies, in contrast, aim to systematically capture returns available from the presence of professional hedging activities in Futures markets. The passive character expresses itself through very low trading frequency and the lack of sophisticated modelling. The system is rather simple (and in most cases publicly known, e.g. the MLM or the sGFII index) and operates on a long time horizon, i.e. several months to a year. Correspondingly, the fees charged are significantly lower.

I also include Currency Trading programs in the category of Managed Futures, as their underlying strategy and trading approaches are often quite similar. Currency strategies include technical trendfollowing, discretionary trading (based on fundamentals), information based short-term trading, complex option arbitrage, interest rate carry, and cross rate arbitrage. Note that some Managed Futures and Currency trading programs are quite similar to Global Macro strategies in that they evaluate broad macroeconomic information and make according 'bets' on certain particular asset moves. Correspondingly, the distinction between some Futures strategies and Global Macro is not always obvious.

Most CTAs trade Futures contracts, some trade options on Futures and a few managers deal with OTC derivatives. Managers are usually broadly diversified by trading in a wide class of Futures across multiple asset classes. Futures and currencies allow significant leverage, as usually only a fraction of the exposure has to be provided by the manager for margin purposes. Margin to equity ratios vary from 5% to about 25%.

Most Futures strategies are 'long volatility', i.e. they profit from rising volatility in financial markets. Being long volatility can be achieved in two different ways: by taking a long position in options, i.e. a straddle; or by implementing a momentum-based trading strategy, e.g. by following moving averages or breakout indicators. The return of most Futures strategies corresponds to a risk premium earned for providing the economic function of price risk transfer in markets with commercial hedging activity (e.g. commodities). Further Opportunistic Futures strategies' returns are dependent on the managers' skills to detect predictable pricing patterns or market inefficiencies.

Futures Active – Systematic Technical

The strategy

Systematic Technical Futures strategies utilize computerized mathematical models to generate buy and sell decisions. Trading is, to a large degree, systematic and occurs mostly in highly liquid markets with low transaction costs. Models are based on quantitative analysis of technical factors and indicators. The most typical examples of this class are trendfollowing or countertrend models, which are based on momentum indicators.[28]

Almost all systematic models have a time horizon or a combination of different time horizons defined by the inherent time constants of their indicators. For long-term models, momentum-based trendfollowing is typically most widely employed. Systematic long-term models are usually rather simple; they use a variety of different moving average (momentum) indicators, which help to detect extended price trends. Most models have been optimized and back-tested for a number of years. The majority of trades executed with this strategy are unprofitable. Nevertheless, such strategies can generate positive returns because they close losing positions quickly ('cut losses') and remain in profitable trades ('let profits run').

Short-term models use a larger variety of statistical tools including momentum and countertrend trading techniques, breakout indicators and pattern recognition. More exotic analysis is sometimes performed with the help of non-linear models, neural networks, genetic algorithms and frequency models. The models try to exploit statistically measurable short-term market inefficiencies.

EXAMPLES

Examples of short-term Systematic Technical trades are:

- short-term trendfollowing and countertrend following with automatic stop-loss limits
- directional volatility positions executed with options
- systematic equity or commodity index (e.g. GSCI) arbitrage
- trading based on a trained (optimized) neural network or other applications of 'artificial intelligence' or non-linear or time series analysis.[29]

Sources of return

The distinction between long-term Systematic Active models and Systematic Passive models can be blurred. Their sources of return are quite similar. As with most Managed Futures strategies, parts of the returns of Systematic Active strategies are based on the risk premium for providing liquidity to Futures and derivatives markets and providing commercial hedgers with the opportunity to transfer their natural price risk. But active models also have a skill component. The correct systematic prediction of trends requires good model development abilities. Short-term model-based trading aims at exploiting market inefficiencies and inhibited information flow in financial markets. Returns are here a function of the manager skill in developing models that detect complex predictable short-term price patterns.

Most Systematic Futures models are of a trendfollowing type and many managers and producers of these models claim that trendfollowing models generate inherent returns as a result of mass psychology, i.e. crowd behaviour (a clear violation of the 'weak' form of the efficient market hypothesis). For most financial markets, however, academic research provides no clear support in favour of these claims for trend persistence in security prices.[30] Likewise, there is a claim for currencies to exhibit serial correlation, but again, this is not convincingly supported by empirical studies.[31]

Risk factors

Managers usually have clear exposure to certain markets. Therefore, the predominant risk of systematic Futures and Currency strategies is *market risk*, i.e. the risk of the market moving against the established position. Trendfollowing strategies in particular are exposed to the risk of steady losses over an extended period of time in non-trending, directionless market environments, which exhibit numerous price reversals ('whip-saw markets'). This is illustrated in Figure 3.9 (left-hand side).

The structure of financial markets changes continuously and models built in the past might not be suited for markets in the future. Systematic models thus bear the *risk of structural changes* in the underlying markets. It often occurs that models that have worked very successfully for a period of time start showing persistent performance problems. Systematic long-term trendfollowing models had excellent performance during the 1980s and early 1990s when financial markets showed strong directional trends. Fewer trends were observed in the later 1990s, and the models accordingly showed much lower returns. In 2000/2001 performance was again good for many Futures strategies. But it has to be noted that the variability of returns between managers increased during 2000–2001, i.e. managers diverged in performance.

Systematic trading strategies rely solely on the functioning of models that were developed as a result of research efforts performed during some past time period. A very important risk factor is *model risk*, which refers to the risk of the model being flawed or unsuited for the current market structure. Most models are optimized on past data, i.e. the parameters of the model are determined such that the model shows the best performance for particular periods in the past. This is a dangerous undertaking and bears the *risk of over-fitting*, also referred to as 'curve fitting'. Provided with a sufficient number of free parameters, every model can be tuned such that it shows excellent performance on any (even random) data set! However, when used with data that the model was not optimized for ('out of sample test'), performance may be significantly worse, sometimes rendering the model useless. The more complicated the model and the more parameters involved, the higher the risk of over-fitting. Simple trendfollowing models bear less risk of over-fitting than complicated 'non-linear modelling approaches' that have a lot of different parameters. The investor should always inquire about the optimization procedure that was undertaken during the development of the model and about the performance on out-of-sample data or during real-time trading.

Systematic Futures and Currency trading bears *operational risk*. Most models are run on computers and their failure or programming errors ('bugs'), electricity breakdown etc. can lead to trading losses. Furthermore, the trading of a large number of different positions bears *execution risk*.

Because approaches are very diverse, it is difficult to determine general market conditions in which all the different models perform consistently well or particularly poorly. Strategies which exploit short-term market inefficiencies perform best in less developed and therefore less efficient markets. Most strategies perform poorly in directionless 'whip saw' market conditions. Long-term trendfollowing models in particular need persistent trends for good performance.

Futures Active – Discretionary

The strategy

Active Discretionary Futures and Currency strategies are characterized by proprietary approaches primarily employing fundamental analysis, sometimes in combination with technical analysis. The most typical examples are directional long-term positions based on fundamental forecasts or short-term trading based on information flow. Trading decisions are largely based on the study of external factors that affect the supply and demand of a particular security or asset.

Most of the Active Discretionary managers have extensive experience with commodity or currency markets. Having typically worked for years in these markets or related environments, e.g. in an oil company, trading corn, trading inter-bank FX markets, the manager's competitive advantage is his knowledge of the essential fundamentals (e.g. worldwide inventory level of a commodity) and his ability to anticipate changes in supply and demand relationships that affect security prices. By monitoring relevant supply and demand factors, a state of dis-equilibrium may be identified that has yet to be reflected in the price of the underlying commodity. Such factors include weather, the economics of a particular commodity, government policies, domestic and foreign political and economic events and changing trade patterns. Most managers have fast access to relevant information which they are able to capitalize on.

Examples of Active Discretionary trades are:

- Directional long-term position based on fundamental analysis, e.g. one currency against another, in a particular commodity, in one country or firm's debt, or in a particular equity market sector (or country).

- Short-term positions based on particular information flow, e.g. corporate currency-hedging activity, a country's central bank policy or the inventory management of particularly influential global corporates.

- Crossrate arbitrage, interest rate carry arbitrage, investing in high-yield currencies.

- Inter-product spread trade between Futures of related commodities, currencies or fixed income products, e.g. soybean versus soybean oil, Euro versus Swiss franc, German Bund versus British gilts.

- Directional volatility positions and other option strategies such as time spreads, i.e. Futures with different maturity times.

- Equity sector arbitrage, i.e. long undervalued sector Futures and short overvalued sector Futures.

- Convexity trades, e.g. long Eurodollar Futures and short Eurodollar forward.

EXAMPLE

An example of an actual trade for an Active Discretionary Futures strategy is the spread trade (long soybean meal and short soybean) grain traders established following the increasing fear of the role of fodder meal and BSE in Europe during 2000.

Sources of return

Similar to Global Macro Hedge fund strategies, Active Discretionary Futures strategies exploit temporary mispricings through superior and faster access to information. The specific skills and experience possessed by Active Discretionary managers in certain markets are the most important source of returns generated. For example, they might have knowledge about the inventory levels of oil or corn producers and can interpret this information accordingly. Their activities often generate the necessary liquidity for commercial market participants to carry out their business in an orderly fashion. This activity is compensated with a corresponding risk (liquidity) premium.

Similarly, the returns of FX strategies can be interpreted as a premium paid by commercial market players for the generation of liquidity and price continuity. In anticipation of the deal flow created by a large transaction of a commercial market participant (that finds no direct commercial counter-party), or the trend induced by an action of a major market player, the speculators adjust the FX rates to create the necessary liquidity. The following serves as an idealized example. A large cooperation has the need to exchange a large sum of money from one currency into another (e.g. Germany-based Siemens wishes to exchange USD 1 billion into EUR). The market anticipates this deal flow and the price shifts accordingly in advance of the transaction, which leads to the company paying a higher price for the desired currency in exchange for the requested liquidity. Further, when major shifts in the supply–demand balance occur due to a macro-economic event (e.g. Mexico crisis 1995), FX traders continue to provide liquidity and price continuity in a fundamentally overvalued/undervalued market. Currency 'carry trades' (investing in high-yield currencies where a return is generated by the interest rate differential) earn a risk premium by assuming exposure to possible currency devaluations of a high-yield currency.

Risk factors

As for most Managed Futures strategies, *market risk* is the dominant risk connected with Active Discretionary Futures trading, i.e. the risk of the market moving against the established positions. Fundamental directional positions are specifically exposed to *event risk*, the risk of a particular external event influencing the position unfavourably (e.g. unexpected cut in interest rates, change of government or unfavourable weather conditions).

Most Active Discretionary Futures and Currencies programs rely on the skill and experience of one or a few key people. On departure or unavailability (e.g. disease or death) of a key person, the trading program might suffer significantly worse performance (*key people risk*). Furthermore, on changing market conditions key people can lose their trading edge. Finally, short-term trading in a high number of different positions bears *execution risk* (e.g. bad fills, slippage).

Most managers perform well in markets that are not entirely information efficient. By way of contrast, Active Discretionary strategies are less successful in very efficient markets.

Futures Passive

The strategy

Equity markets offer investors who are willing to provide capital to companies the possibility of earning a premium (relative to the risk free rate) on their investment. Futures markets also offer inherent returns to investors, but for a different reason. The basic economic function of Futures markets is to act as a risk transfer vehicle. Participants in Futures markets are generally one of two different kinds: hedgers and investors (neglecting the role of arbitrageurs). Hedgers are these commercial producers or consumers of particular commodities who want to transfer their price risk by transferring it to another entity. Investors in Futures markets provide these commercial hedgers with the possibility to transfer their unwanted price risk. Passive Futures strategies follow the hedging patterns of commercial 'natural longs and shorts' (producers and consumers)[32] in Futures markets and systematically take the opposite position.[33]

Demand–supply mismatches in the market between 'natural long hedgers' and 'natural short hedgers' occur frequently. A demand to acquire price stability (or 'price insurance') for either the long or short hedger is almost never completely met by the other side. This gives investors an opportunity to provide the marginal price stability and be compensated accordingly. Investors thus provide 'price insurance' to hedgers. Comparable to an insurance company, which earns a premium for insuring its clients or a bank that lends long term and borrows short term (and thus earns a liquidity and a duration risk premium), the investor should expect a commensurate return. The more extended the supply demand mismatch, the higher the return.

Commercial hedgers naturally follow contrarian strategies, i.e. they are acting against trends. A price increase (or more specifically, a price move out of a certain recent price range) will lead to more natural long hedgers wanting to hedge compared to the number of natural shorts, because they want to lock in a relatively higher price. Inversely, a decrease in prices will motivate natural shorts to hedge/lock in attractive prices. The resulting demand–supply mismatch is a function of the extent of the price move. Investors can take the opposite position of hedgers by investing with the price momentum (i.e. trend). Most Systematic Passive Futures strategies are therefore constructed on the basis of long-term trendfollowing systems. Positions are taken according to a momentum indicator on underlying prices. Another approach is taking positions according to the degree to which the asset is trading in contango or backwardation, which gives an alternative indication of the net direction of commercial hedging activities.

EXAMPLES

Two examples of typical trades of a Passive Futures strategy in crude oil Futures are:

■ The price for crude oil has risen substantially and is currently relatively high. British Petroleum (BP) and other oil producers want to lock in the high price level and sell short crude oil Futures contracts. As a result a demand–supply imbalance occurs in the Futures market for crude oil. The Passive Futures strategy takes the opposite position by going long.

■ The price for crude oil has fallen substantially and is currently relatively low. American Airlines and other airlines are afraid of a potential price increase in oil. They buy energy Futures in the market to protect the airline from possible higher prices, which leads to a general demand–supply imbalance in the crude oil Futures market. The Passive Futures strategy takes the opposite position and builds up a short exposure to energy prices in the Futures markets.

The determinants of commodities prices vary among each other, so the correlation between different commodities is usually low. This enables Passive Futures managers to reach efficient diversification through investing in a broad basket of Futures contracts.

Sources of return

Passive Futures strategies take systematically the opposite position to commercial hedgers and by accepting short-term price volatility they provide necessary liquidity for the Futures markets. In return, the investors receive a premium similar to an insurance company being paid a premium in return for accepting event risk. Thus, the investor generates return by accepting the excessive price risk commercial hedgers are naturally exposed to but unwilling to take.[34] The risk premium earned by Passive Futures strategies can also be referred to as 'commodity hedging demand premium'.

The economic function of risk transfer as provided by investors in Futures markets is entirely different from the function of traditional investment markets (i.e. equity and bond market). The latter is the formation and efficient distribution/allocation of capital to companies and governments. The returns generated by Passive Futures strategies are therefore inherently independent from traditional equity and bond returns.

Risk factors

The predominant risk for Passive Futures strategies is *market risk*, i.e. the risk of the market moving against the established position. As the strategy takes the opposite position of commercial hedgers providing them with an 'insurance' against price adverse moves, it will suffer losses whenever there is a move against the hedgers' natural position.

The strategy sector relies strongly on diversification, similar to insurance companies, which collect premiums over many insurance takers before paying out claims. An important risk factor is *diversification risk*, i.e. the lack of sufficiently broad diversification over different Futures markets. But there is a trade-off between the need for diversification and the available liquidity for Passive Futures strategies. Investing in too many different markets also leads to *liquidity risk*, as the additional Futures contracts may lack sufficient trading liquidity.

Passive Futures strategies bear *model risk*, which is the risk that the model is unsuited to carry out the function of capturing inherent returns in Futures markets. The *execution risk* of the strategy is comparably low. The time horizon of commercial hedgers is in the order of weeks to months, so most Passive Futures strategies have a rather low turnover.

Passive Futures strategies face problems in non-trending, directionless market environments exhibiting numerous price reversals, where trading occurs in a limited price range over an extended period of time ('whip-saw markets'). Contrariwise, persistently trending markets constitute a favourable environment. This is illustrated in Figure 3.9. The strategy sector shows strong performance in volatile and declining equity markets, especially in periods of an equity market crisis (crash), when investors' and hedgers' risk aversion increases and thus risk premiums are high. It therefore offers an excellent diversification to a Long Only Equity portfolio or equity-directional Hedge fund strategies, such as Equity Market Timing and Long/Short Equity.

Unfriendly environment (silver)   Friendly environment (crude oil)

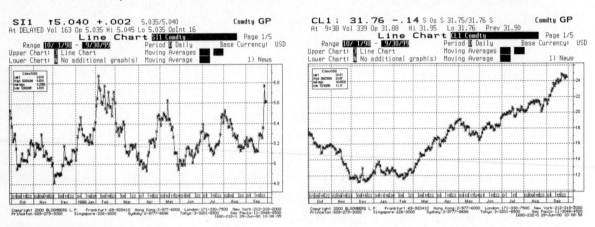

FIGURE 3.9 ■ Profitable and unprofitable environments for Passive Futures strategies (Copyright 2002 Bloomberg LP. Reprinted with permission. All rights reserved.)

Notes

1. Classification schemes with different nuances are presented in 'In Search for Alpha' by A. Ineichen, UBS Warburg (2000) and in 'Alternative Asset Returns: Theoretical Bases and Empirical Evidence' by T. Schneeweiss and J. Pescatore, *Handbook of Alternative Investment Strategies*, Institutional Investors Inc., New York, 1999.

2. It is disputed, whether Long/Short Equity strategies should be classified as opportunistic. There is a great amount of heterogeneity between individual managers in this strategy sector. But characteristically, most managers have a long bias in their strategy, i.e. they maintain a net long exposure. I follow the reasoning of A. Ineichen (2000) here. A different possibility is to introduce a new category on the first level and distinguish the different styles of Long/Short managers by different degree of net exposure (as done by T. Schneeweiss and J. Pescatore, 1999).

3. A description of the different components of a convertible security can be found in 'Market Neutral and Hedged Strategies', published by Hedge Fund Research, Inc. The authors also provide a discussion of Convertible Arbitrage Strategies.

4. For more details about the pricing and characteristics of convertible bonds the reader is referred to *Pricing Convertible Bonds* by K. Connolly.

5. See the article 'Convertible Arb Funds Turn to Default Swaps' by C. Schenk in *Risk Magazine*, July 2001. For credit derivatives generally, see the book by J. Tavakoli, *Credit Derivatives: A Guide to Instruments and Applications*, 2nd edn.

6. See F. Fabozzi in *Fixed Income Analysis* (Chapter II, 2) for more details about valuing bonds with embedded options.

7. A further discussion of the numerous liquidity issues connected to the Convertible Arbitrage strategy can be found in 'Convertible Arbitrage' by M. Boyd et al. in *Managing Hedge Fund Risk* by V. Parker (ed.), Risk Books, 2001.

8. These are often based on quadratic optimization procedures. Quadratic optimization corresponds to the Markovitz construction of efficient portfolios. For more algorithmic details, see H. Markowitz, *Portfolio Selection – Efficient Diversification of Investment*, John Wiley & Sons, New York, 1959.

9. See 'Persuasive Evidence on Market Inefficiencies' by B. Rosenburg et al. in *Journal of Portfolio Management*, Spring 1985, 11, no. 3, p.9.

10. There has been a broad discussion in recent years on extending the standard theory of finance, which is built on the 'no arbitrage' principles, portfolio theory and capital asset pricing models, by what is called 'behavioural finance'. Behavioural finance aims at accounting for market anomalies by considering psychological models of human behaviour. See H. Shefren in *Beyond Greed and Fear: Understanding Behavioural Finance* and the articles by M. Stratman, 'Behavioural Finance: Past Battles and Future Engagements'; and R. Shiller, 'Human Behavior and the Efficiency of the Financial System', in *Handbook of Macroeconomics*.

11. See E. Fama, K. French, 'The Cross Section of Expected Stock Returns'.

12. A thorough description of the different aspects of the Risk Arbitrage strategy is provided in *Risk Arbitrage: An Investor's Guide*, by K. M. Moore, John Wiley & Sons, New York, 1999.

13. The pooling method is no longer accepted under US GAAP for mergers announced after July 1, 2001. In other legislations (e.g. the UK), pooling is still possible, although International Accounting Standards (IAS) provide for pooling only in cases where the acquirer cannot be determined (i.e. the transaction is really a merger of equals).

14. In *Deals, Deals, and More Deals*, by R. Pitaro, there are many examples of historical merger transactions. The book also offers an in-depth discussion of Risk Arbitrage strategies.

15. These are further elaborated in 'The Case for Hedge Funds', Tremont, Partners Inc. and TASS Investment Research Inc., 1999.

16. In 'Measuring the Market Impact of Hedge Funds', W. Fung and D. Hsieh examine the role of Hedge funds during market turbulences of the 1990s.

17. M. Strome in *Evaluating and Implementing Hedge Fund Strategies*, by R. Lake, Euromoney Books, 1996.

18. Credit risk comes mostly in the form of sovereign country risk. For example, the Russian default in the summer of 1998 hurt many Global Macro managers.

19. Ironically, the markets turned strongly in Robertson's favour almost at the same time he made the announcement proving correct his prediction that 'a Ponzi pyramid is destined for collapse'.

20. Some categorize Long/Short Equity completely as a Relative Value strategy, e.g. J. Bernard and T. Schneeweiss in 'Alternative Investments: Past, Present and Future', in *The Capital Guide to Alternative Investments*, ISI publications, 2001. Here, I want to distinguish between market neutral strategies and strategies with a (mostly long) bias.

21. I am trying to resolve the question of whether to classify Long/Short as Opportunistic or Market Neutral by distinguishing Long/Short Equity with net market exposure from Long/Short Equity Market Neutral (the latter is discussed as a 'Relative Value' strategy).

22. An interesting study concerning the price action lag of small and mid-cap stocks is presented in *The Wildcard Option in Transacting Mutual-Fund Shares* by J. Chalmers, R. Edelen and G. Kadlec, Wharton School of Finance, 2000.

23. Note that this statement refers to *sectors*, not to broad markets. Whether statistical properties like trend persistence are present in equity markets (a clear violation of the weak form of market efficiency) is still subject to much discussion. A textbook summary of the discussion on efficient markets with numerous references can be found in Chapter 7 of *Investment Analysis and Portfolio Management* by F. Reilly and K. Brown. A more recent discussion with further references can be found in Dan Sullivan (ed.) *The Chartist Mutual Fund Letter,*

(PO Box 758, Seal Beach, CA 90740). Among the references given here is the seminal paper by Brock, Lakonishok and LeBaron, *Journal of Finance*, December 5, 1992, where the authors found that techniques championed by market timers appeared to provide useful market 'buy and sell' signals. Their study utilized the Dow Jones Index from 1897 to 1986 using two methods: simple moving averages and trading ranges. The moving average method produced the best performance; the trading range break also produced positive returns, which is in sharp contrast to the 'random walk' hypothesis articulated by protagonists of the (weak) form of market efficiency.

Le Baron presents another interesting statistical effect of trend forecasting conditional on volatility in his paper 'Some Relation between Volatility and Serial Correlations in Stock Market Returns', *Journal of Business*, 1992, 65(2), p.199.

24. As discussed in *The Wildcard Option in Transacting Mutual-Fund Shares* by J. Chalmers et al.

25. A discussion about Short Selling in a portfolio context can be found in 'Efficient Sets, Short Selling, and Estimation Risk', by G. Alexander, *Journal of Portfolio Management*, Winter 1995.

26. A good discussion about the issues involved is given in 'Short Selling: A Unique Set of Risks' by A. Arulpragasam and J. Chanos in *Managing Hedge Fund Risk* by V. Parker (ed.).

27. This example is also presented by A. Ineichen; 'In Search of Alpha'.

28. See *Technical Traders Guide to Computer Analysis of the Futures Markets* by C. Le Beau and D. Lucas for more details about technical trading models in financial markets.

29. I generally believe that the methods developed for non-linear time series analysis (a discipline that originated in applied mathematics and theoretical physics) fall short of being applicable to financial modelling.

30. See Chapter 7 of *Investment Analysis and Portfolio Management* by F. Reilly and K. Brown and references therein.

31. One way of reasoning as why currency markets should trend is that central banks attempt to smooth foreign exchange rate movements through intervention, see e.g. R. Arnott and T. Pham, *Tactical Currency Allocation*.

32.   Examples are: 1. Oil: Natural shorts are airline, natural longs are oil producers. 2. Foreign exchange: Exporting companies are natural longs of foreign currency, companies importing raw material from abroad are natural shorts of foreign currency. 3. Interest rates: Firms with a high need of financing (e.g. construction and development companies) are natural shorts of interest rate-linked instruments (bonds), firms with a large amount of liquid capital (e.g. banks) are natural longs.

33.   A detailed description of this type of strategy is presented in L. Jaeger, M. Jacquemai and P. Cittadini, 'The saisGroup Futures Index (sGFI) – A New Passive Futures Investment Strategy', saisGroup Research Paper, http://www.saisgroup.com, *Journal of Alternative Investments*, accepted for publication.

34.   J. M. Keynes originally articulated the theoretical argument for a risk transfer premium in the Futures market. In addition to specifying the theory, however, he also declared that he expected the premium to manifest itself as a consistent downward price bias in the Futures relative to spot prices. He termed this postulated price bias 'normal backwardation'. See J. M. Keynes, *A Treatise on Money*, Volume II, Macmillan & Co., New York, 1930.

CHAPTER 4

Empirical Properties of Alternative Investment Strategies

Attractive risk–reward characteristics and low correlations to traditional assets are features that make investments in Hedge funds and Managed Futures strategies particularly attractive to investors.[1] This chapter provides an overview of empirical risk and return properties of AIS sectors as measured by certain benchmark indices[2] and illustrates the benefits of AIS in a traditional portfolio. Properties of most interest to investors are return, volatility (most often measured in standard deviation of returns), drawdowns, correlation attributes and, as a measure for risk-adjusted performance, the Sharpe ratio. The latter is defined as the ratio between annualized monthly returns less the benchmark return (usually the long-term average of the risk free interest rate, here assumed to be 5%) and annualized monthly volatility.[3]

An interesting additional risk measure included in the following discussion is the kurtosis (fourth moment of the return distribution), which measures the 'tail fatness' of a historical return distribution as compared to the normal distribution. A value larger than zero indicates fatter tails than the normal distribution, i.e. a higher probability of extreme moves.[4] One of the perceived advantages of AIS is that they generally show much lower volatilities than equity investments when measured by the standard deviation (second moment). But many AIS return distributions show negative outliers, which exceed the range of three and more standard deviations more frequently than stocks or bonds. This risk ('tail risk') is of major concern to investors and remains unrecorded if the standard deviation is used for risk quantification only. It is therefore useful to include the kurtosis in the analysis of AIS performance. A value above 5 to 10 indicates significant exposure to tail risk.

Challenges of AIS performance measurement

Before we engage in the detailed analysis of the risk–return properties of alternative investments, some words of caution are necessary. First, the variability of manager performance within strategy sectors is significantly larger than for traditional equity and fixed income investments, which makes benchmark analysis less representative. Second, unlike traditional asset classes (bonds and equities), where performance data and benchmarks are readily and reliably available, the infrastructure and reliability of performance data for AIS are still undeveloped.[5] Several data providers have recently began to emerge, but the data availability and quality does not compare to those of traditional asset classes. For a list of data providers, the reader is referred to the appendix of this chapter.[6] We note at least three important problems specific to measuring AIS performance in the form of an index (or sub-index for particular sectors):[7]

1 *Survivorship bias.* Survivorship bias is the result of unsuccessful managers leaving the industry (and the representative index) and the successful ones remaining. This leads to a bias towards successful managers. The question is whether the database represents the true returns of the strategy sector or the returns of those managers who are successful enough to stay in business.[8]

2 *Weighting within the indices.* Some indices are asset weighted so that funds with more assets under management are given a larger weighting than smaller funds. Other indices are equally weighted giving smaller managers a relatively strong weight. Asset weighting can lead to a few large managers dominating the index (this is especially the case for Short Selling and Global Macro strategies), while equal weighting might be less representative for the average investor. The specific nature of the index should be considered when selecting and comparing indices.

3 *Selection bias.* The selection of the managers and sub-strategies included in the index has a significant influence on the index characteristics. To a lesser degree this also applies to traditional indices (equities and bonds) but the larger degree of peer group performance variability leads to more significant differences in index performances depending on how the particular strategy sector is defined and which managers are included in the index. Furthermore, some managers refuse to be included in any database.

In this chapter, I refer to four different index families: the Credit Suisse First Boston (CSFB)/Tremont indices, the HFR (Hedge Fund Research) indices, the Zurich (formerly MAR) indices for Managed Futures performance and the Parker FX Index for Currency Strategies (see appendix to this chapter for further details). The HFR Index is equally weighted among managers and adjusted for survivorship bias since 1995, while the CSFB Tremont indices and Zurich (MAR) Managed Futures indices are asset weighted and adjusted for survivorship bias since inception. The HFR Index goes back to 01/90 (for some strategies the HFR indices go back to 01/87, but I will only consider the period from 01/90 here) and the Tremont indices started in 01/94. The Zurich (MAR) indices partly go back to the beginning of the 1980s and the Parker indices to 1986, but here also, I will consider the period starting from 01/90 only.

Risk and return

Table 4.1 presents the results of a risk–return analysis for AIS strategy sectors from January 1990 to January 2002 based on monthly data. Returns were calculated as geometric averages (cumulative returns) of the log-differences of consecutive prices. The risk calculation is based on the standard deviation of returns. One can observe that the risk–return properties of Hedge fund strategies are very heterogeneous. Additionally, in Figures 4.1 and 4.2 these performance numbers are displayed graphically in a risk–return plot. I intentionally did not choose to plot the performance properties of individual strategies as risk–return coordinate points, but instead show representative areas of return and risk (namely one standard deviation along the main two axes of each performance 'cluster') to express the variability of manager performance within each sector.

TABLE 4.1 ■ Risk and return of AIS

	Return	Volatility	Max. Drawdown	Sharpe Ratio	Kurtosis
Distressed Securities					
HFR	15.10%	6.38%	−10.78%	1.58	6.53
Long/Short Equity					
HFR	20.22%	9.21%	−9.29%	1.65	1.22
Tremont	13.15%	11.88%	−14.21%	0.69	2.69
Equity Market Neutral					
HFR	11.11%	3.24%	−2.72%	1.88	0.35
Tremont	10.86%	3.17%	−3.55%	1.85	0.05
Event Driven					
HFR	15.90%	6.67%	−10.78%	1.63	6.75
Tremont	11.87%	6.42%	−16.04%	1.07	28.30
Macro					
HFR	17.50%	8.82%	−10.70%	1.42	0.25
Tremont	14.26%	13.28%	−26.78%	0.70	1.33
Market Timing					
HFR	14.49%	6.92%	−5.50%	1.37	−0.61
Regulation D					
HFR*	23.02%	7.18%	−11.99%	2.51	2.04
Relative Value					
HFR	13.58%	4.14%	−6.55%	2.07	8.44
Convertible Arbitrage (HFR)	11.90%	3.39%	−4.84%	2.03	3.61
Convertible Arbitrage (Tremont)	11.06%	4.82%	−12.04%	1.26	5.20
Fixed Income Arbitrage (HFR)	8.59%	4.79%	−14.42%	0.75	9.09
Fixed Income Arbitrage (Tremont)	7.57%	4.76%	−12.47%	0.54	15.22
Short Selling					
HFR	1.43%	22.73%	−53.36%	−0.16	1.44
Tremont	−1.04%	18.27%	−43.64%	−0.33	1.35
Fund of Funds					
HFR	10.97%	6.05%	−13.08%	0.99	4.16
Composite					
HFR	15.83%	7.27%	−11.42%	1.49	3.44
Tremont	11.80%	9.21%	−13.81%	0.74	1.15

TABLE 4.1 (Continued)

	Return	Volatility	Max. Drawdown	Sharpe Ratio	Kurtosis
Managed Futures					
Tremont	4.69%	11.59%	−17.74%	−0.03	1.34
MAR Systematic Active**	6.62%	11.05%	−15.64%	0.15	0.78
MAR Discretionary Active	12.47%	6.87%	−5.60%	1.09	1.13
MAR Trendfollowing	10.29%	16.14%	−20.11%	0.33	1.39
Passive (sGFII)	13.16%	10.02%	−9.09%	0.81	1.19
Currency Trading					
Parker Index	11.11%	9.73%	−8.86%	0.63	3.90
Equity					
MSCI EU (incl. dividends)	8.79%	15.33%	−33.03%	0.25	0.60
MSCI World (incl. dividends)	6.79%	14.65%	−35.32%	0.12	0.63
S&P 500 (incl. dividends)	12.03%	14.52%	−31.41%	0.48	1.13
Bonds					
SSB World (10) Gov't Bonds	6.60%	6.13%	−5.92%	0.26	0.40
Commodities					
Goldmann Sachs Index	3.10%	17.96%	−48.25%	−0.11	1.91

Source: Partners Group
Data: HFR (01.90–10.02), Tremont (01.94–01.02), MAR (01.90–01.02),
*01.96–01.02; **01.92–01.02

Focusing on Global Macro and Long/Short Equity strategies, one can clearly observe that: (1) high returns came at the expense of high risk; and (2) there are significant differences between the HFR and the Tremont benchmarks. For the 12-year study period, HFR show an average annual return for Global Macro funds of 17.5% per annum. Along with these impressive returns came a relatively high level of risk. With 8.9% standard deviation, Global Macro investments ranked among the more volatile in the Hedge funds industry. The strategy has a Sharpe ratio of 1.42 according to HFR. In contrast, the eight-year CSFB Tremont Index for Global Macro shows an average annual return of 14.3%, a volatility of 13.3% and a Sharpe ratio of 0.7. Long/Short Equity strategies showed 20.2% annualized returns, 9.2% volatility and a Sharpe ratio of 1.65 (Tremont: 13.2% returns, 11.9% volatility, 0.69 Sharpe ratio). The kurtosis numbers for Long/Short Equity strategies are slightly higher than those for Global Macro. One reason for

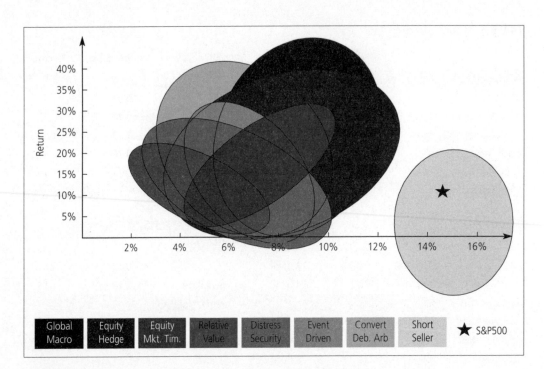

FIGURE 4.1 ■ Risk and Return for Hedge fund strategies (01.90–01.02)

Source: Partners Group
Data: HFR, MAR

the deviation between the two indices for Macro and Long/Short Equity strategies is that they had strong returns during the years 1990–94, a time period not entirely reflected by the Tremont Index, which began coverage in 1994.

It is important to note the large deviation in the drawdown figures between the HFR and Tremont databases for Global Macro, Long/Short Equity, Convertible Arbitrage and Event Driven strategies, for which the different time periods cannot be an explanation. While the ten-year equal-weighted HFR Macro Index shows the most severe drawdown during the period to be –10.7%, the asset-weighted Tremont Index (covering a shorter time period) shows a substantially worse –26.8%. The deviations for Long/Short Equity and Event Driven strategies are less remarkable, but also noteworthy (–9.3% HFR and –14.2% Tremont, –10.8% HFR and –16.0% Tremont respectively). For Convertible Arbitrage, HFR displays the worst draw-

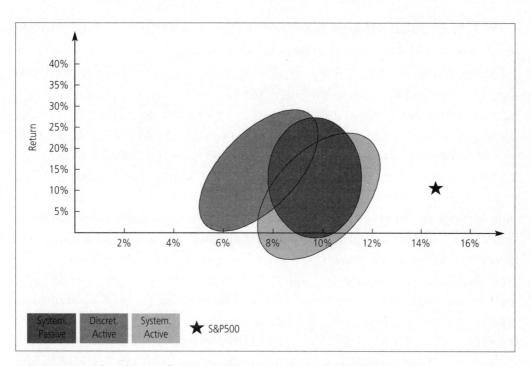

FIGURE 4.2 ▪ Risk and Return for Managed Futures strategies (01.90–01.02)

Source: Partners Group
Data: HFR, MAR

down of –4.9% in comparison to a value of –12.0% for the CSFB/Tremont Index. The wide differences between the two databases for this very important statistic further illustrate the value of understanding the way data is collected and what the information truly represents. My assessment is that the Tremont numbers in most circumstances provide a better understanding of past performance characteristics than the HFR indices. The Tremont data is asset weighted which provides better insights into the performance for the average investor.

Providing slightly lower returns on average, but better stability on the risk side are Market Timing, Relative Value, Distressed Securities and Event Driven strategies. While Market Timing and Relative Value experienced single worst drawdowns of –5.5% and –6.6% (HFR data) respectively, Event Driven and Distressed Securities exhibited drawdowns of about double these amounts. Looking further at kurtosis provides another view on risk: Market Timing (HFR):

–0.6, Relative Value (HFR): 8.4, Distressed Securities (HFR): 6.5, Event Driven: 6.75 (HFR) and 28.3 (CSFB/Tremont). The large kurtosis for Fixed Income Arbitrage (HFR: 9.1, CSFB/Tremont: 15.2), and for Relative Value in general, was largely caused by the events in the fall of 1998.

The worst performing sector during the period is clearly Short Selling. Suffering during a decade of bullish equity markets, short sellers returned an average of 1.4% with a volatility of 22.7% (HFR). The worst drawdown figure of –53.4% sheds further light on the difficulties faced by this sector during the time period considered here. Similar results are reflected by the Tremont Index. It is not surprising, however, that in the 18-month period from April 2000 to September 2001, short sellers were among the best performers in the industry (but they lost significantly again between 10/01 and 01/02).

Equity Market Neutral strategies demonstrated impressive risk-adjusted performance according to both the HFR and Tremont databases. With returns of 11.1% and low volatility of 3.2%, the strategies show a very impressive Sharpe ratio of 1.88 and 1.85 (HFR and Tremont respectively). This strategy has the lowest drawdown overall (–3.55% for Tremont and –2.72% for HFR). The kurtosis for the strategies is zero, indicating low tail risk.

Convertible Debenture Arbitrage ('Regulation D') strategies showed average annual returns of 23.0% and volatility of 7.2%, which gives a Sharpe ratio of 2.51. The worst drawdown stands at –12.0%. An important factor to consider here is the lack of liquidity. The presented volatility is partly the effect of the absence of mark to market pricing. With frequent changes in pricing absent, volatility appears artificially low. The high returns partly represent a liquidity premium the investor receives for accepting a relatively long lock-up period.

The Managed Futures side of the AIS Universe is more homogenous than Hedge funds. The standalone return to risk ratios of Managed Futures strategies are generally not as impressive when compared to Hedge fund strategies. Their main value lies in their correlation attributes and diversification capacities within an overall portfolio. Interesting because of their attractive return and risk properties (and their usually lower fee structure) are Systematic Passive Futures strategies (as represented by the sGFI)[9] with 13.2% return and 10.0% volatility (Sharpe ratio: 0.81). The maximal drawdown of this strategy is –9.1%. Active Discretionary Futures strategies show a 12.5% return, 6.9% volatility and a –5.6% maximal drawdown. Systematic Active strategies demonstrate 6.6% returns and 11.1% standard deviation, with a –15.6% maximal drawdown. The pure trendfollowing strategies show a return of 10.3%, a volatility of 16.4% and a maximal drawdown of –20.1%. For completeness, the Commodity Long Only strategy, as represented by the Goldmann Sachs Commodity Index, is also displayed. This Long Only approach does not take advantage of large swings on the downside and therefore demonstrates only 3.1% returns and a very large 18.0% standard deviation. The worst drawdown of –48.35% is a staggering number that further illustrates the benefits of having the flexibility to go short in the Futures market.

Comparison with equities and bonds

The returns of AIS vary by strategy, but as a whole and individually compare very favourably to the returns of traditional investments. In the equity markets, represented here by the S&P500, the MSCI Europe and the MSCI World, the return to risk ratios are generally lower than their AIS counterparts. The decade of the 1990s saw outstanding unparalleled growth in equity markets, which ended in 2000/2001. Nonetheless, the 12.0% return and 14.5% volatility of the S&P500 does not exactly meet the standard of high return paired with low volatility. In 2000/2001 the S&P500 experienced a 31.4% drawdown. The MSCI Europe Index's average annual return of 8.8% with a volatility of 15.3% is even less inspiring and the MSCI World, with 6.8% returns and 14.7% volatility is below the range of reasonable performance for an investment with this level of risk. The worst drawdowns for the MSCI indices stand at the very intimidating figure of –33.0% for Europe and –35.3% for the MSCI World. Finally, the Salomon Smith Barney World Government Bond Ten Market Index (in US dollar terms) represents the traditional complement to stocks in the form of fixed income (including corporate bonds). Although the volatility level is comparable to Hedge funds (6.1%), the return of 6.6% is about half of the return of the average Hedge fund.

Unconditional correlation properties

Besides the very attractive risk-adjusted return characteristics, one of the most attractive features of AIS is their favourable correlation to traditional asset classes. A correlation matrix with the different strategy sectors and traditional assets is presented in Table 4.2. (The numbers presented here are linear correlations. The use of 'rank correlation' might be more appropriate in many circumstances.) By means of diversification, including AIS in traditional portfolios provides asset managers with the opportunity to produce better returns with lower levels of risk.

Short Selling strategies obviously have the lowest correlation to the equity markets with a –0.64 correlation to the S&P500. The strategy also demonstrates low correlations to the MSCI World and MSCI Europe (–0.6 and –0.48 respectively), as well as a –0.07 correlation to the world bond index. Fixed Income Arbitrage strategies have a slightly negative correlation to equity markets (–0.04) and a significant negative correlation to bonds (–0.28). It should be noted for the discussion of correlations that given the amount of data available (12 years of monthly data), the confidence interval for the correlation coefficient being statistically significant (on a 95% level) is about [–0.15:0.15]. This means that only correlation coefficients smaller than –0.15 or larger than 0.15 are statistically significantly different from zero and correlation coefficients within the interval [–0.15:0.15] can be considered equal to zero.

Equity Market Neutral, Regulation D, Convertible Arbitrage, Relative Value in general, Distressed Securities and Global Macro have the next to lowest correlations to the S&P500. Their correlations to the equity markets are low enough to act as an effective diversifier and hedge, with figures showing 0.11, 0.31, 0.33, 0.37, 0.37 and 0.43 respectively. While not negatively correlated to the equity markets, all have negative or very low positive correlations to bond markets. This property is valuable, as bonds are usually an integral part of traditional portfolios.

The following Hedge fund strategies have rather high correlations to traditional asset classes: Event Driven with a correlation of 0.60, Long/Short Equity with 0.64 and Market Timing with 0.66. Their low correlations to fixed income asset classes gives some validation to their *Hedge* fund classification, but these strategies are not ideally suited from the point of view of diversification and correlation with traditional asset classes, and especially not for an equity portfolio.

TABLE 4.2 ■ Correlations between AIS and traditional investment classes

	CA	FX	DS	LSE	EMN	ED	FIA	GM	EMT	RD	RV	SS	FoF	FSA	FDA	FTF	FP	ME	MW	S&P	SSB	GSC
Convertible Arbitrage	1.00	0.01	0.59	0.46	0.14	0.62	0.13	0.40	0.29	0.21	0.51	-0.37	0.48	-0.09	0.10	-0.09	-0.13	0.24	0.30	0.33	-0.02	0.05
Currency Trading	0.01	1.00	-0.02	0.03	0.17	-0.06	-0.06	0.27	-0.03	-0.05	-0.09	0.18	0.23	0.69	0.40	0.72	0.09	-0.07	-0.03	-0.03	0.13	-0.00
Distressed Securities	0.59	-0.02	1.00	0.57	0.16	0.78	0.37	0.46	0.35	0.37	0.64	-0.48	0.57	-0.26	0.04	-0.20	-0.27	0.34	0.37	0.37	-0.16	0.01
Long/Short Equity	0.46	0.03	0.57	1.00	0.32	0.75	0.08	0.60	0.68	0.57	0.51	-0.76	0.75	-0.08	0.13	-0.08	-0.20	0.53	0.60	0.64	0.03	0.20
Equity Market Neutral	0.14	0.17	0.16	0.32	1.00	0.17	0.06	0.22	0.14	0.13	0.14	-0.14	0.30	0.03	0.10	0.12	-0.01	0.11	0.09	0.11	0.14	0.17
Event Driven	0.62	-0.06	0.78	0.75	0.17	1.00	0.20	0.57	0.48	0.41	0.63	-0.60	0.63	-0.13	0.04	-0.17	-0.24	0.50	0.55	0.60	-0.06	0.04
Fixed Income Arbitrage	0.13	-0.06	0.37	0.08	0.06	0.20	1.00	0.12	0.01	0.13	0.30	-0.04	0.26	-0.14	-0.06	-0.16	-0.14	0.09	0.02	-0.04	-0.28	0.05
Global Macro	0.40	0.27	0.46	0.60	0.22	0.57	0.12	1.00	0.53	0.37	0.37	-0.41	0.71	0.26	0.39	0.27	0.02	0.44	0.44	0.43	0.06	0.02
Equity Market Timing	0.29	-0.03	0.35	0.68	0.14	0.48	0.01	0.53	1.00	0.46	0.29	-0.67	0.51	0.03	0.04	-0.01	-0.18	0.59	0.65	0.66	0.10	0.07
Regulation D	0.21	-0.05	0.37	0.57	0.13	0.41	0.13	0.37	0.46	1.00	0.37	-0.39	0.52	0.01	0.11	-0.09	-0.04	0.38	0.36	0.31	-0.11	0.18
Relative Value	0.51	-0.09	0.64	0.51	0.14	0.63	0.30	0.37	0.29	0.37	1.00	-0.32	0.46	-0.14	-0.02	-0.23	-0.21	0.37	0.37	0.37	-0.12	0.12
Short Selling	-0.37	0.18	-0.48	-0.76	-0.14	-0.60	-0.04	-0.41	-0.67	-0.39	-0.32	1.00	-0.49	0.22	-0.01	0.24	0.26	-0.48	-0.60	-0.64	-0.07	-0.04
Fund of Funds	0.48	0.23	0.57	0.75	0.30	0.63	0.26	0.71	0.51	0.52	0.46	-0.49	1.00	0.09	0.41	0.16	-0.05	0.40	0.42	0.43	-0.08	0.21
Futures Sys. Active	-0.09	0.69	-0.26	-0.08	0.03	-0.13	-0.14	0.26	-0.09	0.01	-0.14	0.22	0.09	1.00	0.47	0.92	0.46	-0.05	-0.01	-0.07	0.30	0.05
Futures Discr. Active	0.10	0.40	0.04	0.13	0.10	0.04	-0.06	0.39	0.04	0.11	-0.02	-0.01	0.41	0.47	1.00	0.49	0.27	-0.09	0.01	-0.06	0.08	0.16
Futures Trendfollow	-0.09	0.72	-0.20	-0.08	0.12	-0.17	-0.16	0.27	-0.01	-0.09	-0.23	0.24	0.16	0.92	0.49	1.00	0.41	-0.17	-0.16	-0.13	0.22	0.08
Futures Pass. (sGFI)	-0.13	0.09	-0.27	-0.20	-0.01	-0.24	-0.14	0.02	-0.18	-0.04	-0.21	0.26	-0.05	0.46	0.27	0.41	1.00	-0.19	-0.23	-0.26	0.07	-0.11
MSCI Europe	0.24	-0.07	0.34	0.53	0.11	0.50	0.09	0.44	0.59	0.38	0.37	-0.48	0.40	-0.05	-0.09	-0.17	-0.19	1.00	0.86	0.69	0.32	-0.08
MSCI World	0.30	-0.03	0.37	0.60	0.09	0.55	0.02	0.44	0.65	0.36	0.37	-0.60	0.42	-0.01	0.01	-0.16	-0.23	0.86	1.00	0.84	0.31	-0.02
S&P 500	0.33	-0.03	0.37	0.64	0.11	0.60	-0.04	0.43	0.66	0.31	0.37	-0.64	0.43	-0.07	-0.06	-0.13	-0.26	0.69	0.84	1.00	0.16	-0.03
SSB World Govt. Bonds	-0.02	0.13	-0.16	0.03	0.14	-0.06	-0.28	0.06	0.10	-0.11	-0.12	-0.07	-0.08	0.30	0.08	0.22	0.07	0.32	0.31	0.16	1.00	0.07
Goldmann Sachs CI	0.05	0.00	0.01	0.20	0.17	0.04	0.05	0.02	0.07	0.18	0.12	-0.04	0.21	0.05	0.16	0.08	-0.11	-0.08	-0.02	-0.03	0.07	1.00

Source: Partners Group
Data: HFR (01.90–01.02). MAR (01.94–01.02)

In the Managed Futures Universe, non-to-negative correlation properties are more widely observed. All are either negatively correlated or show zero correlation to the S&P500. The Passive Futures strategy sector has a statistically significant negative correlation of –0.26 to the S&P, followed by trendfollowers (–0.13) and Discretionary and Systematic Active strategies (–0.06 and –0.07 respectively). The correlation factors of the last three are not significantly different from zero. Furthermore, Managed Futures strategies demonstrate rather low correlations to bond markets with figures ranging between 0.07 and 0.3. With these correlation properties to equity and fixed income investments, Managed Futures generally serve as an excellent hedge (i.e. diversifier) within the global portfolios of investors.

AIS also display interesting correlation properties among themselves. Short Selling strategies have negative correlations to all other Hedge funds and Regulation D strategies have low correlations to Relative Value, Macro and Event Driven strategies (correlation numbers for illiquid strategies might be biased due to the infrequent marking to market)[10]. Market Timing strategies have low correlations to Distressed Securities and Relative Value strategies. Relative Value and Macro strategies also have low correlations to one another. The correlations between Managed Futures and Hedge funds also range from negative to zero. Passive Futures strategies, for example, are positively correlated to only one Hedge fund strategy (Short Selling).

As a final note on correlations, I would like to outline the variability of correlation characteristics (which makes the application of quantitative optimisation techniques very problematic). Figure 4.3 displays the rolling 12-month correlation between the S&P500 index and the HFR Composite. For illustration the 12-month rolling return of the S&P500 is also displayed. One can observe the large fluctuations in the correlation figures ranging from about 0.3 to above 0.9.

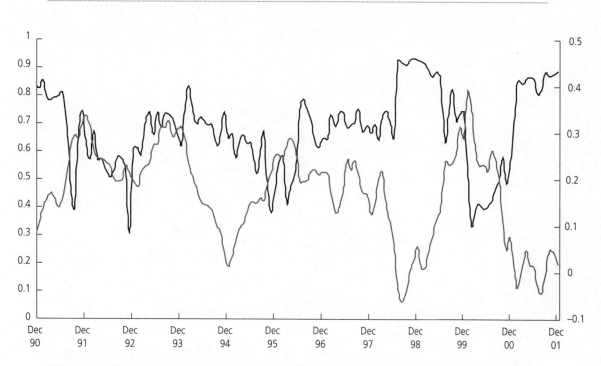

FIGURE 4.3 ■ Rolling 12-month correlation between the S&P500 and the HFR Composite Index (black) and the 12 month rolling return of the S&P500 (grey)

Conditional correlation properties

The correlation properties presented thus far do not tell the entire story about diversification benefits. What investors really want is positive correlation in periods when equity and bond portfolios advance, and negative correlation in periods when the value of traditional investments decline. This can be measured by looking at *conditional correlation*. Conditional correlation is defined as the correlation between two different assets measured only during particular periods. It can be particularly useful in evaluating a portfolio's sensitivity to extreme market moves. Figure 4.4 displays the correlation of various AIS in different equity market condition, as represented by the performance of the S&P500, while Figure 4.5 presents a different view on the same subject of conditional correlations by showing the performance of selected strategies during the months of worst S&P performance.

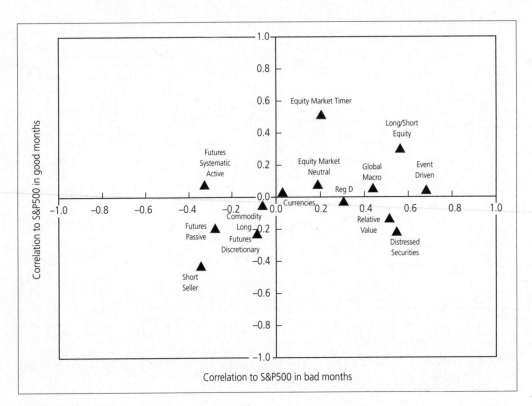

FIGURE 4.4 ■ AIS Conditional Correlation Properties

Source: Partners Group
Data: HRF, MAR

Systematic Active Futures strategies provide an example of favourable conditional correlation. The strategy has a positive correlation of about 0.2 with the S&P500 during periods when the S&P500 is up and a negative –0.37 correlation when the index is down. This property serves as an excellent hedge in an equity portfolio. Note that the confidence intervals for statistical significance are about [–0.2:0.2] for positive S&P500 return periods, and [–0.25:0.25] for negative S&P500 returns.

Systematic Passive Futures strategies also display interesting conditional correlation features, posting a negative –0.3 correlation to the S&P500 when the index is down and a correlation that is statistically not different from zero (–0.17) when the index is up. While the returns are not necessarily correlated in advancing equity markets, the strategies' returns can very well serve to hedge against losses in declining equity

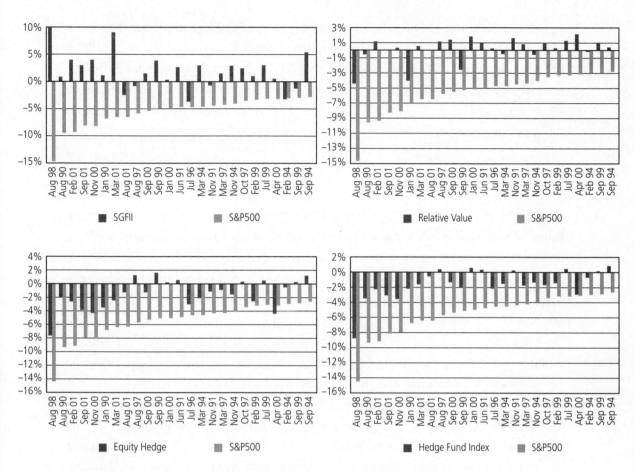

FIGURE 4.5 ▪ Performance of selected strategies during equity down months

Data: HFR, partners Group

markets. This is especially useful in periods of great market volatility and uncertainty (e.g. August/September 1998, fall 2000, early 2001, September 2001). Equity Market Timing strategies, in contrast, are highly correlated to the equity markets in periods of rising equity market (0.55) and almost uncorrelated in poor market periods (0.14). This property is equally desirable for an investor. Returns in positive equity market periods are not sacrificed, while losses in declining equity markets are avoided.

Positive correlation in up markets and in down markets is a feature of most Long/Short Equity strategies. Event Driven, Distressed Security, Relative Value and Macro strategies move in line with equity markets during periods of declining equity markets, but are largely uncorrelated to the S&P500 in advancing equity markets. Short Selling strategies are naturally negatively correlated to the S&P500 in both advancing and declining equity markets. Convertible Debenture Arbitrage (Reg D), Currencies, Discretionary Futures and Long Only Commodity strategies show no statistically significant conditional correlation, either in rising or in falling equity markets.

Behaviour in extreme market situations

During the last ten years or so there has rarely been a year without a move in the range of ten standard deviations in one or more financial or commodity markets. Investors have been faced with a variety of extreme market environments (e.g. Japanese stock market crash, Gulf War, oil price boom, recession, bond market crash, Mexico crisis, Asian crisis, Russian default, Brazil crisis, TMT crash, WTC terrorist attacks). For the following discussion, I selected five such periods in order to illustrate the behaviour of AIS during extreme market turmoil: the rising interest rates (bond crash) in early 1994, the Asian crisis in 1997, the Russian default crises in 1998, the 'TMT crash' in 2000/2001 and the terrorist attacks in September 2001.[11] The performance of each strategy sector during these periods is displayed in Table 4.3. I also included the performance of the average fund of funds as a best indication for the return provided to investors in multi-manager AIS portfolios. Finally, the performance of the two traditional asset classes (equity and bonds) is given:

1　From February to April 1994 the US and European yield curves shifted upwards by about 150 basis points within the short period of two months, after the FED unexpectedly raised interest rates. This led to major losses in traditional bond portfolios. Within the AIS Universe, Global Macro and Convertible Arbitrage managers suffered most from this unusual interest rate move, with losses of –10.7% and –4.6%, respectively. Long/Short Equity managers lost –2.9% and Active Futures returned between   –3.0% (systematic) and –5.0% (discretionary). Fixed Income Arbitrage and short sellers on the other side made significant gains with +3.6% and +16.2%, respectively. The average fund of funds lost –5.6% due to the high exposure to Global Macro strategies most AIS portfolios had at the time.

2 During the Asian crisis following the devaluation of many Asian currencies in the second half of 1997, all AIS earned significant positive returns led by Futures strategies (Passive +14.0%), Long/Short Equity (+13.5%), Regulation D (+13.8%) and Risk Arbitrage (+9.9%). Fixed Income Arbitrage with +1.7% displayed the lowest returns of all strategies. Fund of funds returned 6.2% on average.

3 The market crisis following the Russian default in August 1998 is also referred to as a 'Hedge fund crisis'. The average fund of funds lost −11.6% in the three-month period from August to October! This is mainly due to large allocations in Fixed Income Arbitrage strategies (−13.2% from August to October 1998) in many AIS portfolios at that time (the strategy had shown very high performance in the two-year period preceding August 1998). Distressed Security strategies also lost significantly (−12.4%). But the period also had some clear winners. Futures strategies returned +8.9% (Systematic Active), +4.8% (Systematic Passive) and +1.0% (Systematic Discretionary).

4 The equity market downturn and the burst of the technology bubble ('NASDAQ crash') that started in March 2000 and led to a decline of 30.5% in the S&P500 during the following 19 months is largely seen as one reason for the tremendous increase of investors' interest in AIS. Interestingly, the performance of an average fund of funds was actually negative (−2.6%) during this period! Again, this was caused by the high exposure in many funds of funds to a strategy sector that lost significantly; this time it was the Long/Short Equity sector that lost −7.9% in the 18-month equity bear market until September 2001. But the period also saw a number of very successful strategies. Relative Value strategies provided very high returns to investors (more than +20% for Convertible Arbitrage and Equity Market Neutral, and +7.6% for Fixed Income Arbitrage). Futures strategies also had a period of good performance (ranging +7.3% to +28.7%). But the stars of the industry were short sellers with +95.6% return (according to HFR). Note that the performance numbers for Short Selling strategies deviate significantly between different data providers (CSFB/Tremont shows a return of about +43.7% during this period). This can be explained by the fact that short selling managers are not very numerous, and the information reported by each index depends strongly on what managers included and how they are weighted in the index (see preceding

discussion). Global Macro strategies were able to make a comeback. Note also here that the CSFB/Tremont numbers (+28.8%) are significantly different from the HFR numbers (+4.0%) presented in Table 4.3. A possible explanation here again is the different weighting scheme. The Tremont indices are asset weighted, which puts most emphasis on just a few large Hedge funds.

5 Finally, the month of September 2001 proved to be another real stress test for AIS, which the industry, generally speaking, passed well. The average fund of funds lost less than –2% compared to –8.2% for the S&P500 and +0.7% for bonds (Lehman US Government Bond Index). Long/Short Equity, Fixed Income Arbitrage and Risk Arbitrage lost –3.8%, –2.9% and –3.1% respectively, while Futures again served as an excellent hedge in the AIS portfolio with returns of +2.9% (Systematic Passive).

TABLE 4.3 ■ AIS returns in extreme market environments

	Bond Crash 02.94–04.94	Asian crisis 07.97–12.97	Russian default 08.98–10.98	TMT Crash 04.00–09.01	Terrorist attack September 01
Convertible Arbitrage	–4.62%	5.67%	–4.69%	20.74%	0.72%
Fixed Income Arbitrage	3.58%	1.70%	–13.18%	7.57%	–2.92%
Equity Market Neutral	1.94%	7.31%	–1.48%	21.43%	2.27%[4]
Risk Arbitrage	0.70%	9.91%	–2.00%	13.78%	–3.05%
Distressed Securities	–1.38%	6.98%	–12.43%	8.32%	–1.02%
Regulation D	N/A	13.83%	2.08%	–7.42%	–1.22%
Global Macro	–10.70%	8.88%	–5.93%	3.98%[2]	2.72%
Long/Short Equity	–2.85%	13.50%	–2.38%[1]	–7.89%	–3.78%
Equity Market Timing	–2.08%	8.01%	5.72%	–1.68%	–0.96%
Short Selling	16.15%	1.97%	4.15%	95.56%[3]	3.22%
Futures Systematic Active	–2.98%	4.60%	8.91%	7.34%	0.19%
Futures Discretionary Active	–4.98%	4.53%	0.99%	13.09%	0.83%
Futures Systematic Passive	0.71%	14.00%	4.81%	28.65%	2.87%
Fund of Funds	–5.59%	6.23%	–11.60%	–2.62%	–1.76%
S&P500	–6.37%	9.63%	–1.96%	–30.54%	–8.17%
Lehman US Government Bond Index	–9.34%	12.55%	6.62%	18.72%	0.74%

[1] 7.65% in 08.98

[2] 28.76% for the Tremont index

[3] 43.72% for the Tremont index

[4] For Stat. Arbitrage: –1.95%

Benefits of AIS in a traditional portfolio

Risk–return and correlation properties have already given a clear indication of the benefits of AIS in a generic traditional portfolio. In order to demonstrate the effects of including AIS in a traditional portfolio of bonds and equity, Figure 4.6 presents the efficient frontiers of a traditional portfolio with and without investments in Hedge funds and Managed Futures. For the representation of a traditional portfolio, the S&P500 Index, the MSCI World Index, the MSCI Europe Index and the Salomon Smith Barney (SSB) World Government Bond Index were selected. For Hedge fund representation, the HFR Composite Index as an equally weighted basket of managers from all different Hedge funds strategies was chosen. For comparison I also included an efficient frontier analysis with the HFR Fund of Funds Index (FoF) instead of the HFR Composite Index. Finally, for Managed Futures strategies, I chose the Zurich Managed Futures Index and the sGFII. It should be noted that the quantitative portfolio optimization techniques applied are subject to certain assumptions about the risk and return inputs (see Chapter 7 for a more detailed discussion on the pitfalls of portfolio optimization of AIS portfolios).

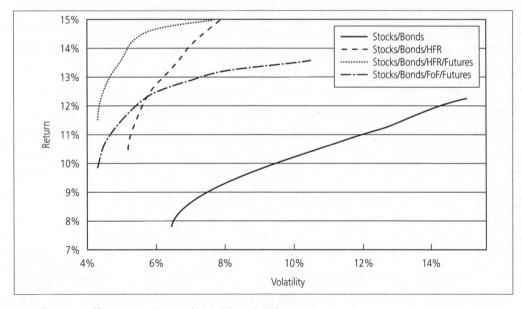

FIGURE 4.6 ■ Efficient Frontier Analysis with and without AIS

Data: Time period: 01.90–01.02. HFR, MAR and SGFII were taken for AIS; MSCI, S&P and SSB bond index were taken for traditional asset classes (see text)

The traditional portfolio displays annual returns ranging from just over 7% to 12% (the S&P500 return), with a volatility ranging from about 6% to 14.5%. The top right corner of the curve is a result of the equity contribution of higher return and higher risk. On the bottom left corner of the curve, the efficient frontier displays the contribution of bonds to the portfolio; risk is minimized with returns being sacrificed as well.

The efficient frontier of the traditional portfolio changes dramatically when combined with AIS. The addition of Hedge funds to a portfolio of equity and bonds reduces the levels of volatility to a range from 4.7% to 7.4%. This substantial drop in volatility occurs simultaneously with a dramatic rise in returns to a greatly improved range of 10.4% to 15%. When Managed Futures are further added to the equity, bond and Hedge fund portfolio, the risk levels are even more reduced, while the returns are enhanced along the efficient frontier (the two efficient frontiers meet in the point of highest return, which is the HFR return). The result is that the efficient frontier curve for the traditional portfolio plus Hedge funds and Managed Futures stretches from 11.5% to 15.0% in the return dimension, with only 3.8% to 7.4% volatility. The lowest level of return of the portfolio enhanced with Hedge funds and Managed Futures is only slightly lower than the highest level of return for the traditional portfolio without AIS. The same can be said for the risk dimension. The highest risk point of the curve combining equity, bond, Hedge funds and Managed Futures is only about 1% higher than the lowest risk level for the traditional portfolio without AIS, which corresponds to a 100% bond portfolio.

Also interesting is the comparison if the average fund of funds performance instead of the HFR Composite is used. This combination also shows a significant improvement compared to equities and bonds only, but compared with the analysis using the HFR Composite Index, the portfolio with fund of funds has lower return with about the same level of risk. The extra layer of fees that must be paid to fund of funds managers explains a part of this difference.

Summary of empirical properties

The broad range of AIS demonstrates very attractive risk–reward characteristics. Strategies with negative, zero and low correlations to traditional assets and/or to each other offer attractive capacities for diversification and efficiency enhancement within an investor's global portfolio.

It is interesting to look at how AIS investors fared during times of market turmoil. Although quite diverse in their returns, Hedge funds and Managed Futures generally showed much better performance than traditional investments during these periods. Interestingly, in difficult market environments funds of funds have shown much worse returns than the average strategy sector (even after accounting for the extra fee level). I believe this performance pattern mirrors the fact that AIS allocators tend to behave in a pro-cyclical way, over-weighting the best performing strategy sectors of the recent past. With too much money flowing into these strategies they are often the first to experience problems during market turmoil. Futures strategies generally performed well during these critical periods. This justifies their presence as a 'hedge' in a multi-manager AIS portfolio.

AIS investments generally have a meaningful impact on the efficient frontier for investors who usually hold traditional assets such as stocks and bonds only. For periods when traditional markets suffer, some AIS display consistently positive returns. All the benefits of AIS work dramatically to improve the efficient frontier of the traditional portfolio, producing significantly higher returns with substantially lower risk.

Appendix: Data providers for AIS

Altvest, New York (www.altvest.com) tracks 13 strategies from a database that allows managers to input their own data. Each fund is assigned to the category in which the largest percentage of its assets is invested. There are no performance criteria for inclusion in the index. Index results are based on reports from more than 1,400 Hedge funds in a database of 1,800 funds. Data goes back to 1993. Altvest is owned by InvestorForce and the website requires registration in order to gain access to the indices.

Capital Markets, EACM (www.eacmalternative.com), is based on 100 funds selected to be representative of 13 strategies, arranged in five clusters. The index is an equally weighted composite of unaudited performance information provided by the funds. EACM bases its results on the same funds from month to month, allowing no manager who had a bad month to avoid inclusion. Funds are assigned categories on the basis of how closely they match the strategy definitions. Names of the funds are not disclosed. The index is rebalanced annually. It was launched in 1996 with data going back to 1990. Capital Markets is owned by Evaluation Associates.

Credit Suisse First Boston/Tremont (www.hedgeindex.com) covers nine strategies and is based on 340 funds, representing $100 billion in invested capital, selected from a database of 2,600 funds. It is the only asset- (capitalization-) weighted Hedge fund index. The CSFB/Tremont Index discloses its construction methods and identifies all the funds within it. CSFB/Tremont accepts only funds (not separate accounts) with a minimum of $10 million under management and an audited financial statement. If a fund liquidates, its performance remains in the index for the period during which the fund was active in order to minimize survivorship bias. The index was launched in 1999, with data going back to 1994. It incorporates the TASS+ database.

Hedge Fund Research (www.hfr.com) includes 29 categories plus subtotals. The index is equally weighted and based on 1,100 funds, drawn from a database of 1,700 funds. Funds of funds are not included in the composite index. Funds in the database represent $260 billion in assets. The index was launched in 1994 with data back to 1990. Funds are assigned to categories based on the descriptions in their offering memorandums. The indices aim at eliminating the survivor bias problem by incorporating funds that have ceased to exist.

Hedgefund.net (www.hedgefund.net) covers 31 strategies arranged into three subtotals. Called the Tuna Indices, they are updated from a database of 1,800 Hedge funds and funds of funds. The data goes back to 1979 and managers select their own categories. HedgeFund.Net is operated by Links Securities LLC, an NASD registered broker–dealer and owned by Links Holdings and Capital Z Investments.

Hennessee Group (www.hedgefnd.com) reports 22 investment-style categories. The indices were created in 1987 and first published in 1992. Results are based on 450 funds, including 150 in which Hennessee clients are invested, from a database of 3,000 funds. Assets of $160 billion are represented in the index. Each reporting fund is placed in the category that reflects the manager's core competency.

LJH Global Investments (www.ljh.com) tracks 16 different equally weighted indices, each composed of approximately 50 managers. It is the only index that presents performance exclusively in graph form. To be included, funds must have an audited statement and have passed some level of LJH due diligence. Funds are assigned to categories based on LJH's screenings. The index is rebalanced quarterly or semi-annually, depending on the strategy. For a fee, LJH provides data on index components.

MAR Futures (www.marhedge.com) reports especially on the performance of Managed Futures strategies in each of 15 categories, ten of which are combined into four sub-medians. The variety of Zurich (formerly MAR) index databases contains 1,300 funds. Managers usually select their own categories. The firm's website identifies the number of funds and assets in each category. MAR, the former publisher of the index, sold its database business to Zurich Financial Services in spring 2001.

A new index from **Morgan Stanley Capital** was announced to be available in the second half of 2001. It will not be investable initially, although the option remains under consideration. Morgan Stanley Capital claims that its index will be 'institutional-brand quality' and that it will be 'different'. The database for the new index will come from Financial Risk Management in London, an institutional asset manager investing in Hedge funds.

The Parker Currency Trading Index (http://www.parkerglobal.com/fxindex.htm) is a performance-based equally weighted benchmark that measures the returns of global currency managers. In addition to the Parker FX Index, there are two style-driven sub-indices: the Parker Systematic Index and the Parker Discretionary Index. The former tracks those managers whose decision process is rule based and the latter tracks those managers whose decision process is judgmental. The Parker FX Index currently includes 43 programs managed by 37 firms located in the USA, Canada, UK, Ireland and Switzerland. The 43 programs manage over $8 billion in currency assets and include a combination of 33 programs that are systematic and ten programs that are discretionary. Disciplines include technical, fundamental and quantitative.

Van Hedge Fund Advisors International (www.vanhedge.com) is derived from the performance of an average of more than 750 funds separated into US and off-shore funds covering 14 strategies and combined into a separate global index. There are no performance or size criteria and funds are assigned to categories based on their offering memorandums and interviews with the individual managers.

Zurich Capital Markets (http://www.zcmgroup.com) provides the Zurich Hedge Fund indices in partnership with TRS Associates to track the performance of various Hedge fund strategies. They differ from existing Hedge fund indices by focusing only on those funds/managers most likely to be considered for investment by institutional and other sophisticated investors. Focusing is on those funds/managers that: (1) are strategy pure in their style; (2) have a two-year minimum performance track record; and (3) have sufficient assets under management to demonstrate organizational and managerial infrastructure, scalable strategies and the ability to raise funds from sophisticated investors. Highly leveraged strategies and strategies involving complex derivatives are excluded. There is no requirement that these funds be open to new investments, because the indices themselves are not designed to be directly investable and are constructed only to reflect the returns of a particular Hedge fund strategy. The indices are equally weighted.

Notes

1.　There are numerous empirical studies showing the benefits of AIS in traditional portfolios. Please refer to 'The Benefits of Alternative Investment Strategies in the Institutional Portfolio' by L. Jaeger, saisGroup Research Paper, 2001, available on http://www.saisgroup.com; 'The Benefits of Hedge Funds' by T. Schneeweiss and G. Martin, Lehman Brothers Publications, 2000; 'Portfolios of Alternative Assets: Why not 100% Hedge Funds?' by R. McFall Lamm Jr., *The Journal of Investing*, Winter 1999; 'The Performance of Hedge Funds: Risk Return, and Incentives', Ackermann et al., *Journal of Finance*, 1999.

2.　An excellent and more detailed discussion of the empirical properties of AIS is provided by A. Ineichen, 'In Search of Alpha', October 2000.

3.　The Sharpe ratio, however, is not the only and arguably not the most appropriate measure for risk-adjusted performance. There is a large variety of different performance measures. Please refer to Dacorogna et al., 'Effective Return, Risk Aversion and Drawdowns', *Physica A*, January 2001, 289, p.229–48 for an excellent discussion and further references.

4.　Kurtosis is most often defined as $k \int \left(\frac{x-m}{\sigma} \right)^4 dx$ (where m is the mean, σ the standard deviation and k a normalization factor). The kurtosis of the standard normal distribution is three. In the numbers presented here, kurtosis is defined as $k \int \left(\frac{x-m}{\sigma} \right)^4 dx - 3$.

5. See 'Performance Characteristics of Hedge Funds and Commodity Funds: Natural versus Spurious Biases' by W. Fung and D. Hsieh in the *Journal of Financial and Quantitive Analysis,* 2000.

6. See also the work by Schneeweiss Partners, *A Review of Alternative Hedge Fund Indices.*

7. A discussion of the different issues in AIS index construction is also presented in 'Hedge Fund Indices' by G. Crowder and L. Hennessee, *Journal of Alternative Investments,* Summer 2001; see also 'The Benchmark Bane' in *The Economist,* August 31, 2001.

8. See also the article by G. Amin and H. Kat, 'Welcome to the Dark Side: Hedge Fund Attrition and Survivorship Bias over the Period 1994–2001'.

9. sGFI stands for 'saisGroup Futures Index', a systematic Passive Futures strategy index developed by the author and his partners at saisGroup (now Partners Group). Please refer to the following article for further details about this index: L. Jaeger, P. Cittadini and M. Jacquemai, 'The saisGroup Futures Index (sGFI) – A New Passive Futures Investment Strategy', available on http://www.saisgroup.com.

10. See the article by C. Asness et al., 'Do Hedge Funds Hedge?'

11. The study was published in German in the *Neue Zürcher Zeitung* (Jan 8, 2002): 'Hedge Funds in Marktturbulenzen'.

CHAPTER 5

Risk in Alternative
Investment Strategies

Alternative Investment Strategies entail the search for 'alpha' combined with the proper management of the underlying risks. Whereas for traditional investments, sector and instrument selection next to portfolio diversification are the key performance drivers, for AIS it is strategy sector selection together with downside risk management, which are the most critical determinants of investment performance. In Chapter 3, I outlined the return drivers and risk characteristics of the single AIS sectors. In this chapter, I discuss general risks and the strategy-specific risk management principles of AIS. In Chapter 7, I go on to outline the top down sector and bottom up manager selection process in an integrated risk management framework for the AIS portfolio. Important here will be the distinction between 'pre-investment' risk management ('top down' strategy allocation, 'bottom up' manager due diligence, portfolio diversification) and 'post-investment risk management' (monitoring, active risk control).

Risk factors in AIS investments

AIS investments are inherently more complex than traditional investments. Hedge funds and Managed Futures trade a wide spectrum of different asset classes and instruments and include features such as leverage, Short Selling, complex derivatives trading, spread positions and low liquidity. While also present in traditional portfolios, many risk factors are more difficult to analyze in an AIS context because of their complex interaction with each other.[1]

▪ *Market risk*: Market risk is the risk of loss due to unexpected and adverse price moves or changes of volatility in the broad markets or single sectors.

▪ *Credit risk*: Credit risk is the risk of counter-parties defaulting on their obligations or of changes in the market's sentiment about the probability of their default.

▪ *Liquidity risk*: Liquidity risk is twofold: (1) The risk of loss due to the (temporary) inability to unwind a position at a normal bid/ask spread; (2) the risk of not being able to fund investment leverage. Liquidity risk in AIS is magnified by a certain herding behaviour of AIS managers in times of turbulence.[2] An example is October 1998, when many Hedge funds exited their yen carry trades simultaneously, which led to a 15% rise of the Japanese currency against the US dollar (a normally extremely liquid market) within just a few hours.

▪ *Common factor risk*: Common factor risk is the risk inherent in some, but not all, securities. (e.g. industry-specific risk, geographic risk, etc.).

▪ *Operational risk*: Operational risk is the risk of failure of internal systems, technology, people, external systems or physical events.

▪ *Event risk*: Event risk is the risk of an extraordinary political or economic event, e.g. unexpected election outcome, military events, sovereign default.

▪ *Corporate event risk*: Corporate event risk is the risk of loss due to an exposure to a particular firm and a specific event affecting its value, e.g. surprise announcements like earnings revisions, mergers or changes of management.

▪ *Model risk*: Model risk is the risk of a model mis-specification, which can lead to incorrect valuation of a financial instrument or the model not being suitable for the particular trading approach.[3]

An AIS risk manager has to understand the complex relationship between market risk, manager risk, liquidity risk, counter-party risk, pricing risk and leverage.[4] Liquidity risk is often connected to the leverage employed by the fund. While it is still current practice to consider market risk, credit risk and liquidity risk separately, risk experts increasingly argue that risk management should treat these risks in combination.

Because Hedge funds and Managed Futures have a much higher transaction turnover and usually fewer back-up staff compared to traditional asset managers, operational risks (e.g. exceeding position limits or erroneous execution) can be significantly higher. Further, many Hedge funds depend on systematic quantitative models for buy and sell signal generation. Inappropriate models can expose AIS investments to model risk. AIS are also subject to event risk of many different kinds. The summer/fall of 1998 showed that tumultuous financial markets can affect Hedge funds just as negatively as traditional investments.

But AIS risks extend beyond the risks shared with traditional investments. Investors and risk managers must consider the following additional risks:

- *Lack of transparency*: Despite growing investor awareness of its importance, there remains strong resistance against transparency in the AIS industry. There are good reasons why investment and trading activities at financial institutions (banks, insurances, brokers, pension funds) are generally subject to disclosure to clients and regulatory authorities. The same logic should apply to the trading activities of AIS managers; however, transparency in AIS is far from universal. Lack of transparency and insufficient investor control are among the main reasons for the following risk factors.

- *Manager risk*: AIS returns are to a high degree a function of the individual AIS manager's skill. Much discretionary decision-making power is concentrated in one or a few individuals. Overconfidence, in extreme cases hubris, is one of the most important origins of unexpected losses encountered by single AIS managers. The legal set-up of a Hedge fund gives the manager almost unlimited freedom in their investment process. Typical disclosure documents provide for broad manager authority along the lines of the following:

The program's objective is to achieve substantial long-term capital appreciation while offering an efficient diversification investment vehicle to traditional assets such as bonds, equities or real estate based on the systematic application of computerized trading strategies or fundamental models. There are no restrictions or limitations to the markets, exchanges, futures, options and forward contracts that can be traded by the advisor.

The wide freedom provided to the manager creates idiosyncratic risks such as single-person dependency, style drift and 'bets'.

▪ *Leverage risk*: For AIS investments, leverage is not always undesirable and in some cases even necessary to achieve return targets. An excessive amount of leverage can be disastrous, however. In volatile markets, AIS easily becomes a captive of leverage. Leverage risk has two components: volatility and financing. To the same degree that leverage enhances returns, it also increases investment risk. The problems of leverage become apparent with the advent of the unexpected, when leverage can quickly turn moderate losses into investment disasters. For strategies that use external financing for leverage, sudden unavailability of financing can cause significant problems. A single margin call on a position can destroy an entire portfolio, if the manager is forced to sell at an inopportune time. It should be noted that prime brokers tend to change their haircut policies and withhold financing exactly at those moments when it is most needed.

▪ *Counter-party risk*: There are numerous incidences where counter-parties' change of policies and withdrawal of funding support caused severe losses to AIS funds. This usually occurs in stress situations, when several risk factors act simultaneously. The story of MKP Capital Management LLC, a mortage-backed Securities Arbitrage manager, provides an illustrative example of counter-party risk in combination with leverage, liquidity and legal risks. The manager was forced to liquidate a significant part of his $370 million fund in October 1998, when the prime broker, Salomon Smith Barney (SSB), stopped accepting certain securities as collateral for MKP's margin payments and at the same time refused to give credit to MKP for unrealized returns generated by securities held in SSB's account. Furthermore, according to the lawsuit filed by MKP, SSB refused to confirm the trades that the manager was able to negotiate in the process of the liquidation, claiming lack of administrative support for the heavy trading volume. The fund ended up losing hundreds of millions of dollars. Three years after the event the case is still with the courts.[5,6]

■ *Risk of asset–liability mismatch*: The investor should make sure that the investments of the AIS manager are liquid enough to fulfil redemption obligations to investors. It is possible for Hedge funds to have a mismatch between portfolio liquidity and redemption policies.

■ *Capacity risk*: Most AIS strategies have limited investment capacity, i.e. they can only handle a certain amount of money without significantly diluting their performance. Investors might not be able to invest with the managers they find most attractive. High quality managers tend to close their program quickly. The investor should be aware of the capacity limits of the strategy. Some managers dislike rejecting new investors' money when their capacity limit is reached.

■ *Fraud risk*: In an unregulated industry with about 5,000 Hedge fund products offered, a certain number of these unavoidably involve fraud. Although a rather rare occurrence, fraud in the form of false performance reports and audits or Ponzi schemes have in the past resulted in significant losses for investors. The names John Natal (Cambridge Fund) and Michael Berger (Manhattan Fund) are linked with Hedge fund fraud.[7]

■ *Data risk*: Unlike traditional asset classes, where performance data and benchmarks are readily and reliably available, the infrastructure of performance data for AIS is still rather undeveloped and reliability of the data is low.[8] The results of performance studies for AIS often depend on the database used (see Chapter 4 for a more detailed discussion). AIS data is biased in several different ways. It usually does not go back far into the past and is largely drawn from the period of the exceptional equity bull market in the late 1980s and 1990s. The resulting bias can be illustrated by strategies containing 'short option' or 'short volatility' elements, which generate steady returns containing a certain but low probability of large losses. Losses may simply not yet have been observed during the measurement period. Further, the survivorship bias (i.e. the bias due to liquidated strategies dropping out of the pool of reported managers) can lead to reported performance being 2–3% higher than actual returns. Finally, not all AIS managers disclose their performance to reporting services (see Chapter 4 for a more detailed discussion).

■ *Performance measurement risk*: Traditional equity or bond managers' performance is usually measured against specific benchmarks (indices). In contrast, AIS are considered 'absolute return' investments, i.e. they do not have explicit performance benchmarks. Benchmarks as used in traditional asset management are unlikely to be developed for AIS. Their definition and use requires (a) an unambiguous classification of the strategy universe, (b) a good representation of the investment universe benchmarked and (c) the possibility of being replicated. These requirements cannot easily be applied to AIS investments.[9]

The emphasis of AIS managers is on how much absolute return their strategy generates. Although the focus of many managers has shifted from absolute return targets to quantifying performance in terms of 'risk-adjusted returns', the best way of measuring risk-adjusted return is still the subject of intense discussion.[10] Many investors and managers use the Sharpe ratio or one of its variations. The Sharpe ratio has its set of difficulties as a performance measure, however.[11] Most investments that earn premiums for taking particular risks, and they can be exposed to asymmetric payoffs (similar to a 'short option' position). Sharpe ratios are unsuited for measuring the risk-adjusted performance of investments with skewed return distributions, because the standard deviation does not account for risk appropriately in this situation (see Chapter 2). Choosing inappropriate criteria for non-benchmarked performance measurement imposes the risk of introducing performance targets that do not match the investment objectives. The examination of the performance track record of individual managers has to be complemented with other types of analysis. A track record should serve as a basis for questioning the past rather than for predicting future performance.

■ *Pricing risk*: The pricing and NAV calculation for investment funds is not guided by unique standards. Some Hedge fund strategies trade illiquid instruments, which cannot be reliably priced on a regular basis and whose market values the manager usually estimates himself. This leaves generous space for performance smoothing. In some cases, the securities may be so illiquid that they are not mark to market for several months. Thus, there may be significant lags between reported returns and 'real' returns.[12] An interesting survey on NAV calculation and fair value practices used in the broad investment industry[13] displayed that 13% of all funds (including Mutual funds, Hedge funds and others) make some kind of adjustment to the prices they receive from their valuation sources. This percentage is likely to be significantly higher for Hedge funds only. The most frequently made adjustments mentioned are write-downs for liquidity, price adaptations to time zone and proprietary pricing models for complex derivative instruments.

- *Portfolio risk*: As discussed, the risk profile of AIS can differ considerably from traditional investments. The amount of variation in Hedge fund returns that can be explained by the risk factors used in common asset-pricing models is rather low.[14] It is therefore difficult to map AIS investment risks onto standard risk factors like equity, fixed income, FX, commodity risk or credit risk. As a result, if included into the traditional portfolio, the heterogeneous nature of AIS strategies makes it more difficult to obtain an overall picture of portfolio risk.

- *Legal risk*: Hedge fund managers can find themselves in situations where they are unable to enforce their claims other than through a lengthy legal process. This is mainly true for very illiquid strategies such as Distressed Securities or Regulation D strategies. Another aspect of legal risk concerns the relationship between the investor and the fund. Due to the litigious nature of the US legal system, offering memorandums for Hedge funds are almost always one-sided in favour of the AIS manager. The legal documents, which should be carefully read and understood by the investor prior to investment, are the fund prospectus, subscription agreement, investment management agreement and advisory contracts.

- *Administrative risk*: The Hedge fund investor relies strongly on the quality and responsibility of administrators and auditors in controlling the assets and the accuracy of financial statements. Often some basic infrastructural requirements for the performance of these tasks are not present in offshore locations that many AIS managers choose as fund domiciles, including independent mark to market pricing (which is too often left in the hands of the Hedge fund managers) and the auditing of financial statements. The case of the 'Manhattan Fund' provides an illustrative example, where the fund manager, Michael Berger, was able to deliver false account statements to the administrator and auditor for an extended period of time.

■ *Regulatory risk*: Most AIS funds are registered offshore. The choice of domicile for a Hedge fund or Managed Futures fund is critical. Changing regulatory or tax requirements can be damaging to investors' interests.

■ *Systemic risk*: Systemic risk involves the contagious transmission of a sudden shock due to the financial system's exposure to one or more failing institutions. This shock might result in damage to the financial system to such an extent that the economic activity in the wider economy can suffer. It is feared that the large size of a single Hedge fund can expose the wider financial market to systemic risk. The near collapse of LTCM is often referred to as an example of systemic risk.

Risk from an investor's point of view

Most AIS investors are not able to devote sufficient resources to the selection of strategies and managers and to the necessary degree of risk management. They therefore rely on a professional fund of funds manager to cope with the details of the various risks outlined above. Therefore, many private and institutional investors have a broader perspective on risk and are possibly concerned about the following issues when investing in AIS (in order of least to most impact on the investor's portfolio):

1 *Investment underperformance*: While the risk of investment performance falling short of expectations can never be entirely eliminated, it can be reduced by a thorough manager due diligence and strategy allocation process through which the best trading talents are picked within the most attractive sectors.

2 *Inappropriate strategy sector allocation*: Inappropriate sector allocation may lead to a risk–returned profile that is unsuited for the investor. This type of risk can be minimized if clear investment objectives, (risk-adjusted) performance targets and well-defined risk parameters are established and used as the drivers of the sector allocation process. Further, sector allocation should not be static; it must be subject to ongoing review.

3 *Severe decline in account value*: This is (besides fraud) the greatest fear of investors. A sharp and significant drop in the portfolio value can be caused by all of the following:

■ a deviation from the stated strategy (style drift or an unexpected 'bet' by the trading manager)

■ an existing risk factor that the investor did not understand or recognize (most often an event or a market behaviour that was not anticipated)

■ risks that were known and accepted as part of the investment strategy.

In order to cope with the risk of severe loss, continuous monitoring of exposure and risk is necessary. In addition to allowing for the early recognition of deviations from a stated strategy ('style drifts') and the identification of undesired 'bets', exposure and risk monitoring can help detect previously unknown risks (particularly in extreme market environments). However, risks as a result of previously known and accepted risks cannot be entirely eliminated.

4 *Fraud*: This is a risk in any investment, but due to the specific focus on individual trading managers and the participation in private and mostly unregulated investment vehicles, this risk is more severe for AIS investments compared to traditional investments. Fraud can occur in many different ways ranging from rather mild forms (e.g. undisclosed kickbacks to third parties) to very severe forms (e.g. manipulated performance statements). Exposure to fraud is the ultimate nightmare for investors. In many cases of fraud the investor loses all or a large portion of his investment. A good safeguard is to know the individuals involved and to check every detail of their background. Continuous monitoring of the manager's trading activity decreases fraud risk significantly. Detailed reading of the fund's offering memorandum is essential. Ultimately, the best way to safeguard against fraud risk is to separate the trading manager from the money, i.e. establish a managed account.

From an investor's perspective, the gradations between fraud and bad business practice, between malicious intent and ineptitude may not be so relevant. Investors would like to avoid any kind of irregularity that can potentially harm them. One irregularity is a breakdown in the integrity of a manager. The initial due diligence and constant monitoring should uncover potential irregularities before they occur.

Effective risk management begins with the ability to control. In the process of the institutionalization of the AIS industry and in light of the increasing number of AIS investors with fiduciary responsibility, investing in a 'black box' must be considered more and more unsuitable. The risk manager should have regular knowledge about the activities of the AIS manager. At the same time, long redemption periods make control impossible. Ideally, if the allocation is sufficiently high, the AIS allocator should make an investment with an AIS manager through a managed account, which provides him with daily transparency and the highest possible level of liquidity (which, of course, ultimately depends on the traded securities).

Risk factors of the different AIS sectors

As discussed in Chapter 3, the degree and type of risk varies substantially among strategy sectors. Global Macro, Long/Short equity, Short Sellers and Futures/Currency strategies are strongly exposed to broad market risk, while credit risk is an important element of the risk profile for Distressed Securities and Regulation D strategies. Some Relative Value (Convertible Arbitrage) and Event Driven strategies (Risk Arbitrage and Distressed Securities) are highly exposed to corporate event risk. Liquidity risk requires significant attention for Fixed Income Arbitrage, Regulation D and Distressed Securities strategies.

AIS strategies are often distinguished in terms of their exposure to market risk (equity, interest rates, FX, commodities) and credit risk.[15] Sometimes liquidity risk is added as an extra dimension. Figures 5.1–5.10 introduce a further differentiated view on AIS risk and illustrate the various risk types for each of the strategy sectors using a scale from zero to five (zero represents no sensitivity to the risk factor and five represents maximal sensitivity). The illustration is of rather a descriptive nature here and should serve its illustrative purpose.

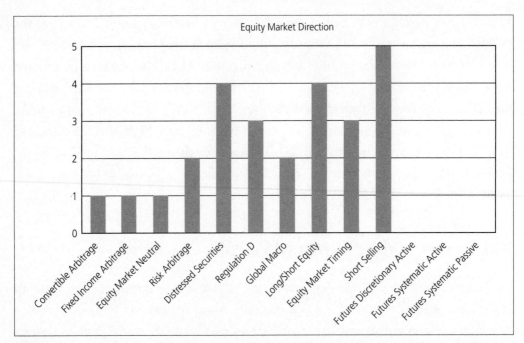

FIGURE 5.1 ■ Directional market risk: Sensitivity to falling (for Short Selling: rising) stock markets

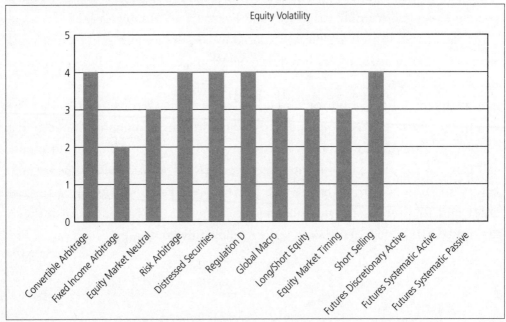

FIGURE 5.2 ■ Non-directional equity risk: Sensitivity to stock market volatility (note that Convertible Arbitrage usually displays an inverse sensitivity to equity volatility)

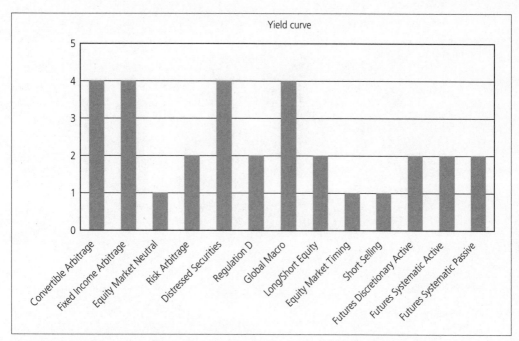

FIGURE 5.3 ■ Yield curve risk: Sensitivity to parallel shift in interest rate term structure

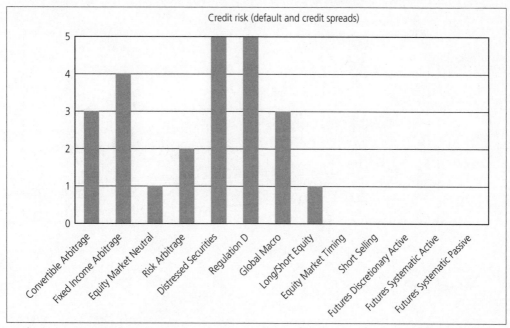

FIGURE 5.4 ■ Credit risk: Sensitivity to increasing default probability and widening credit spreads

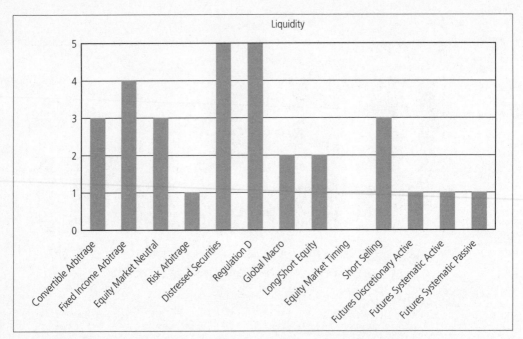

FIGURE 5.5 ■ Liquidity risk: Sensitivity to liquidity decreasing in financial markets

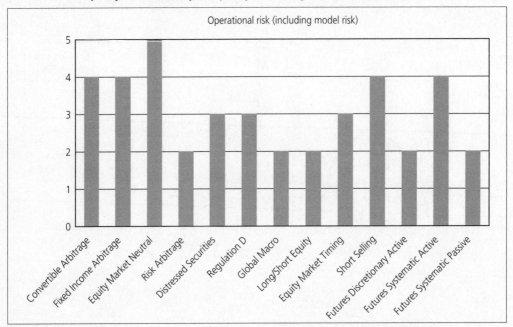

FIGURE 5.6 ■ Operational risk: Risk of failure due to internal systems, technology, people, external systems or physical events (including model risk)

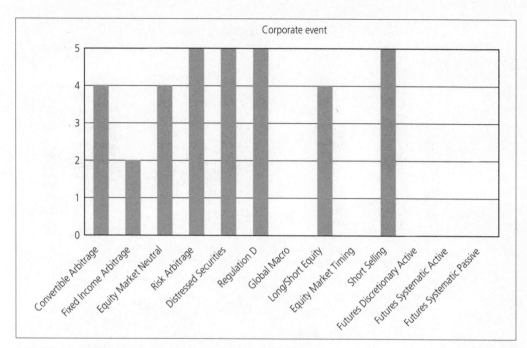

FIGURE 5.7 ■ Idiosyncratic equity risk: Risk of corporate event

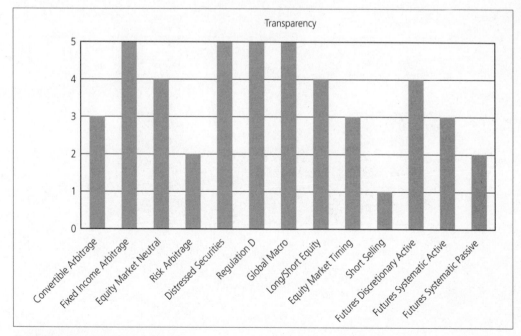

FIGURE 5.8 ■ Lack of transparency

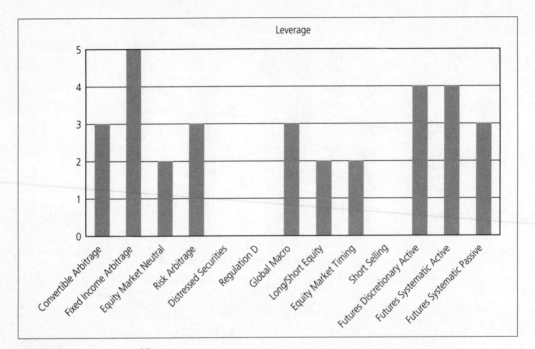

FIGURE 5.9  Leverage risk

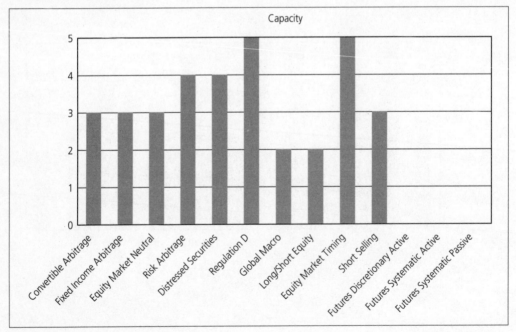

FIGURE 5.10  Capacity constraints

Broad equity market ('beta') risk comes in two forms: directional (price) and non-directional (volatility) risk (Figures 5.1 and 5.2). Next to the 'beta' risk (also called 'systemic risk'), financial market theory (the CAPM) differentiates the idiosyncratic (residual) portion of equity risk, which is denoted 'corporate event risk' in Figure 5.7. Interest rate risk is a function of possible yield curve shifts (Figures 5.3). Credit and liquidity risk (Figures 5.4 and 5.5 respectively) often appear simultaneously (except in the case of short sellers, where liquidity risk represents the risk of a 'short squeeze'). Figures 5.6, 5.8, 5.9 and 5.10 display the different strategies' exposure to operational risk, the risk of insufficient transparency, leverage risk and the degree of capacity constraints.

Directional and corporate specific equity market risk ranges from high for opportunistic equity strategies (Long/Short Equity, Short Selling) and certain Event Driven strategies (Regulation D, Distressed Securities) to low or non-existent for most Futures strategies. By making bets on the direction of certain equity market sectors and other financial markets (e.g. currencies) Global Macro strategies are directly exposed to directional price risk (in equity, fixed income, FX markets). Convertible Arbitrage, Equity Market Neutral and Fixed Income Arbitrage in contrast bear little exposure to directional price moves in the broad equity markets and Risk Arbitrage strategies find themselves in an intermediate range for directional equity risk. But some Relative Value strategies (Convertible Arbitrage and Equity Market Neutral) are exposed to changes in the volatility of equity markets as well as corporate event risk. Note that Convertible Arbitrage carries an inverse sensitivity to equity market volatility, performing well in periods of increasing volatility and showing lower returns in periods of decreasing volatility.

Yield curve risk is most prevalent for Fixed Income Arbitrage strategies, which tend to also be exposed to credit and liquidity risk. The most illiquid strategies, namely Distressed Securities and Regulation D, also come with significant credit risk. Operational risk in the form of model risk is present in those strategies that rely on pricing and technical trading models, which are mostly Relative Value and Futures strategies. Finally, the strategies with the lowest capacities are the illiquid Event Driven strategies (Distressed Securities, Regulation D) and Equity Market Timing. This last strategy is facing increasing problems in its operation due to the fact that Mutual fund managers are less willing to accept market timers trading in their funds.

Risk management principles for the different AIS sectors

An understanding of AIS risk and risk management principles on a strategy-by-strategy basis is important for three reasons. First, it provides the allocator with the possibility to decide during the sector allocation process which risks he is willing to bear for an appropriate expected return and to avoid the ones he is unwilling to accept. Second, it allows the AIS allocator to critically review a manager's own internal risk controls as part of the manager due diligence process. Third, it enables the allocator to monitor and control risk on the portfolio level more effectively (see Chapter 7 for a more detailed discussion).

Active risk management generally includes measures such as establishing maximal position sizes, maintaining defined allocations to sectors and asset classes, keeping a minimum number of different positions, and applying strict position stop-loss limits. But the most important element of risk management on the level of the individual strategy as well as the multi-manager portfolio is diversification. While multi-manager funds reach diversification by investing with a variety of strategies, individual AIS managers diversify by trading their particular strategy in various instruments and asset classes. The following presents the most important risk management guidelines for each strategy sector.

Convertible Arbitrage

Convertible Arbitrage is a 'long volatility strategy'. The strategy is naturally exposed to 'vega' risk, i.e. the risk of unexpected changes in volatility. This risk is generally not hedged other than through sector and issuer diversification. But most managers seek to implement a delta neutral hedge, i.e. they avoid exposure to price moves of the stock. For this purpose the manager has to determine the appropriate number of stocks to be sold short against the long convertible position (as determined by the hedge ratio). Scenario analysis and stress tests are performed to determine how prices and hedge ratio behave under different market scenarios. Besides delta hedges for the equity component, interest rate derivatives (options, futures, swaps) are used to hedge exposure to changes in interest and foreign exchange rates (if relevant). Recent developments in credit derivatives enable Convertible Arbitrage managers increasingly to hedge credit risk through total return swaps credit default swaps and credit options.[16] This still happens mostly on security baskets, as individual credit default protection for below investment-grade securities remains costly. But as the credit derivatives markets are developing, single issuer protection might become more easily available in the future. Convertible Arbitrage managers who build up an expertise in trading credit derivatives can potentially build up a real edge in their sector.

Convertible Arbitrage managers have to perform in-depth, traditional fundamental analysis on the issuing company's stock and debt. Credit analysis is especially important in cases where credit quality is low. The focus of most managers has traditionally been on financial ratios (earnings per share, ROE, Altman's Z-score, interest rate coverage, balance sheet leverage etc.). Recently, quantitative credit risk models have evolved which can aid the risk manager in the analysis of default risk (see Chapter 6 for a discussion of these models).

Diversification is an important component of Convertible Arbitrage risk management. The manager can diversify across industries, sectors, credit qualities and moneyness of convertible securities (out-of-the-money convertibles are more duration sensitive, while in-the-money convertibles bear higher equity sensitivity). The manager should stress test the portfolio for sensitivities to interest rate risk (rho risk), vega (volatility) risk, spread widening and credit default risk and equity price moves. Setting stop-loss limits and maximum sizes for exposures to individual companies can further control risk.

Convertible Arbitrage managers have to deal with liquidity risk. The manager has to be aware of funding risk, the exposure to short squeezes and possible decreases of short rebates, especially in situations of financial market turmoil, when spreads increase and liquidity dries up. 'Flight to quality' can become a serious issue at moments when the extension of credit, including the financing provided by prime brokers, is rationed and investors avoid riskier assets in favour of higher quality issues. A good relationship with the prime broker decreases these financing and 'shorting' risks. Leverage control constitutes an important guideline for risk management. The manager should always consider the following question: 'In extreme circumstances, can the position be unwound, and at what price?'

Fixed Income Arbitrage

Knowledge about the present and the possibility of future portfolio exposure and risk (VaR and stress tests respectively) is extremely important for the Fixed Income Arbitrage manager in order to be able to react to developments in financial markets in a timely fashion. The continuous analysis of the strategy's risk profile requires very sophisticated quantitative tools. 'Variance-based VaR', 'multiple standard deviation' and '95% confidence interval' approaches are insufficient for assessing the market risk of a typical Fixed Income Arbitrage strategy. It is the '5% tail risk' that requires the risk manager's particular attention. Monte Carlo simulation, extreme market stress tests (e.g. the scenario of the emerging market/Hedge fund crisis of 1998, unexpected cuts/raises of interest rates by the Fed or sovereign default), and Extreme Value Theory (a concept widely applied in insurance mathematics) are examples of more appropriate risk analysis tools.

A Fixed Income Arbitrage manager relies strongly on his counter-parties as lenders as well as borrowers. A thorough due diligence of their creditworthiness as well as their reliability is necessary. A variety of portfolio credit risk tools have been developed recently (see Chapter 6). The strategy can easily become a captive of extreme leverage, where a single margin call on a position can destroy an entire portfolio. The liquidity risk has to be controlled by ensuring sufficient funding and maintaining appropriate leverage levels. Generally, managers try to eliminate interest rate risk by structuring their portfolios to be near zero duration (except when managers execute a particular view on the future shape of the yield curve). Convexity risk is less often hedged.

Fixed Income Arbitrage managers often employ sophisticated quantitative models to identify pricing anomalies. These models require constant reassessment to ensure that the required level of accuracy is maintained. Accurate understanding and valuation of prepayment options for mortage-backed securities (MBS) is the key to appropriate risk management for MBS strategies. The main tool here is an appropriate option-adjusted spread (OAS) model. OAS is the yield spread that has to be added (to a binomial model or Monte Carlo simulation) in MBS valuations accounting for the optionality of prepayment.[17] Prepayment risk is usually difficult to hedge.

Equity Market Neutral

The key to risk management for Equity Market Neutral strategies is diversification. Exposure should be spread widely across industries and sectors. Managers have to narrow down the number of stocks considered for trading to 200 to 1,000 out of the tens of thousands of companies listed on international exchanges. For this, they use criteria such as sectors, size, liquidity and market depth, ability to short and corporate event risk. Statistical Arbitrage managers usually trade more liquid stocks, because their turnover is generally high and positions need to be readily bought and sold. Corporate event risk requires special attention. Most managers avoid stocks involved in mergers or restructuring, buyback programs or heavy (legal) insider trading (e.g. employee stock plans). Particularly 'hard to borrow' stocks are also excluded from the list of eligible stocks. Important features of risk management are stop-loss limits and maximum sizes for individual positions. As for Fixed Income Arbitrage, the '5% tail risk' calls for the particular attention of the risk manager, who should also consider the correlation features of specific stocks and sectors. In most circumstances variance-based VaR with 95% confidence intervals is insufficient to assess the risk of a typical Equity Market Neutral strategy.

Once the 'eligible stock list' is defined, the manager begins the process of selecting the individual stocks to be included in his portfolio. The investment decision-making process might require an in-depth fundamental analysis of companies. For Statistical Arbitrage strategies this often happens based on factor models. Many Statistical Arbitrage managers have no qualitative component to their decision-making process, i.e. they use quantitative models exclusively. These rely mostly on past statistical properties of single stocks and stock sectors. Most market neutral Long/Short Equity managers, on the other hand, perform discretionary evaluations or use a qualitative discretionary overlay on top of quantitative analysis. They review the buy and sell lists to identify specific factors that models cannot cover, such as pending mergers, late breaking news, rumours or simply faulty data.

Models and discretionary techniques do not work equally well in all sectors, so managers have to select the sectors for which their valuation models and analysis techniques work best. High-tech stocks require different valuation approaches from low tech, utility or railway companies. Sophisticated quantitative models that are employed to rank stocks relative to one another and to identify equity price anomalies require constant monitoring and reassessment to ensure their predictive accuracy. Continuous structural changes of financial markets usually affect the predictive quality of the models and necessitate their frequent re-evaluation and dynamic refinement. The manager has to determine when to drop certain factors of the model that have lost their predictive power and when to include new ones. Out-of-sample testing should always follow model optimization in order to limit 'over-fitting'.

Portfolio construction is a very important component of return and risk management for Equity Market Neutral strategies. Managers often utilize sophisticated computer algorithms, so called quadratic optimization procedures, for this purpose. Such optimizers are widely commercially available (BARRA, Mathlab, etc.), but some managers construct their own proprietary tool sets. Constant portfolio monitoring is necessary to ensure neutrality against the exposures that strategy seeks neutrality against (e.g. market beta, sector or industry, size, P/E levels etc.).

With a high position, turnover efficient and reliable execution and back office facilities are necessary to cope with operational risks (e.g. execution risk). The relationship to the prime broker is important for ensuring continuous funding of leverage, the availability of shorting capacity and protection against 'short squeezes'.

Risk Arbitrage

Risk Arbitrage can be seen as equivalent to writing a put option on a merger deal. The primary risk of the strategy is the deal risk arising from financial, legal or regulatory challenges to a merger going through. When a merger actually fails, the long position usually drops significantly. In order to avoid a single deal failure spelling disaster for the entire portfolio, diversification across a number of mergers is the first principle for risk management in Merger Arbitrage. Many managers use position limits on individual deals in the portfolio. Some managers spread risk across different industry sectors, while others have particular expertise in one industry sector. In this case, the investor should seek diversification within his AIS portfolio through diversification across various managers with different sector focuses. Concentrating on deals in the late stage of the merger transaction process decreases deal risk, but also decreases the deal premium spread (expected return).

Many managers enter into positions related to announced deals only and do not speculate on possible merger candidates prior to their announcement.

Risk Arbitrage managers have to perform in-depth analysis of all the issues involved in the merger and constantly monitor the evolution of the merger process in order to control the deal risk. This includes the financial situation of the two companies (earnings, balance sheet leverage, growth etc.), regulatory issues, shareholder resistance and the development of the deal premium (spread). Important parts of the due diligence and risk control process are studies of the financial statements, interviews with management, attending anti-trust court hearings, analysis of market sentiment and stock market valuations, studying trade data sources and past justice department and anti-trust agencies' enforcement policies.

Most Risk Arbitrage managers use some leverage. Leverage control generally constitutes an important guideline for risk management, especially in periods of decreased deal flow. Taking equal size long and short positions usually controls exposure to the broad equity market. In some cases the precise value of the merger transaction is unknown or changes occur in the course of the transaction. In those cases, delta neutrality should be monitored diligently. Liquidity is usually not a major risk factor, if the involved companies have sufficient market capitalization. In the case of smaller deals the manager should monitor whether the stocks are traded with sufficient liquidity. The ability to sell the acquirer short can be dampened by the stock being 'hard to borrow'.

A note on VaR: VaR techniques are difficult to apply to Risk Arbitrage strategies, as the prices of the two stocks (especially the stock of the acquired company) detach from their price history once a merger has been announced. The deal specific character of a contemplated transaction generally makes VaR-based quantitative risk analysis less useful. Nevertheless, recent efforts by CMRA[18] are directed towards developing a 'database that will allow investors to apply value-at-risk to portfolios with investments in Merger Arbitrage Hedge funds'.

Distressed Securities

Distressed Securities strategies are exposed to a very unique set of risks, mostly company specific. Liquidity is inherently low, as restructuring negotiations and/or bankruptcy proceedings often stretch over an extended period of time with uncertain outcome. Therefore, diversification across a broad range of companies is an important part of risk management. Once invested, however, liquidity constraints impose limitations on active risk management. Nevertheless, constant monitoring or involvement in the ongoing restructuring process or bankruptcy proceedings is important.

Managers must engage in in-depth fundamental analysis of individual companies in the pre-investment phase and should have extensive experience in assessing troubled companies. Credit risk, the probability and default and the impact of an actual default must be assessed in a 'bottom up' analysis. Quantitative credit risk models are of limited use, as most of these models are not specifically designed for distressed investments and do not distinguish sensitively enough in the range of high default probability.

In order to value equity and debt securities of troubled companies, the analyst often prepares both a 'going concern' valuation and a valuation based on liquidation and then assigns probabilities to possible outcomes. In the case of a debt security, this includes an assessment of the debt's collateral and other terms. In addition to looking at recent and projected financial results, other factors such as liquidity, competence of management, credibility of restructuring plans and company strategy and external market factors should be taken into account. Bankruptcy laws in relevant jurisdictions and the impact of a bankruptcy must be assessed along with any other relevant legal issues. The valuation of the specific securities also requires an assessment of the ranking of debt or equity claims relative to other stakeholders as well as an analysis of specific legal issues that may impact the enforceability of the claim.

Convertible Debenture Arbitrage (Regulation D)

Similar to Distressed Securities or Private Equity investments, Convertible Debenture Arbitrage strategies are exposed to a unique set of risks, mostly specific company and liquidity risks. Until SEC registration takes place, there is basically no liquidity for the investment and no guarantee can be given that SEC registration will eventually occur. This severely constrains the possibilities of pre-registration active risk management once an investment is made; therefore, diversification across a broad range of companies is critical to control risk.

Based on 'bottom up' analysis, the financial condition, the firm's management competence and its credit risk (the probability of default) must be assessed prior to investment. The financial analysis should consist of a review of historical financial performance, the company's current pro forma income statements, Z-score and ratio analysis (mostly focusing on current ratios and liquidity ratios) and an assessment of the appropriate valuation. Recently developed credit risk models based on the 'Merton model' (for more details about structural credit risk models, see Chapter 6) can provide for a quantitative assessment of the probability of default for the company. Further firm and management evaluation should include due diligence on management quality and experience, personal background checks, industry and competitive analysis, supply capacity/supplier agreements, client/buyer analysis and performance trends of the firm and its industry. Finally, 'downside' assessment of the impact of a possible bankruptcy along with the relevant legal issues should be completed.

Once registration with the SEC is completed, the converted parts of the debenture become freely tradeable. If the conversion price is floating, the manager is largely hedged against a declining stock price. An analysis of post-registration risk should include historical liquidity analysis (e.g. volume, bid–ask spreads), historical volatility, short interest, share overhang, market makers and specialists who are actively trading the stock and institutional and insider ownership and their recent activity. The manager also has to assess the nature and investment approach of other possible investors in order to evaluate the risk that the company enters into a 'shorting death spiral', i.e. too many investors shorting the stock at the same time to hedge their exposure.

Global Macro

Global Macro managers invest very opportunistically in a variety of different asset classes and instruments. It is difficult to describe general risk management guidelines for this strategy, as the risk profile of Global Macro strategies generally extends over the wide range of AIS risks (market risk, liquidity risk, event risk, corporate risk, foreign exchange, operational risk, credit risk, fraud risk, regulation risks, legal risk, model risk). Knowledge about current and possible future portfolio exposure and risk (VaR and stress testing respectively) provides the manager with the ability to react in a timely fashion to undesired risk exposure. The key risk management tool, however, is effective diversification across asset classes and instruments. This includes exposure limits and risk buckets. Many managers impose stop losses on individual positions. Leverage limits are important for controlling risk.

Long/Short Equity

Long/Short Equity strategies face broad equity market risk to the extent of their net market exposure. Determining the net exposure is one of the key issues of the Long/Short strategy sector and requires solid macroeconomic research. The manager can mitigate the broad market risk by monitoring the relevant macro factors in relationship to stock market valuations and adjusting the net long and short exposure accordingly. In bull markets exposure is usually net long, but in bear markets net long exposure should be avoided. Sector risk can be reduced or eliminated by trading pairs, i.e. the manager takes a long position in a company with a favourable outlook in a certain industry and sells short a stock with less favourable outlooks in the same industry. These two positions offset each other in case the entire sector experiences a downturn.

Most managers predefine a certain set of stocks to pick their positions from. Often 'liquidity filters' are employed which take the form of required minimum free float market capitalization or trading volume, before actual fundamental research is performed. Stocks with large capitalization have the advantage of being more liquid. But at the same time more analysts follow large cap stocks, i.e. the manager is less likely to have any informational advantage. Small cap stocks usually involve more risk, as they are unknown and have unproven earning streams. Generally, the choice of a stock universe and an 'investment theme' has great influence on the risk profile of the particular strategy.

Picking a stock for a long or short position means taking on specific company risks such as unexpected change of profit margins and earnings (or earnings outlooks), unfavourable industry trends, discontinuity of management, emergence of new technologies, unfavourable international trends, loss (gain) of market share, changing commodity prices, mergers and others. Diversification across positions in various sectors is of key importance and ensures that the manager's portfolio is not too strongly affected by events related to individual companies or industries. The construction of an efficient individual portfolio requires that careful attention be paid to correlations between stocks.

A key tool for managing the company-specific risk is thorough fundamental research that allows the manager to make predictions about the company's future earnings and stock price based on all currently available information. Important research sources are journals and newspapers, data providers (Bloomberg, Reuters etc.), industry contacts and conference calls with management, company visits, reports provided by brokerage houses and the internet. Technical analysis can be employed to determine the price momentum of the specific stock or to support a fundamental view.

For the individual long and short positions, stop-loss limits and profit targets are important risk management measures. They enforce discipline in situations where the stock does not behave as expected or profit targets have been reached. Further, as most managers employ leverage in order to increase their return potential, this leverage has to be controlled. Finally, Long/Short Equity strategies are exposed to the risk connected to short selling. A good relationship with the prime broker and a solid short selling experience base are necessary to minimize common 'short selling risks' (e.g. 'short squeeze', ability to borrow stock).

Equity Market Timing

Equity Market Timing strategies are among the least complex strategies in the AIS universe. Usually, rather simple indicators determine whether to enter or exit a position. Standard VaR or volatility-based approaches can be used for the monitoring of market risk. Diversification across various equity sectors and industries is important for risk reduction. A risk management measure used by some Equity Market Timing managers is the adjustment of position size according to current market or sector volatility. Studies by LeBaron[19] have shown that trend persistence in equity markets is conditionally correlated to volatility. Trends tend to be more persistent in periods of lower volatility but are more likely to revert at times of high volatility.

The manager has to be certain that the selected instruments, mostly mutual funds or stock basket, have the desired exposure to the market or sector. This is not always guaranteed, as most mutual funds do not frequently disclose their current holdings. Furthermore, most Mutual fund managers are resistant to allowing market timers to use their funds. The manager must ensure that he can get into the fund at the time he wants to with no time delay. This requires a good relationship with the Mutual fund firms. Because many Equity Market Timing strategies switch positions frequently, the manager has to guarantee reliable trade execution.

Short Selling

Short Selling strategies are exposed to the same risk factors as 'long only' investment strategies and require similar risk management approaches with respect to broad market risk and specific stock risk/corporate event risks. Sound macroeconomic and sector-specific research and fundamental analysis of individual stocks are important elements of risk management. This has to go along with diversification across different stocks and sectors.

In addition to the general equity investment risks, there are particular execution and liquidity issues associated with Short Selling. Short Selling strategies are subject to a unique set of risks related to the fact that managers have to borrow stocks before selling them ('borrowing risk'). Borrowing risk can be greatly reduced through the appropriate choice of and a strong relationship with a prime broker. Important parameters are the prime broker's capability to lend stock, his buy-in policy and his funding practices. A good prime broker is proactive in securing stocks to loan out to the short seller and communicates changing stability of the borrowing process quickly enough for the short seller to react.

Short Selling strategies face a particular form of portfolio risk through an inverse relationship between performance and exposure. A loss in a short position leads to a larger overall portfolio exposure to the losing position. Short sellers have to manage this dynamic risk vigilantly. Rigorous adherence to maximum position size limits is one way to mitigate this risk. Stop losses are often used to control the risk in individual stocks. However, especially in volatile periods, stop losses can have an undesired side-effect. Other market participants who know about the stop loss can artificially induce the necessary short-term price move to trigger them.

Managed Futures

The risks of Managed Futures strategies (Active Discretionary, Systematic Active, Systematic Passive) and the appropriate approaches to risk management are generally quite similar, so they all will be treated in the same subsection. The number one risk management principle for a Managed Futures portfolio is diversification. Most active as well as passive strategies invest in a large number of different Futures markets. This ranges from trading the most liquid 20–25 Futures contracts to investing in more than 100 markets across commodities, equities, fixed income and foreign exchange. Note that there is a trade-off between diversification and liquidity. A large universe of contracts includes those which are less liquid. Unwinding larger positions in these markets might become difficult, especially at times of high market volatility. Liquidity risk and the relevant liquidity indicators such as transaction volume and bid–ask spreads should in this case be constantly monitored. Another useful measure for risk control is volatility-dependent allocation, where the weight of the different contracts in the portfolio is determined by their historical (or implied) volatility.

Quantitative analysis such as VaR and stress tests are important risk monitoring tools for Futures strategies. Besides portfolio VaR, the large number of positions in different asset classes necessitates the consideration of VaR on various aggregation levels (e.g. commodities only) to detect undesired risk concentrations. Some managers apply limits on the notional exposure or risk to a single market/risk factor (this is referred to as 'risk budgeting'). Risk budgets can be based on VaR or stress test losses. Limits on employed leverage (margin to equity ratio), stop losses and profit targets constitute further useful risk control measures for Managed Futures strategies. For contracts traded in different currencies, FX futures and options can be used to hedge unwanted currency risk (however, currency exposure remains unhedged in most strategies).

Systematic Managed Futures strategies rely on models that are the results of past research efforts. These might be flawed or unsuited for current market structures. Generally, model development should be guided by four principles:

1 The more complex the underlying model, the higher the risk of 'over-fitting' ('curve fitting'). The parameter optimization of models should be limited to only a few parameters, which, if feasible, are chosen identically for each traded market.

2 Choosing exactly those parameters which give the best performance without consideration of the performance for nearby parameters is another recipe for over-fitting. The optimal parameters should be located on a 'plateau' in parameter space rather than on an isolated 'performance peak'.

3 A strict distinction between in-sample and out-of-sample data is essential. Performance for optimization periods (in sample) and for model testing periods (out of sample) should be compared and found not to be too different from each other.

4 The target function of the optimization should be selected carefully. Risk-adjusted performance measures are generally better suited than gross returns.[20]

Fully systematic trading approaches are widespread, especially among Managed Futures strategies. But it is important to note that these principles of model optimization and addressing model risk equally apply to model-based strategies in other AIS sectors.

By way of contrast, non-model-based strategies (Active Discretionary) often rely on the skill of one or several key persons. Appropriate backup should be available should one of these people become unavailable. While some mostly Passive Futures strategies have rather low turnover, there are strategies with hundreds of trades per day. This requires efficient in-house execution and back-office facilities.

Portfolio diversification

Diversification is the most rudimentary, but at the same time one of the key elements of portfolio construction and risk management in finance. Modern portfolio theory[21] (MPT) states that correlation properties are the key to efficient diversification in an investment portfolio. In the investment practice the calculation of efficient frontiers is the most important application of MPT. Numerous studies[22] (see also Chapter 4) have shown that due to low correlations to traditional assets, AIS investments offer attractive possibilities for diversification and efficiency enhancement in an investor's global portfolio. At the same time, the performance and correlation properties of AIS differ widely across the strategy sectors.[23]

A note of caution is necessary upfront: quantitative optimization for AIS portfolios can be quite useful in determining the scope for improvement from adding AIS to a global traditional balanced (equity and bond) portfolio, however, it shows its limitations if used for determining the right AIS sector allocation within a multi-manager AIS portfolio. The results of Markowitz-type optimizations are very sensitive to the return and risk assumption used in the calculation. The availability and reliability of AIS performance data leaves much to be desired, as discussed in detail in Chapters 4 and 7. Data is available only for a limited time frame and is biased due to the specific market circumstances in the 1990s (bull equity markets). The performance of the different strategy sectors is very heterogeneous and generally far from stationary, i.e. the mean return, standard deviation and the correlations, all important inputs to portfolio optimization programs, vary substantially with respect to chosen time periods, market environments and individual managers. Taking average performance numbers over a time period of a few years as representative for the strategy sectors in the portfolio optimization does not account sufficiently for this variability. Performance and correlation properties between the different strategies remain an important consideration in setting up an AIS portfolio, but experienced AIS portfolio managers do not apply quantitative portfolio optimization on a sole basis, rather they combine it with qualitative considerations.

The diversification of equity risk in the traditional portfolio is one of the main motivations for investing in AIS. But for this very purpose, certain combinations of strategies are better suited than others. For example, Relative Value and Managed Futures strategies show generally lower correlations to equity markets than most Opportunistic strategies. Chapter 4 introduced the concept of conditional correlations, which provides a powerful tool for examining the effectiveness of portfolio diversification.

Figure 5.11 shows an example of two different sets of strategies (encircled) and their past correlation properties *conditional to equity market directions* (compare with Figures 4.4 and 4.5). The figure illustrates clearly that the second set provides better diversification in periods of negative equity performance than the first. The first portfolio consisting of Long/Short Equity, Global Macro, Event Driven and Distressed Securities is biased towards an environment of rising equity markets and shows weaknesses during periods of negative equity market performance. In contrast, the combination of Managed Futures, Equity Market Timing and Relative Value strategies (Convertible Arbitrage, Fixed Income Arbitrage, Equity Market Neutral) shows strengths in various equity market environments. In periods of falling equity markets, Managed Futures tend to perform well[24] and

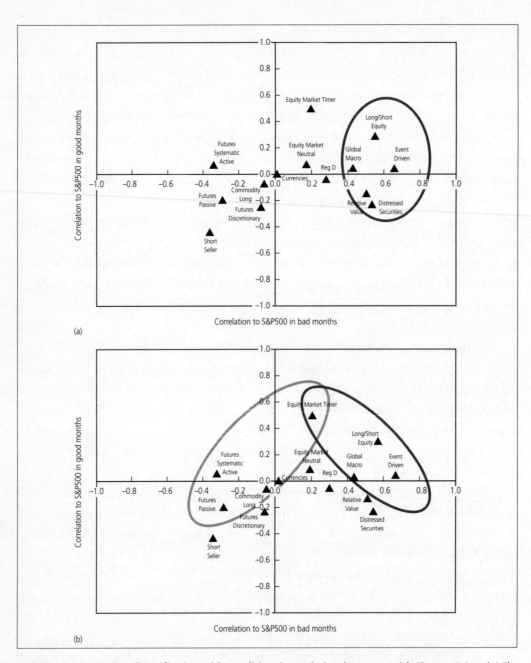

FIGURE 5.11 ■ Testing diversification with conditional correlation (compare with Figures 4.4 and 4.5)
(a) Example for a portfolio with strong equity correlations in falling markets
(b) Example for a diversified portfolio

Equity Market Timing strategies are almost uncorrelated to equity markets. In periods of rising equity markets, Equity Market timers show strong performance, while Managed Futures are uncorrelated. Relative Value strategies generally display low correlation to equity market directions in 'normal periods' but tend to be highly correlated in times of market turbulence (not shown in Figure 5.11).

Another example is the following: A combination of Convertible Arbitrage and Risk Arbitrage can provide favourable correlation properties *conditional to equity market volatility*. Convertible Arbitrage strategies show above average performance during periods of increasing equity market volatility, when Risk Arbitrage strategies struggle. Low volatility periods bear inverse performance behaviour. Risk Arbitrage is attractive, Convertible Arbitrage less so.

Another important analysis refers to the returns and correlations conditional on different bond market performance. Generally, a systematic study of conditional returns and correlations in various market environments (e.g. with respect to equities, bonds, FX) can lead the AIS investor to similar insights as multi-factor models of returns.

Statistical analysis and correlation studies are only one way to approach the subject of AIS portfolio diversification. Another approach, which aims at supplementing the results of statistical studies on past performance data, is based on fundamental economic reasoning and looks more closely at the economic reasons and sources of AIS returns. Understanding the return generation process for each strategy can help to reach efficient portfolio diversification. As discussed in Chapters 2 and 3, individual strategies can have very different performance drivers, as they represent different economic functions in financial markets. The following list builds on the discussion in Chapter 2 and summarizes the classification of the AIS in terms of economic functions:

▪ *Capital formation* (providing capital to companies): *Equity Market Timing, Long/Short Equity*. The primary purpose of equity markets is the formation and efficient distribution of capital needed by companies to foster innovation and economic progress. Investors provide the needed capital and ensure its efficient allocation to the most promising businesses.

- *Risk transfer* (taking risk from commercial hedgers): *Managed Futures*. The investor provides commercial hedgers with the necessary liquidity to perform their hedging activities. Similar to insurance companies, they are compensated with a risk premium.

- *Relative Value Arbitrage* (making markets more efficient): *Convertible Arbitrage, Risk Arbitrage, Fixed Income Arbitrage* and *Equity Market Neutral*. Arbitrageurs[25] take advantage of relative mispricings or differences in credit, liquidity or other risk factors of different but generally closely related securities. This provides financial markets with a higher degree of efficiency and a less erratic price formation process.

- *Providing liquidity* (taking positions in less liquid markets and instruments): *Distressed Securities, Regulation D*, some *Fixed Income Arbitrage*. Managers invest in less liquid instruments and earn a liquidity premium, thus providing a market for instruments less frequently traded.

- The economic function for *Global Macro, Short Selling* and some *Long/Short Equity* strategies is less clear. The returns of these are based on the manager's skills in forecasting stock price developments and acting quickly rather than earning particular risk premiums. Usually, these strategies involve a higher degree of speculation.

Low statistical correlations to equity and other markets as well as between different AIS sectors usually find their theoretical explanation in different economic functions of the corresponding strategies. So for the example just discussed: the set of Equity Market Timing (economic function: capital formation), Futures (economic function: risk transfer) and Relative Value (economic function: market efficiency) contains strategies with very different return generation processes. Next to statistical correlation features, the AIS allocator should consider the economic sources of returns for the purpose of AIS portfolio diversification.

Notes

1. See the article by L. Rahl, 'Risk Budgeting: The Next Step of the Risk Management Journey – A Veteran's Perspective', in L. Rahl (ed.) *Risk Budgeting: A New Approach to Investing*.

2. See also the study 'Hedge Funds and Financial Markets Dynamics', by B. Eichengreen and D. Mathieson.

3. This risk is sometimes classified as operational risk, but in our context it should be seen as a risk type on its own.

4. See also report issued by a group of five Hedge fund managers, 'Sound Practices for Hedge Fund Managers', section 'Recommendations: Risk Monitoring'.

5. Personal communication with M. Perkins, MKP. See also 'Prime Brokers Can Make and Break Hedge Funds' in *Pension & Investments*, September 3, 2001.

6. For more recent developments in the relationship between Hedge funds and their prime brokerage counter-parties, see the article by Patel and Navroz, 'Courting the Hedge Funds' in *Risk Magazine*, November 2001.

7. See the article 'Hedge Fund Disasters: Avoiding the Next Catastrophe' by D. Kramer in *Alternative Investment Quarterly*, October 2001.

8. See Chris Clair, 'Hedge Funds Suffer Without a Benchmark', *Pension & Investments*, June 11, 2001.

9. See also the work by W. Fung and D. Hsieh, 'Benchmarks of Hedge Fund Performance: Information Content and Measurement Biases'.

10. Dacorogna et al. in 'Effective Return, Risk Aversion and Drawdowns' in *Physica A*, January 2001, provide an excellent presentation of different performance measurements.

11. See the articles 'Life at Sharpe's end' and 'Measure for Measure' by H. Till in *Risk and Reward*, September and October 2001.

12. A study 'Do Hedge Funds Hedge?' by C. Asness et al. examines the effect of these liquidity-induced lags on correlation and performance properties of Hedge funds.

13. Capital Market Risk Advisors, 'NAV / Fair Value Practices Survey Results', July 2001, available on http://www.cmra.com.

14. See B. Liang, 'Hedge Funds: On the Performance of Hedge Funds' in *Financial Analysts Journal*, July 1999.

15. See the discussion in 'TSS(II)-Tactical Style Selection: Integrating Hedge Funds into the Asset Allocation Framework' by Crossborder Capital, published by Hedge Fund Research, August 2000.

16. See the article 'Convertible Arb Funds turn to Default Swaps' by C. Schenk in *Risk Magazine*, July 2001.

17. See F. Fabozzi in *Fixed Income Analysis* (Chapter 11, 2) for more details on OAS models.

18. CMRA stands for 'Capital Markets Risk Advisors'; see article by G. Polyn, 'Value-at-Risk for Merger Arbs' in *Risk Magazine,* April 2001, p.6.

19. See the publications by B. LeBaron, 'Forecast Improvements using a Volatility Index' and 'Some Relation between Volatility and Serial Correlations in Stock Market Returns'.

20. See the work by Pictet et al., 'Real Time Trading Models for Foreign Exchange Rates', where possible target functions for model parameter optimization are discussed.

21. Modern Portfolio Theory (MPT) is a topic in almost all finance textbooks and university classes. For an introduction into MPT refer to *Investment Analysis and Portfolio Management* by F. Reilly and K. Brown.

22. See the article 'The Benefits of Hedge Funds' by T. Schneeweiss and references therein.

23. For a discussion of diversification within a multi-strategy portfolio, see J. Park and J. Strum, 'Fund of Fund Diversification: How Much is Enough?, *The Journal of Alternative Investments*, Winter 1999. See also R. McFall Lamm, 'Portfolios of Alternative Assets: Why not 100% Hedge Funds?', *The Journal of Investing*, Winter 1999, pp.87–97.

24. This statement applies when interest rates remain constant or fall. CTA actually struggles when interest rates rise. See the discussion in Chapter 4 and also the work by M. Caglayan and F. Edwards, 'Hedge Fund and Commodity Fund Investment Styles in Bull and Bear Markets'. The authors of this article found that CTAs have higher returns than Hedge funds in bear markets and generally have a negative correlation with equity returns in periods of falling markets.

25. I am not referring to arbitrage in the strictest meaning of the word here (which is 'generating a profit without risk'): With 'Relative Value Arbitrage' I generally mean 'buying relatively undervalued securities and selling overvalued securities'. There is a risk involved, specifically, the risk that the undervalued securities become even cheaper and the overvalued ones more expensive.

CHAPTER 6

Tools and Principles of Modern Financial Risk Management

Although there is no unique and widely accepted definition of risk in financial markets, on a very general level, risk is the result of holding an investment (exposure) combined with the uncertainty about future price developments (with risk factor variability). Investment decision makers can control exposure, while uncertainty is by nature uncontrollable. Risk measurement starts with the analysis of these two components. Exposure analysis is the categorization of investment positions by risk factors, and uncertainty is often described by statistical estimates of future price variability, i.e. volatility (as measured, for example, by the standard deviation of historical returns).

It is acknowledged among risk professionals that the widespread perception of risk and volatility as equivalents leads to a very incomplete picture of financial risk. Statistical measures of volatility most often do not capture all the risks an investor is facing (e.g. extreme market moves). Therefore, the emergence of various risk quantification tools (such as VaR) notwithstanding, qualitative considerations remain important for the complete assessment of risk, as some risk factors defy accurate quantification. This is particularly true for AIS, where the wide range of investment instruments and trading techniques exposes the investor to more numerous and more complex risks compared to traditional investments (see Chapter 5) and therefore makes risk quantification all the more challenging.

The foundation of effective risk management is a general risk policy outlining what types of risk are acceptable and which are to be avoided. The policy must be supported by appropriate tools that allow for monitoring and control and, importantly, by the actions and attitudes of key personnel. In the end, risk *management* must be more than just risk quantification or risk measurement; it must involve specific actions, which directly influence the investment decision-making process and which ensure that corrective action is taken when risk exceeds permitted levels.

This chapter aims at introducing the reader to the state-of-the-art financial risk management tools and principles, including a discussion of their strengths and shortcomings. It cannot claim complete coverage of this extensive subject. Numerous articles, books and encyclopaedias have been published over the years[1] and it is almost impossible to cover them all. The interested reader is advised to read the references provided. They are, naturally, selective.[2]

The emergence of quantitative tools for risk management

During the last decade the role, importance and spectrum of tools for risk analysis and risk management have evolved dramatically. The fallout from numerous financial fiascos, combined with the emergence of powerful quantitative models and strong computing capacities, have led to what the financial profession regards as a 'risk management revolution'. Today, the theory of risk management is considered as a distinct field of its own within the world of finance.

The emergence of the 'Value-at-Risk (VaR)' changed the scope and character of applied financial risk management. Developed initially as a concept for market risk, it is now used for a variety of risk types (e.g. credit risk, liquidity risk, operational risk as well as firm-wide risk). Although it is difficult to pinpoint the precise origin of VaR, it is undisputed that two events helped to bring this approach to the attention of investment professionals globally. One is the Group of Thirty Report in July 1993[3] and the subsequent use of VaR as a measure for market risk by financial market risk managers and regulators (that ultimately defined the 1996 amendments, in particular the 'internal models approach', to the Basle accord for the minimum capital requirements by internationally active commercial banks), and the other is the introduction of RiskMetrics by J.P. Morgan in October 1994.

The emergence of VaR has led to new problems, however. Most VaR calculations rely on certain assumptions which, at best, only approximate reality. Theoretical discussions about VaR are ongoing, but it is widely accepted that VaR can actually be quite misleading unless used with care. Much intellectual energy is currently being dedicated to the development of more robust risk analysis tools than VaR.

On the application side, risk managers can today choose from numerous commercial software tools with varying degrees of sophistication. The large, and, for some, overwhelming, variety of available tools is a blessing and a curse at the same time. Too often the key decision makers in financial institutions receive risk information which is either too complex or too voluminous to allow for efficient decision making and control. An important part of risk management is the presentation of risk information in a manner such that the key decision takers can understand and act on the presented information.

Pre-VaR risk management: Traditional risk measures and 'modern' portfolio theory

On the most basic level, risk management consists of breaking down a portfolio by holdings and analyzing risk on an instrument-by-instrument basis. Then exposures on different aggregation levels (e.g. instrument, asset class, region, sector) are measured and risk levels are quantified. Traditionally, volatility describing past fluctuations and future uncertainty of security prices (usually quantified by the standard deviation of returns) is the most important measure of risk. A further risk measure often used for interest rate-sensitive portfolios (bonds) is duration (defined as the weighted average time to maturity of cash flows).[4] Such exposure analysis and volatility/duration measurement on distinct aggregation levels is still widely used today.

'Modern' portfolio theory (MPT) provided a new approach to portfolio risk analysis ('modern' is not quite accurate; the origins of MPT go back to the works of H. Markowitz in the early 1950s, and W. Sharpe in the early 1960s). MPT does not look at the volatility of individual positions, but considers the extent to which individual holdings contribute to overall *portfolio* volatility. While a complete discussion of MPT is beyond the scope of this book, this topic is extensively covered in most financial textbooks.[5]

While not immediately resulting in a conceptual change of how risk is measured (MPT still assumes risk can be completely described by the standard deviation of returns), MPT set the stage for risk management on the portfolio level (and specifically the development of VaR) by introducing the concept of 'correlation'. MPT introduced the idea that highly volatile instruments may add no risk to a portfolio, if they correlate negatively with the rest of the portfolio (i.e. if they are added to the portfolio, the resulting portfolio volatility remains equal or decreases). For the calculation of correlations (and volatilities) the literature offers a rich universe of methods.[6]

Value-at-Risk (VaR)

VaR is today the most widely used quantitative analysis tool for financial risk. It describes the maximal portfolio loss for a given confidence level over a specified trading horizon. Mathematically speaking, VaR characterizes the tail (extreme quantile) of the portfolio return distribution.[7] Despite a number of pitfalls (see later), VaR has introduced a new dimension of risk analysis into the financial community. The magic of VaR is that it introduces a uniform measuring system for the various instruments in a portfolio by providing a method for comparing risk across security and asset classes (prior to VaR, an investor was unable to quantify the risk of a combination of a $1 million position in US equity and a $1 million position in short duration German Government Bonds). The two important parameters that a risk manager has to define for VAR are the time period and the confidence level (e.g. 99% for a one-day horizon). VaR can be calculated on a variety of different aggregation levels within the portfolio (fund-wide risk attribution, asset classes, sectors, instruments, trading managers, geographic regions).

In most respects VaR is a natural progression from MPT, but there are also important differences:

■ MPT interprets risk in terms of the standard deviation of returns, while VaR describes risk as the maximum likely loss.

■ The variance–covariance approach of MPT is just one of several methods to calculate VaR (others are the Monte Carlo method and the historical method).

■ VaR can be applied to a range of different risks beyond market risk, while MPT is limited to market risk. The concept of VaR can even be used for firm-wide risk management.

■ VaR offers a wider frame for the incorporation of more complex statistical methods such as non-normal returns.

While VaR is conceptually and intuitively quite simple, the technical details of its calculation can be rather involved depending on the heterogeneity of the portfolio and the distributional assumptions made. Detailing the technical aspects of portfolio VaR calculation is beyond the scope of this book[8] but a short overview is provided in the following.

The three main elements of standard VaR calculation are:

■ mapping the portfolio positions to risk factors

■ calculating the risk factor covariance matrix

■ determining the VaR method and calculating VaR.

Mapping risk factors

Risk factor mapping is the decomposition of individual securities into components over which the risk manager has control (the exposure) and exogenous influences he cannot control (the risk factors). A risk factor is a variable which affects directly the future value of a security (e.g. interest rates, equity market valuations, FX rates etc.). The prices of thousands of worldwide available financial securities are influenced by common risk factors.

The dependency of a security on risk factors (the security's 'sensitivities') is expressed by a 'pricing function' which can depend on the VaR method employed (see below). Note that the concept of risk factors and sensitivities is not new. Sensitivities have been used for the analysis of yield curve risks as well as in option theory for many years (examples are the 'value of a basis point move' or the 'Greeks').

VaR calculations should account for every important risk factor in the portfolio, which can be quite numerous (>1,000). The following provides a broad categorization.[9]

- *Equity indices*: The risk of an equity position can be separated into two components, the sensitivity to one or several relevant market/sector indices and an idiosyncratic residual risk. With a sufficient number of stocks in the portfolio, the latter is diversified away. Commonly employed equity risk factors are broad market or specific sector risks, expressed as 'sensitivities', or in the language of the 'Capital Asset Pricing Model', 'betas'.

- *Yield and credit spread curves*: Fixed income risk arises from potential moves in interest rate term structures (yield curves) and credit ratings. Each currency has its own yield curve. Credit risk is expressed in terms of the spread to a 'risk-free' (i.e. not defaultable) reference bond or probability of default. A portfolio exposure to yield and spread curve risk can be described by certain representative maturity points on the yield and credit spread curves (e.g. one-month, six-month, one-year, two-year, five-year, ten-year, 15-year and 30-year maturities).[10]

- *Foreign exchange rates*: Foreign exchange spot rates are risk factors in portfolios that hold positions in currencies different from the investor's home currency. For positions in FX forwards and futures, the two underlying yield curves define additional risk factors. The interest rate parity theorem provides the exact relationship between the spot rates, the forward rates and the two interest rates.

- *Commodities*: Spot commodity positions are exposed to single risk factors, the respective commodity prices. Similar to yield curves defining risk factors related to interest rates, commodity Forward and Futures contracts define a term structure for each commodity which is determined by the costs of carry (mostly related to interest rates) and the 'convenience yield'.

One of the most common approaches to mapping positions to risk factors is via the use of a security's cash flow. This method assumes that all instruments can be represented by defined cash flows to the investor at present or specified times in the future (note that this assumption is invalid for options). The cash flows are attributed to specific risk factors and discounted to present value at the prevailing interest rates. A simple example is given by the cash flows of a (default free) bond with yearly coupon payments and principal payback in ten years. The risk factors are represented by the interest rates at various maturities on the yield curve. The present value of the cash flow to the investor in a given year (coupon payments in years one to ten and

principal payback in year ten) is uniquely determined by the x-year interest rate. Cash flows that fall in between two maturity points are split between the two nearby points. A second commonly used approach is the sensitivity approach, which is based on directly determining the portfolio's sensitivity to changes in each risk factor.[11]

Calculation of covariance matrix

The next step in the calculation of VaR consists of estimating volatilities and correlations of the risk factors. Making the standard assumption that security returns are multivariate normally distributed, the correlation matrix (together with the vector of expected returns) uniquely determines the distribution of portfolio returns, and therefore portfolio VaR. There are various methods for calculating volatility (variances) and correlations (covariances). The following approaches are most common (the RiskMetrics Technical document (1996) provides a discussion of the details):[12]

▪ Equally weighted moving average of squared returns (variance) and cross-products of returns (covariance).

▪ Exponential moving average of squared returns and cross-products of returns with specified decay parameter. This is the method chosen by RiskMetrics and many others. The decay parameter most often chosen is 0.94 for daily observations and 0.97 for monthly observations.

▪ The family of ARCH models: ARCH (autoregressive conditional heteroskedastic) and GARCH (General ARCH) models were developed in the early 1980s and have become a starting point for sophisticated volatility and correlation forecasting models.[13] The exponential moving average model can be seen as a special case of a GARCH model.

Calculation of VaR

After attributing cash flows to risk factors and calculating the risk factors' covariance matrix, VaR can be calculated using several methods which differ mainly in respect to two factors.

1 *Assumptions regarding security valuation as a function of risk factors*: A determination must be made as to how to model the sensitivity of security

prices to changes in risk factors. The industry distinguishes between local valuation and full valuation methods.

2 *The distributional assumptions made*: The industry distinguishes between parametric (mostly normal) distributions versus historical distributions.

The three most popular VaR methods are:

■ *Parametric approach*: The idea behind parametric VAR models is to approximate the pricing function of each instrument (i.e. the relationship between each instrument and the risk factors), in a way that an analytical formula for VaR can be obtained. The simplest parametric approach is the 'delta method', also referred to as 'variance–covariance-based VaR'.[14] Assuming normal return distributions and a *linear* relationship between risk factors and the securities in the portfolio, the returns of the portfolio themselves are conditionally normally distributed (here 'conditional' refers to the standard deviation of this distribution changing over time depending on the most recent volatility). The covariance matrix of risk factors determines the standard deviation of portfolio returns. The method possesses the charm of simplicity, but is severely flawed in circumstances where the assumption of linearity does not hold. An enhancement of the delta method is the 'delta–gamma' method, where second-order approximations are added to the security pricing function. Both the delta and delta–gamma methods are 'local' valuation methods, as only the mark to market values of the portfolio positions enter into the valuation of the portfolio (and no other price scenarios).

■ *Monte Carlo simulations*:[15] The Monte Carlo method is a 'full valuation' method based on simulating the behaviour of the underlying risk factors through a large number of draws produced by a random generator. Using given pricing functions, the values of the portfolio positions are calculated from the simulated values of risk factors. A possible non-linear relationship between security and risk factors is fully accounted for. The positions in the portfolio are fully revalued under each of the random scenarios. Every random draw of risk factor values thus leads to a new portfolio valuation. A high number of iterations (several thousand) provides a simulated return distribution of the portfolio, from which the VaR value can be determined. (The number of iterations necessary can be somewhat reduced by 'deterministic sampling', i.e. pseudo-random selection of values to ensure that the full spectrum of relevant scenarios is selected.) The underlying distribution of the randomly generated risk factor values can theoretically be chosen freely, but in most cases the simulation draws from a normal distribution. The random values are transformed such that the empirical correlations between the risk factors are recognized (mathematically, this is achieved through a 'Cholesky decomposition' of the correlation matrix). The use of non-normal distributions can quickly lead to complex mathematical problems.[16]

■ *Historical simulation*: Instead of simulating return distributions, the distribution is determined by looking into the past. The historical method is also a full valuation method and relies on the (unconditional) historical distribution of returns by applying past asset returns to the present holdings in the portfolio. The values of the portfolio positions are fully evaluated for each historical return by the use of the specified pricing functions. This method has the advantage that no explicit assumptions about the underlying return distribution have to be made. The problem of the method is that it relies on historical price behaviour, which might no longer be relevant in current market environments.

It was mentioned that the full security re-valuation employed by the Monte Carlo as well as the historical method requires specific valuation models or pricing functions. These models have to be correctly adjusted, which happens by calibrating the model parameters to the market prices of specific benchmark instruments. Further, as long as normally distributed draws are used, the Monte Carlo method does not address the issue of non-normally distributed asset returns. The dependence and correlation structure of non-normal multivariate distributions is still the subject of intense research. Stretching out beyond the normal distribution very quickly leads to intractable mathematical problems, as non-normal multivariate distributions are much more difficult to deal with (see the section on Extreme Value Theory later in this chapter).[17]

Because of complex and non-linear (option) positions that are present in most AIS portfolios, the variance-based method can be quite misleading and should be avoided. Historical simulations are attractive as they make no distributional assumptions, but the results depend strongly on the historical period chosen for the analysis. The Monte Carlo approach is usually the most reliable method, but is at the same time computationally the most intense.

VaR: Back testing and model verification

It is important to realize that the VaR figures any model generates are subject to error. These errors have various sources (sampling error, model error, human error etc.). It is essential that the VaR numbers themselves are monitored on a regular basis. As VaR values are not directly observable in the markets, this can only happen by checking whether the calculated numbers are consistent with the subsequently realized returns. The most obvious way to do this is by investigating how often losses exceed the calculated VaR levels, and whether such losses occur significantly more or less frequently than indicated by the chosen confidence level. More advanced tests take into account the sizes of losses exceeding VaR. There are a number of different tests available.[18] Their common problem is that due to sparse data, they tend to have a limited ability to distinguish between good and bad models. Bad models are too often qualified as good ones.

The problems of VaR

VaR cannot cover all aspects of risk. It provides useful information about portfolio risk under normal market circumstances, but does not address the extreme left tail region of the return distribution (which becomes important in the case of extreme market moves and turbulences). This is one of several problems with using VaR as a sole risk quantification tool.

1 VaR measures potential losses that occur fairly regularly (e.g. once in 20 or once in 100 days). It does not provide information about the extreme left tail of the profit and loss (P&L) distribution and the expected size of an experienced loss that exceeds VaR. Often it is the rare but extreme losses that are of most interest for a risk manager. For the past 15 years, at least one major market has moved by more than ten standard deviations in almost every year. Examples include the 1987 stock market crash, the 1990 Nikkei crash and High Yield tumble, the 1992 European currency crisis, the 1994 US interest rate hike, the 1995 Mexico and South America crisis, the 1997 Asian

crisis, the 1998 Russian crisis and the fall of LTCM, the 1999 Brazilian crisis and the 2000/2001 high-tech market downturn. These are market environments where VaR fails to accurately account for risk.

2 VaR relies heavily on its assumptions. One major challenge in implementing VaR is the specification of the probability distribution of extreme returns. As mentioned earlier, in most VaR schemes the risk manager chooses a normal return distribution with a stationary (i.e. structurally stable) covariance matrix of risk factors. These can be good assumptions on some days and poor ones on other days. Unfortunately, the latter are the moments when VaR is most needed. Much has been written about the assumption of normality of the returns, which is the most important of all assumptions made by VaR models. It is well known in mathematics that the covariance matrix (next to expected returns) uniquely describes a multivariate normal distribution. The assumption of normality makes it easy to calculate VaR from the standard deviation at any desired confidence level by simply multiplying the latter by a z-factor (1.65 for the 95% confidence level and 2.33 for the 99% confidence level). There is strong empirical evidence, however, that security returns are non-normally distributed.[19] Non-normal return distribution can be considered by investigating higher moments, specifically the skewness (unsymmetrical distribution) and kurtosis ('fat tails'). The characteristics of VaR using non-normal distributions are still subject to intense research.[20]

   VaR based on full revaluation (like the Monte Carlo and historical method) depends on the particular pricing models employed for the valuation of financial instruments. Many derivative instruments are not very actively traded, so they have to be marked to model rather than marked to market.

3 VaR relies on estimates of correlations and volatilities. These are usually based on historical data. It is assumed that historical returns are approximately stationary, i.e. their behaviour will not change structurally in the future. In reality, correlations and volatilities are unstable and change constantly. Correlation and volatilities in specific market environments (also called 'conditional correlation/volatilities') can be quite different from their average

('unconditional') values. Especially in times of financial crisis, volatility increases well above historical averages and correlations tend to be significantly higher than in normal market environments. Events tend to happen discretely rather than continuously. In other words, the events that expose the investor to extreme risks are often not predictable from historical time series. Further, like all statistical measures, correlations and volatilities have statistical errors. The smaller the sample of observation, the greater their impact. VaR depends on how volatilities and correlations are calculated from past data. Calculations based on equally weighted historical returns can deviate from the results of exponentially weighted schemes.

4 VaR only captures certain systematic risk factors, such as market (equity, bond, FX, commodity) or credit risk. VaR does not measure non-systematic risk, which can present itself in a variety of disguises: idiosyncratic (e.g. corporate event) risk, liquidity risk, credit spread risk, operational risk, political risk, model risk. With a generally higher degree of non-systematic risk in their portfolios, VaR is less likely to provide reliable approximation of total risk for AIS investors. Event Driven strategies, such as Distressed Debt or Merger Arbitrage strategies, provide good examples of this. They are exposed to a large amount of deal- or company-specific risk that cannot be reliably described by VaR.

5 VaR has an important and widely criticized theoretical shortcoming: It is not additive with respect to sub-portfolios, i.e. the VaR of a portfolio consisting of two sub-portfolios can be larger than the sum of the single VaR values of the two sub-portfolios. Thus, VaR does not qualify as a 'coherent risk measure'.[21]

Risk managers should be sceptical about breaking down risk into one number. Risk has many dimensions and different degrees of severity. It is undisputed among theoreticians and practitioners of risk management that VaR needs to be supplemented by other analysis tools suited to cope with non-systematic risks and extreme market conditions. VaR alone is not a sufficient means to quantify potential unacceptable losses.

Variations of VaR

There are other risk measures which are related to Value-at-Risk.

- *Marginal and Incremental VaR*: Marginal VaR expresses the amount by which the value of portfolio VaR is increased upon inclusion of a particular position or sub-portfolio. Incremental VaR is a related concept and measures the sensitivity of the portfolio risk to very small (incremental) changes in the portfolio holdings. Incremental VaR is additive (Marginal VaR is not), i.e. the sum of Incremental VaRs of individual positions equals the Incremental VaR of the sum of the positions. Incremental and marginal VaR can be used to evaluate the impact of a particular position or an individual trading manager on the risk structure of the entire portfolio.

- *Expected Shortfall (Conditional VaR):*[22] Expected shortfall is the mean value of the portfolio loss, conditional on the loss exceeding VaR (or any specified threshold). It provides important information about the left tail of the P&L distribution. Conditional VaR is a coherent risk measure, i.e. (among other properties) it is sub-additive. Expected shortfall has desirable features for portfolio optimization algorithms, in which risk is minimized under given constraints (in particular, it is a convex function of portfolio weights).[23]

- *'Lower partial moments' (LPM)*: A generalization of risk measures that includes Expected Shortfall as a specific sub-case, are 'lower partial moments' (LPM). A set of lower partial moments can be defined by the nth power of the loss exceeding a certain threshold:

$$LPM(n) = E[(\text{return} - \text{threshold})^n] \quad \text{for (return < threshold)}$$

For n=1 this measure reduces to the Conditional VaR. For n=2 and the threshold equals the expected return, this measure reduces to the semi-variance, i.e. the variance with only returns below the expected return taken into account (the square root of which is often referred to as 'downside deviation'). The use of lower partial moments in the (multivariate) portfolio is generally more difficult, because the portfolio risk measured by LPM is not composed of the individual securities' risk and correlations only. Thus, although LPM capture more specific measures of risk, they are not as convenient to estimate or to derive analytical solutions for.

Stress testing and scenario analysis

Scenario analysis consists of applying predetermined changes to the values of risk factors and determining the resulting changes of portfolio value as a result. Scenarios can be applied independently to each instrument/asset class or in consideration of risk factors'correlations. The latter is more useful, as it accounts for co-movement in risk factors other than those considered directly in the scenario. Stress tests make use of extreme scenarios in order to ascertain coverage of the impact of large price changes in financial markets. Such tests give insight into the portfolio behaviour under extreme and low probability, but, nevertheless, plausible market conditions, which are outside the predictive capability of any statistical model. Stress tests are usually performed by applying an appropriate stress event and observing the resulting portfolio re-valuation. The choice of stress scenarios is the crucial factor in performing these tests. Stress scenarios should include:

■ *Appropriately sized shocks*: Extreme events are characterized by large moves, which should be accounted for in scenario definitions.

■ *Test for asymmetries in return distribution*: Skewed distributions are omnipresent in financial markets.

■ *Test for correlation breakdown*: Extreme events usually lead to very different correlation structures in financial markets. Investments that are uncorrelated in normal market environments can be highly correlated during times of financial crisis.

■ *Stressing different combinations of asset classes separately and in combination*: The best way to perform stress tests is to include all assets in the scenario and apply realistic correlations between instruments to define the full impact of a specific scenario. For example, the behaviour of bonds, commodities and foreign exchange rates during turmoil in equity markets should be considered through certain assumptions about their correlations to stocks.

Scenario selection is the most important and most difficult part of stress testing and is much more an art than a science.[24] Three different sorts of scenarios can be distinguished:

■ *Historical scenarios*: The replication of past events is a rather simple way to define a scenario. Examples are the stock market crash in 1987 or the emerging market crisis (Russian default) in 1998.

■ *General user-defined market scenarios*: In order to incorporate current market structures rather than relying on historical events, the risk manager can define specific changes to different risk factors (e.g. a drop of 15% in the broad equity markets or a parallel shift of 100bp in the US dollar yield curve).

■ *Portfolio-specific scenarios*: The particular portfolio in consideration can guide the definitions of scenarios. Risk managers should examine the impact of extreme losses in particular positions in the portfolio or the result of a sudden change in their correlations. Portfolio-specific scenarios can include expert views on certain subsets of risk factors and the possible future correlation scenarios between core risk factors.[25]

The second part of stress testing is the re-valuation of the portfolio based on chosen scenarios. The valuation is usually based on the same models as used for the Monte Carlo simulation. The stress test result is obtained by calculating the difference between the portfolio value after the stress test and the current portfolio value.

Extreme Value Theory

Academics as well as practitioners in financial markets generally agree that financial risk factors are not normally distributed. They exhibit fat tails, i.e. extreme events are more likely to occur compared to what the normal distribution suggests. But accurate prediction of extreme events is of central importance to risk analysis. As discussed, most VaR models have rather poor predictive capabilities for the tails of the P&L distribution. Even historical simulations are subject to sampling problems in the tails, as extreme events do not occur sufficiently regularly to apply valid statistical judgement. In order to cover the fat-tailed distribution of financial risk factors, a non-normal probability distribution is more appropriate to work with. A first alternative choice is the student-t distribution, which shares some attractive properties with the normal distribution. Mathematically speaking, it falls into the class of 'elliptical distribution', i.e. the correlation matrix uniquely describes the dependence structure of multivariate t-distributions (see below).[26]

The mathematical description of extreme events requires a solid mathematical foundation and is outside the scope of this book. The following explanations should serve the purpose of a short overview only. The interested reader is asked to study the references provided for a more in-depth discussion. An understanding of the mathematical discussion that follows is not essential to the further comprehension of this book.

The 'central limit theorem' provides the foundation for the statistics of normally distributed events, as it describes the 'Gaussian' (normal) distribution as the generic form of the 'middle part' of many probability distributions. The 'Fisher-Tippett theorem' in contrast provides the generic form of the asymptotic tails for a wide class of probability distributions.[27] The theorem is central to the mathematical discipline of Extreme Value Theory (EVT), which provides the theoretical foundation for the analysis of leptokurtic (i.e. fat-tailed) distributions. The three generic distributions for extreme events (the 'extreme value distributions') are those defined by the 'Frechet', 'Gumbel' and 'Weibull' distributions and all three are represented by the 'Generalized Extreme Value (GEV) distributions', a framework in which each distribution can be characterized by what statisticians refer to as the 'tail exponent'. The empirical models based on EVT are usually calibrated to the extreme ends of the distributions and do not cover the more common events.[28] Risk managers therefore sometimes work with a mixture of different distributions for the different regimes.

Non-normal marginal (i.e. univariate) distributions for individual asset returns in a portfolio lead to very complex mathematical problems, when the corresponding multivariate portfolio distribution is examined. As already mentioned, for multivariate normal distributions the correlation matrix uniquely defines the dependency structure between the individual processes (asset returns),[29] which makes them very handy in practical applications. In financial markets, however, the statistical properties of extreme events are too complex to be covered by the assumptions of statistical normality. Multivariate normal distributions cover the dependency structure of rare events insufficiently. Compared to what is empirically observed in financial markets, joint extreme events of individual processes (asset returns) occur too seldom in normally distributed multivariate processes. For non-normal (generally 'non-elliptical') distributions the correlation matrix does not describe the dependency structure of the multivariate process adequately. Two strongly dependent variables could have a low or even zero (linear) correlation, which can be illustrated with the following simple example: Consider a normally distributed random variable X and the random variable $Y=X^*X$. Although they are perfectly dependent (as they can be determined from each other with deterministic certainty) their (linear) correlation is zero!

Alternative measures for statistical dependency, especially for the dependency of rare events, are the subject of intense research.[30] One approach is to quantify dependency through conditional quantiles. These describe the likelihood that one variable will take on extreme values conditional on another variable. A further method is rank correlations, which can be used as a more reliable correlation measure. They are computationally simple enough to be used by practioners. The general theory of 'copulas' provides a way to separate the joint multivariate distribution into two different parts: the marginal univariate distributions and the dependence structure, called the 'copula'.[31] The joint multivariate distribution can be described as a convolution of the copula function and uniformly distributed marginal distributions. Copula theory provides the possibility of including more complex dependence structures into a Monte Carlo setting.[32] It should be noted, however, that introducing non-normal distributions into financial risk management is a difficult and complex undertaking. Most commercial risk management software providers do not offer users the possibility of dealing with this degree of complexity.

After determining the tail properties of the portfolio distribution, VaR can be estimated as a quantile of the corresponding extreme value distribution.[33] Studies have shown that VaR calculated on the basis of EVT is considerably higher than normal VaR.[34] In other words, VaR calculated on the basis of standard (normal) volatilities and correlations often severely underestimates real risk.

Liquidity Risk

Liquidity Risk takes two different forms: asset liquidity and funding liquidity risk. Asset liquidity risk describes the potential inability to sell a position at fair value because of insufficient trading activity. In order to examine the potential impact of insufficient asset liquidity, a risk manager should run scenarios using prices that are discounted from current market prices, i.e. 'liquidation values' rather than fair value. Liquidation values should reflect the likely impact on prices upon forced liquidations. The discount depends on the position size relative to trading volume and bid–ask spreads.[35]

Funding risk is of central concern to AIS managers. A lack of funding can contribute to a crisis situation where the Hedge fund has to liquidate positions to raise cash, either because the fund must post margin with its counter-parties (usually as the result of a loss) or because of redemptions by investors. The manager should constantly track the fund's cash positions (cash and short-term securities of high credit quality) and its borrowing capacities (margin rules and credit lines) on the one side and the potential need for liquidity on the other. The level of liquidity required is dependent on the nature of the instruments traded (e.g. Futures require much less cash than other instruments), the level of leverage and risk (as can be measured by VaR, scenario analysis or stress testing) and redemption policies. Possible funding liquidity measures include the cash/equity ratio, the VaR/(cash plus borrowing capacity) ratio and the worst historical drawdown/(cash plus borrowing capacity) ratio. Hedge fund managers should have good communication lines with their credit providers, giving them sufficient access to information about the fund's risk and liquidity levels.

Credit Risk

While the decade of the 1990s saw tremendous advances in the modelling of market risk, more recently, quantitative credit risk modelling has emerged as a major focus of risk management. Important advances in the analysis of credit risk have led to the proliferation of a new breed of sophisticated quantitative credit models. These models build on the extensive mathematical modelling of default and loss probabilities for single obligors as well as correlations between obligors. Several commercially available approaches have received a great deal of attention, of which the five most prominent are:[36]

▪ CreditMetrics (JP Morgan)

▪ CreditMonitor (KMV)

▪ RiskCalc (Moody's)

▪ CreditRisk+ (Credit Suisse Financial Products, now Credit Suisse First Boston)

▪ CreditPortfolioView (McKinsey).

To the practitioner, the seemingly disparate collection of new approaches may be confusing and should be interpreted as a warning sign of the early developmental stage of the technology.[37] Credit risk imposes new dimensions of complexity, as return distributions are largely non-normally distributed and sufficient diversification is reached only after including hundreds or thousands of positions in the portfolio. While a variety of theoretical modelling approaches have been developed, the empirical testing of these models is still in its infancy.[38]

The goal of credit risk analysis is to calculate the probability distribution for credit losses in order to define a 'Credit VaR' similar to 'Market VaR'. But modelling credit risk is significantly more complex than market risk, as there are numerous factors driving the value of debt. Additionally, credit and market risk can be highly interrelated. One of the most critical issues in modelling credit risk is the data input (past default rates, recovery rates, observed correlations between different obligors etc.). The three main elements of credit risk are exposure, default probability (including market sentiments about its possible changes) and loss following default, which is expressed by recovery rates. Default probability is assessed by the credit rating (for debt rated by agencies) or quantitative models (e.g. the Merton model; see later). Finally, exposure is defined by the investor or modelled through scenario simulations (e.g. for OTC swaps where future exposure is not certain at present).

The expected loss and the distribution of losses can be estimated through probability distributions of default and the resulting loss following default. Loss following default is composed of the net exposure to the firm and the forecasted recovery rate in case of default. This is a function of the debt-issuing firm's asset value versus the face value of its liabilities. Research into recovery rates is a rather undeveloped area in credit risk management and one where consensus in approach is less clear.

While all three elements are important variables in evaluating credit risk, none is more important than the default probability. Prior to default, there is no way to distinguish unambiguously between firms that will default and those that will not. At best the risk manager can make a probabilistic assessment of the likelihood of default for individual firms.

Two general frameworks for calculating default probabilities have evolved, each with different approaches modelling the 'economics of default'. The first method, which is referred to as 'structural modelling', was pioneered by Merton and describes the firm's liabilities as contingent claims issued against the firm's underlying assets.[39] According to Merton, default happens for an explicit reason – the value of the firm's assets falls below the face value of the debt (in which case the debt holder receives the value of the remaining assets). Making rather simple assumptions as to the capital structure of the company, assuming no liquidation costs and constant interest rates, the payoff to a bank making a loan is isomorphic to writing a put option on the assets of the borrowing firm (equivalently, equity of the firm can be seen as a call option on the firm's assets). Given this framework, it is not surprising that the Black–Scholes (BS) option pricing formula is at the heart of all structural models. There are numerous extensions of the basic model introducing more realistic capital structures.[40] Three of the most popular credit risk models, KMV CreditMonitor, JP Morgan's CreditMetrics and Moody's RiskCalc, fall within the extended class of Merton-based structural models. And although McKinsey's CreditPortfolioView and CSFB's CreditRisk+ do not rely on explicit modelling of the firm's asset value, they can be summarized under a similar generalized framework.[41]

A second class of models abstracts completely from the economics of default. These models, summarized under the term 'reduced form' models, try to estimate the risk neutral probability of default from prevailing credit spreads quoted in the market. No reference to the cause of default is made.[42] This approach relies on the availability of high-quality data for credit spreads, a prerequisite that is often not fulfilled. The deeper and more liquid the market, the better the reduced-form models are expected to work. Reduced-form models are not applicable to the obligations of small and micro cap firms with no publicly traded debt.

Other risks

The development of risk management tools in recent years has mainly been geared towards market and credit risk analysis. It remains more difficult to quantify other risks. Pushed by regulators, the financial community is now turning to operational risk, which in many cases has proven to be an important cause of large financial losses (e.g. Sumitomo: $2.6 billion loss, Barings: $1.3 billion loss, Daiwa: $1.1 billion loss, all three in 1997). Most of these losses can be attributed to a combination of exposure to market and credit risk along with failures of controls. Operational risk can be defined as the risk of losses due to people (employees), processes (errors in internal systems or model, hedging errors), technology (IT programs or data), external factors (human factors outside the firm) or physical events (weather, theft etc.). Besides the regulatory capital charges to internationally active financial institutions for market and credit risk, which were established in 1998 and 1996, the Basel Committee has now proposed the establishment of capital charges for operational risk.[43] As a consequence, the measurement of operational risk is currently the subject of intense discussions and new models are under development.[44] The various approaches can be broadly classified into 'top down' and 'bottom up' models. While top down models measure operational risk at the broadest level (i.e. firm wide or even industry wide), bottom up models start at the individual process level within business units.

The focus on operational risk is generally geared towards larger financial institutions, where processes and the interaction between different units can be rather complex. Hedge funds are usually smaller and less complex from an operational viewpoint. Nevertheless, operational risks are quite similar. Human error, model risk and exposure to technology risk are equally present in most Hedge fund operations. Some Hedge funds exploit market inefficiencies with very small price margins. Here, frequent execution errors can quickly erase otherwise lucrative returns. Methods that are used to measure operational risk include the following quantitative and qualitative elements:[45]

- *Audit oversight*: Review by an external auditor (or audit department of the same firm in the case of large organizations).

- *Critical self-assessment*: Each business unit or key person identifies the nature and size of operational risk.

- *Key risk indicators*: Audit scores, staff turnover, trade volume etc.

- *Earnings volatility*: This includes business and macroeconomic risks and might be less relevant for AIS managers.

- *Causal networks*: Causal networks describe how losses can occur from a cascade of different causes, which are linked to each other through conditional probabilities. Most causal networks are based on Bayes' theorem and Bayesian statistics.[46]

- *Actuarial models*: Actuarial models combine loss frequencies with loss severities to generate losses distributions. Most actuarial models estimate the distribution of losses, i.e. the loss frequency and loss severity distributions, from historical data. Assuming that frequency and severity of losses are independent, these two distributions can be combined into the distribution of aggregate losses through what is called 'convolution' in mathematics. In practice, the calculation of aggregate losses is often performed through numerical simulation. With a loss distribution at hand, one can define an 'Operational VaR'.

- *Extreme Value Methodology*: Most operational loss distributions are non-normally distributed and show fat tails. Some promising methods from the

Extreme Values Theory (EVT, see earlier) have lead to interesting applications for operational risk analysis. Many of the developments and applications of EVT in the field of finance originated within the insurance industry, where due to the nature of the business the focus is much more directly on extreme event risk.

Once operational risk is measured and quantified, it has to be controlled. Operational risk management consists of various procedures and control mechanisms. The following provides a list of some of the most important elements:

- *Separation of functions*: This is one of the key risk management principles and applies equally to large and small institutions. Responsibility for trading should be separated from clearing, accounting and risk management functions.

- *Incentives*: The compensation of the people responsible for accounting and risk management should be independent from the success of trading or asset management activities. Generally, the incentive structure within the firm should encourage people to ask the right questions and express concerns openly.

- *Monitoring*: Control policies and compliance rules should be in place to ensure that objectives are carried out. Policies and procedures should spell out expectations regarding the integrity and ethical behaviour of employees.

- *Risk-adjusted performance compensation*: Traders and asset managers should be compensated based on risk-adjusted performance, e.g. RAROC ('risk-adjusted return on capital').

- *Involvement of senior management*: Senior management should set clear risk management guidelines and capital policies and enforce those efficiently.

- *Dual entries and reconciliation*: Entries and final positions should be matched from different sources. Each counter-party needs to confirm the trade tickets.

- *Price verification*: Prices should be obtained from several external sources. The institution should have the capability to value a transaction in house before entering it.

- *Authorizations*: All counter-parties should be provided with a list of personnel authorized to trade.

■ *Internal and external audits*: Auditors provide useful information on potential weaknesses.

Enterprise-wide risk management

Best risk management practices in the industry have evolved from the lessons of the financial disasters in the 1990s. Financial institutions have realized that it is in their best interest to promote a set of guidelines to forestall further regulatory action. In 1993 the Group of Thirty (G-30) issued a report,[47] which provides 24 sound risk management principles and became a milestone for risk management. The failure of Barings Bank was followed by an in-depth report from the Bank of England.[48] Finally, the failure of Long-Term Capital Management (LTCM) led to some very useful lessons, especially for the Hedge fund industry. In the wake of this event, the Counter-party Risk Management Policy Group (CRMPG) was established to strengthen financial risk management practices.[49] Chapter 7 provides a further discussion of these reports.

The interaction of various types of risk requires particular attention, as different sources of risks (market credit, credit risk, operational risk) are not acting isolated from each other. The industry increasingly focuses on 'integrated risk management' or 'firm-wide risk management'. The major elements of risk management at the enterprise level are analysis, integration, data and reporting.[50] The focus on 'firm-wide risk management' is a recent development and the challenge ahead is the extension of risk management beyond the sole monitoring of traditional credit or trading exposure. The establishment of feedback loops between senior management and individual business and trading units allows for a proactive response to risk assessment.

A general note: The 'catastrophic risks', i.e. the risks that can lead to failure of the entire firm, are not the most complex to detect from an analytical standpoint. They are usually due to failures in the organizational structure of the firm. Many institutions put analytical efforts at the centre of risk management attention, which leads to the focus being on providing answers to questions that have already been answered with ever more detail and sophistication. But digging more deeply into one spot does not ensure that one is digging at the right spot.

Active risk management

Much of the discussion about risk management centres on the question of how to measure or analyze risk. However, a critical dimension to risk management is the decision-making process after the analysis of risk. In order properly to control risk and achieve the objective of maximizing risk-adjusted returns, risk management has to be integrated into the investment decision-making process. Risk management entails monitoring exposures and risks *and* using the risk measures to allocate risk optimally among different assets and strategies with refinements and modifications undertaken when necessary. The optimal allocation of risk among different AIS requires the assessment of which risks should be borne for which level of expected return. The allocator should define the acceptable risk level within the portfolio and judge current risk as measured by VaR, stress tests or other risk characteristics against it.

The important initial step in effective risk management is setting up a diversified portfolio. The theory of modern portfolio management (MPT) and the resulting quantitative tools are well known by most portfolio managers. But the quantitative optimization of AIS portfolios bears a number of pitfalls and significant qualitative analysis is needed on top of the quantitative tools for the set-up of a well-diversified portfolio (see Chapter 7 for more details). Risk limits on individual instruments, sectors or managers/traders ('risk budgeting' or 'risk bucketing')[51] serve the purpose of avoiding excessive one-sided exposures in a portfolio. Stop-loss limits help to control losses due to sudden unexpected strong price moves.

Risk management requires action. Action must be taken in cases where: (a) risk limits are exceeded; (b) it is decided that exposure to certain risk factors should be reduced; or (c) external events demand cutting certain risky positions. This requires reliable quantitative tools and a good understanding of the relationship between risk levels and market developments. 'Marginal risk' analysis can be useful to mitigate deteriorating effects in case of an unfavourable event.

One of the most important principles of risk management is the separation of responsibilities between risk takers and risk managers. Risk management should be an independent function that is implemented and directly supervised by a senior management. The decision-making power for risk control should be put into the hands of those who oversee the risk analytics and not those who take the risk. The principles that apply to large institutions apply equally to AIS managers, even though they often operate within the structure of a small firm without independent risk management, where risk manager and trader are often one and the same person. Many Hedge fund managers implement independent risk management through strict adherence to predefined risk principles such as stop losses, risk limits, maximal exposure to single asset classes etc. This corresponds to how many AIS managers interpret their success. Asked about the reasons for their success many answer: 'Investment discipline.'

Risk analysis systems in practice

The development of a fully operative risk analysis system that enables the user to perform the sort of calculations discussed (VaR calculations, stress tests, scenario analysis etc.), is a very complex undertaking. The three critical issues are the build up and maintenance of a database for historical volatility and correlation analysis, the definition of relevant risk factors and the construction of pricing models.

Many Hedge funds want access to enhanced risk analysis but lack the financial and human resources to build a full risk analysis structure themselves or to run and maintain an externally purchased system. A common solution for many AIS managers is the complete outsourcing of their risk analysis to external service providers.

The demand for quantitative risk analysis tools and the increased availability of computational power in recent years has led to a number of firms specializing in providing risk services to investment managers. AIS managers have become an important part of their client base. Similarly, most prime brokers have begun offering risk services to their AIS clients as a value-added service in return for obtaining their attractive execution and clearing business.

Communication between service provider and investment manager happens increasingly through the internet. With its emergence, many firms have web enabled their software and run their services on an ASP ('application service provider') basis.[52] An ASP is a service that hosts and runs specific applications for a number of different customers. While this occurs in most cases with little customization, some AIS managers do request tailor-made analytics. An example for an ASP implementation of a risk analysis system offered by a prime broker is PrimeRisk at Credit Suisse First Boston, which is based on Algorithmic's RiskWatch.[53]

Outsourcing risk analysis has several advantages for the AIS manager:

- He does not have to set up his own system for the risk analysis and valuation computation of very complex instruments.

- He does not have to gather all the data required to model risk appropriately.

- He does not have to hire full-time risk management staff.

- He gains credibility when an independent third party not involved in marketing his products performs the risk analysis.

- He gains access to risk analysis techniques that until recently only the big investment firm could afford to operate.

But there are problems with outsourcing risk analysis. One might not know exactly the nature and the origin of the risk analysis output. Like any number-crunching exercise, it is difficult to interpret numerical results if one does not know precisely the calculations behind them. It is therefore essential for the AIS risk manager to have an understanding of the risk systems, their underlying features and the models used for the calculations.

Readers of financial magazines are confronted with a growing number of advertisements for risk management services and increasingly these target particularly the AIS manager. The seemingly disparate collection of risk service suppliers and software vendors may be confusing for practitioners. In the following, I provide a list of some key players in this market (the URLs are included in parentheses for further information). A description of the individual systems is, however, beyond the scope of this book:

Algorithmics (http://www.algorithmics.com)

Askari (http://www.askari.com)

Barra (http://www.barra.com)

BlackRock Solutions (http://www.blackrocksolutions.com)

Financial Engineering Associates (http://www.fea.com)

GlobeOp's (http://www.globeop.com)

Imagine Trading System (http://www.imagine-sw.com)

Measurisk (http://www.measurisk.com)

Misys (formerly MKIRisk) (http://www.misys-ibs.com)

Kiodex (http://www.kiodex.com)

Kronos (http://www.krns.com)

Panalytix (http://www.panalytix.com)

PrimeRisk (Credit Suisse First Boston: http://www.primerisk.csfb.com)

Reech Capital (http://www.reech.com)

Reuters (http://about.reuters.com/risk)

RiskBox (http://www.riskbox.com)[54]

RiskMetrics (http://www.riskmetrics.com)

Summit Systems (http://www.summithq.com)

SunGard's Opus, Infinity, Panorama (http://www.risk.sungard.com)

Ubitrade (http://www.ubitrade.com).

Wilshire (http//www.wilshire.com)

As the market for risk services is subject to constant change, the list of service providers is necessarily incomplete (also some vendors might disappear from the market). In January 2002, the firm Capital Market Risk Advisors (CMRA) completed a review of risk management systems for investment managers, Hedge funds, funds of funds, plan sponsors, endowments and foundations.[55] *Risk Magazine* frequently publishes software and vendor surveys, which describe the latest developments in this particular field of financial technology.[56]

Notes

1. Despite being a few years old, the original technical RiskMetrics documents ('RiskMetrics', 1996 and 'CreditMetrics', 1997) provide an excellent discussion of the fundamental market and credit risk principles and models. In 2001, the company came out with a new edition of the document for market risk: 'Return to

RiskMetrics'. A broader coverage of different risks and further references are presented in *The Professional's Handbook of Financial Risk Management* by M. Lore and L. Borodovsky (eds) and the GARP Association (General Association of Risk Professionals).

2. An excellent textbook designed for the candidates of the FRM (Financial Risk manager) examination of the GARP association (http://www.garp.com) is *The FRM Handbook 2001/2002* by P. Jorion. This book introduces the main concepts of modern risk management and provides numerous references.

3. See: Group of Thirty, Derivatives, 'Practices and Principles', New York; the report is available on the IFCI web page risk.ifci.ch, maintained by the International Finance and Commodities Institute (IFCI), a non-profit Swiss organization.

4. The concept of duration is discussed in almost all textbooks about finance, e.g. *Investment Analysis and Portfolio Management* by F. Reilly and K. Brown.

5. See, for example, *Investment Analysis and Portfolio Management*, by F. Reilly and K. Brown.

6. For a good overview, see J. Hull, *Options, Futures, and other Derivatives*, 4th edition, Prentice Hall, 1999, Chapter 13. The ARCH/GARCH approach is well covered in the review paper by T. Bollerslev, R. Chou and K. Kroner, 'Arch Modelling in Finance', *Journal of Econometrics*, 1992, 52, pp.5–59.

7. VaR is discussed in all textbooks about risk management, e.g. *Mastering Value at Risk: A Step-by-Step Guide to Understanding and Applying VaR* by C. Butler.

8. There exist numerous publications covering this topic. I recommend the discussion provided in the RiskMetrics Technical Document (the one from 1996 is more detailed than the 2001 version). P. Best also provides a good overview of the subject in Chapter 5 of *Implementing Value at Risk*, 1998.

9. The RiskMetrics Technical Document provides a discussion of the individual risk factors. For commercially available risk management software, the technical documents usually include a discussion of the risk factors used and the details of the pricing and mapping procedure.

10. The construction of yield curves is discussed in detail in Chapter 2 of *The Professional's Handbook of Financial Risk Management* by M. Lore and

L. Borodovsky (eds). *The DataMetrics Technical Document* by A. Malz also provides a detailed explanation of how to construct a yield curve from a set of bond and swap prices.

11. More details about both methods are described by P. Best in *Implementing Value at Risk*, p.114.

12. For more information and a discussion of the quality of different volatility and correlation forecasts, see the article 'Volatility and Correlation Forecasting' by C. Alexander in *The Handbook of Risk Management and Analysis* by C. Alexander (ed.), 1996.

13. See the article by T. Bollerslev et al., 'Arch Modelling in Finance', *Journal of Econometrics*, 1992, 52, pp.5–59.

14. This method is often called the 'RiskMetrics VaR' method, as this was the original method introduced by RiskMetrics in the early 1990s. Today, RiskMetrics also offers other parametric VaR approaches as well as Monte Carlo-based and historical simulation-based VaR.

15. In *Beyond Value of Risk* (Chapter 5) Kevin Dowd presents a good discussion about the different aspects of Monte Carlo approaches.

16. See P. Embrechts et al., 'Correlation and Dependency in Risk Management: Properties and Pitfalls'.

17. An excellent paper about non-normal distributions is given by P. Embrechts et al. in 'Correlation and Dependency in Risk Management: Properties and Pitfalls', ETHZ Working Paper, 1998; see http://www.math.ethz.ch/~mcneil/pub_list.html. A shorter version appeared in the journal *Risk*, May 1999, pp.69–71. Further, an overview treatment of the issues involved with non-normality is presented in the RiskMetrics document 'Return to RiskMetrics, 2001, Appendix A.

18. A good overview of the different available methods of VaR testing and further references is provided by K. Dowd in *Beyond Value at Risk*, Appendix to Ch. 2.

19. See, e.g., the article 'Evaluating Value at Risk Models using Historical Data' by D. Hendricks or the article by H. Hauksson et al. 'Multivariate Extremes, Aggregation, and Risk Estimation'.

20. There are many articles about this topic. Please refer to the article 'Portfolio Value at Risk with Heavy Tailed Risk Factors' by P. Glassermann et al., 2000,

which also provides further references.

21. The concept of 'coherent risk measure' as well as a discussion on other desirable theoretical properties of risk measure is discussed in the article by P. Artzner et al., 'Coherent Risk Measures'.

22. A good discussion of conditional VaR can be found in S. Uryasev and Tyrrall Rockafellar, 'Optimization of Conditional Value at Risk', under http://www.ise.ufl.edu/uryasev/roc.pdf.

23. For more details see the following articles: S. Uryasev and T. I. Rockafellar, 'Optimization of Conditional Value at Risk'; P. Krokhmal, J. Palmquist and S. Uryasev, 'Portfolio Optimization with Conditional Value-At-Risk Objective and Constraints'.

24. In early 2000, the Bank of International Settlement (BIS) initiated a survey of stress tests scenarios employed by risk managers. Please refer to the article by I. Fender and M. Gibson in *Risk Magazine*, May 2001, p.50, for the details and results.

25. An interesting discussion on the effect of correlation in stress tests is presented in 'A Stress Test to Incorporate Correlation Breakdown' published in the *RiskMetrics Journal* in May 2000.

26. Glassermann et al. present some interesting VaR calculations with the student-t distribution in their article 'Portfolio Value at Risk with Heavy Tailed Risk Factors'.

27. A good reference for the mathematical properties and theorems of extreme value theory can be found in P. Embrechts et al., *Modelling Extremal Events*, Springer, 1999. See also A. McNeil, 'Extreme Value for Risk Managers', in *Internal Modelling and CAD II,* Risk Books, 1999, pp.93–113 and *Extremes and Integrated Risk Management* by P. Embrecht (ed.).

28. A good presentation on the measurement and modelling of operational risk is presented in 'Modelling and Measuring Operational Risk' by M. Cruz.

29. This generally applies to 'elliptical distributions', i.e. distribution with a density function that is constant on ellipsoids (which include the normal and the student-t distribution). For more details see the excellent discussion by P. Embrechts et al. in the article 'Correlation and Dependency in Risk Management: Properties and Pitfalls!'.

30. The following two articles provide good discussions of the subject and include numerous references: P. Embrechts et al., 'Correlation and Dependency in Risk Management: Properties and Pitfalls', and H. Hauksson et al., 'Multivariate

Extremes, Aggregation, and Risk Estimation'.

31.   For an introduction to copula theory, see *An Introduction to Copulas* by R. Nelson.

32.   For further reference, see 'Understanding Relationships Using Copulas' by E. Frees and E. Valdez.

33.   For an overview and further references for tail index estimation and applications of EVT to financial risk analysis, see J. Danielsson and C. de Vries, 'Value at Risk and Extreme Returns', Tinbergen Institue discussion paper, TI, 98-017/2, 1998. Downloadable from http://www.fee.uva.nl/BIEB/TIDPs/TIDP98nr.htm. The paper proposes an interesting semi-parametric approach, where smaller risks are captured by the non-parametric empirical distribution function (historical method) and larger risks are modelled parametrically by an estimation of tails exponents.

34.   S. N. Neftci, 'Value at Risk Calculations, Extreme Events, and Tail Estimation', *The Journal of Derivatives*, Spring 2000, p.23 and the paper by J. Danielsson and C. de Vries, 'Value at Risk and Extreme Returns'.

35.   See the article by D. Cosandy in 'Adjusting Value-at-Risk for Market Liquidity', *Risk Magazine*, October 2001, p.115 for an interesting discussion on how to quantify liquidity risk.

36.   A. Saunder presents an overview of the different approaches in *Credit Risk Measurement*, Wiley Frontiers in Finance, 1999. The author introduces the different models mentioned earlier, but also gives a rather extensive literature list covering the most recent academic and non-academic research results.

37.   A. Hickman and U. Koyuoglu demonstrated in an excellent research paper that all these different models can be considered as quite similar once simplified to one systematic risk factor. They are shown to effectively produce the same result. This lead the Basel Commission to embrace credit risk modelling and base their new framework for a revision of the 1988 Basel Accord on Internal Rating-Based (IRB) capital requirements. See U. Koyluoglu and A. Hickmann, 'Reconcilable Differences', *Risk Magazine*, October 1998.

38.   An interesting survey on empirical studies can be found in J. Bohn, *A Survey of Contingent Claim Approaches to Risky Debt Valuation*, Haas School of Business,

1999. See also by the same author: *Empirical Assessment of a Simple Contingent-Claims Model for the Valuation of Risky Debt*, Haas School of Business, 1999.

39. R. Merton, 'On the Price of Corporate Debt: The Risk Structure of Interest Rates', *Journal of Finance*, 29, p.440 (June 1974).

40. For further information and references, see M. Crouhy, D. Galai and R. Mark, 'A Comparative Analysis of Current Credit Risk Models', *Journal of Banking and Finance*, 2000, 24, pp.59–117; M. Gordy, 'A Comparative Anatomy of Credit Risk Models', *Journal of Banking and Finance*, 2000, 24, pp.119–49; and the work by the Basel Committee on Banking Supervision, 'Credit Risk Modelling: Current Practices and Applications', Basel, 1999, available on the BIS homepage: http://www.bis.org.

41. CreditRisk+ actually makes no assumptions about the economic reason for default and for that reason might be better classified as a 'reduced form' model. But the model does not require any credit spread data, as reduced models do. The general assessment of the default rate distribution for an individual firm is quite similar to the one in structural models, where CreditRisk+ assumes an Γ-distributed default rate distribution. See also 'CreditRisk+', Credit Suisse Financial Products (now CSFB), 1997.

42. See F. Longstaff and R. Schwartz, 'A Simple Approach to Valuing Risky Fixed and Floating Rate Debt', *Journal of Finance*, 1998, 50, pp.449–70; D. Duffie and K. Singleton, 'Modelling the Term Structure of Defaultable Bonds', Stanford University Paper, 1998; and Gregory Hayt, 'How to Price Credit Risk', *Risk Magazine*, January 2000.

43. Discussions about this subject are ongoing. The propositions for operational risk charges in the new amendment of the Basel Accord provide a good perspective on the difficulties of quantifying operational risk. See the 'Overview of the New Basel Capital Accord' by the Bank for International Settlement, January 2001 and the discussion in *Risk Magazine*, March 2001.

44. See the articles by M. Crouhy et al., 'Operational Risk'; D. Wilson, 'Operational Risk' in *The Professional's Handbook of Financial Risk Management* by M. Lore and L. Borodovsky (eds); A. Brewer, 'Minimizing Operations Risk', in *Derivatives Handbook* by R. Schwartz and C. Smith (eds). The book *Operational Risk: Measurement and Modelling* by J. King provides a wide coverage on the subject of operational risk management.

45. Compare with P. Jorion in *The FRM Handbook 2001/2002*.

46.   For an introduction to Bayesian statistics, see *Bayesian Theory* by J. Bernardo and A. Smith.

47.   Group of Thirty, 'Derivatives: Practices and Principles', New York, 1993, available on the IFCI website http://risk.ifci.ch.

48.   Bank of England, 'Report of the Board of Banking Supervision Inquiry into the Circumstances of the Collapse of Baring', HMSO Publication, London, 1995, available on the IFCI website http://risk.ifci.ch.

49.   *Counterparty Risk Management Policy Group*, 'Improving Counterparty Risk Management Practices', CRMPG, New York, 1999.

50.   For more details see the article by D. Williams, 'Selecting and Implementing Enterprise Risk Management Technologies' in *The Professional's Handbook of Financial Risk Management* by M. Lore and L. Borodovsky (eds).

51.   A more detailed discussion about the risk budgeting methodology can be found in *Risk Budgeting: A New Approach to Investing* by L. Rahl (ed.).

52.   How Hedge funds increasingly use ASP-based risk management services is discussed in the article 'Hedge Funds look to Cultivate Technology Roots', *Risk Magazine*, August 2001. See also the article by A. Favell, 'To ASP or not to ASP' in *Risk Technology*, October 2001.

53.   See the article by A. Favell, 'To ASP or not to ASP' for more details about the Prime Risk application.

54.   RiskMetrics and Tremont have recently banded together to form a joint venture. They announced the release of a 'transparency product' in the first half of 2002.

55.   Highlights of this work were published in *Risk Magazine*'s Institutional Investor Supplement in December 2001 (downloadable from the website www.cmra.com). A detailed comparison of the systems is available at www.risksystems.info.

56.   See the January 2001 software survey by C. Davidson in *Risk Magazine*, January 2001 or the 2000 and 2001 Vendor surveys in the August 2000 and August 2001 editions, respectively.

CHAPTER 7

Active Risk Management in Multi-Manager AIS Portfolios

The discussion so far has centred on investment features, risk profiles and risk management principles of individual strategies (Chapters 2, 3 and 5), the benefits of AIS in a traditional portfolio (Chapter 4), the generic risks of AIS investments (Chapter 5) and the variety of risk management tools available in today's investment market (Chapter 6). It is time to bring these different aspects together and discuss the risk management principles that govern asset allocation, the monitoring and controlling process and investment management. In this chapter I describe the elements of sound AIS portfolio risk management practices starting with a discussion about the importance of transparency, liquidity, leverage control and investment structure. The remainder of the chapter is then dedicated to outlining an integrated investment and risk management approach for multi-manager AIS portfolios. The chapter concludes with the description of active risk control in the AIS portfolio.

The AIS industry's current best practices for risk management

As a result of various investment disasters, in particular the failure of Long-Term Capital Management (LTCM) in September 1998, a lot of effort has in past years been dedicated to defining sound risk management principles for the AIS industry. The market crisis of 1998 created a heightened awareness among market participants of the need for better risk analysis and management tools including Monte Carlo VaR, stress testing, leverage control and liquidity assessment. In April 1999 the President's Working Group on Financial Markets published its report entitled 'Hedge Funds, Leverage and the Lessons from Long-Term Capital Management'. The report requested that a group of Hedge fund professionals drafts and publishes a set of sound practices for risk management and internal controls in Hedge funds. Consequently, five large Hedge fund managers[1] developed and published a document addressing this request.[2] The report is a detailed description of AIS risk management principles and provides a good reference for investors and AIS managers. The reader is strongly recommended to examine the report. To summarize, the report states that managers must understand the sources of returns and identify and quantify the types of associated risk. Hedge fund managers take investment risks in order to earn commensurate returns and they are responsible for setting, allocating and controlling the risk levels. The report emphasizes that Hedge fund risk managers should closely monitor the interrelated exposure to market risk (including asset liquidity), funding liquidity risk, credit risk (debt investments, counter-party risk) and operational risk. An extended appendix is dedicated to risk-monitoring practices. Some key risk management issues discussed are: Monitoring tools (VaR, scenario analysis, stress tests, back testing), funding risk, counter-party risk and leverage.

In July 1993 the Group of Thirty published a guideline report entitled 'Derivatives, Practices and Principles'.[3] One of the main objectives of the report was to establish 'best practices' in addressing the risks inherent in the use of derivatives. The presented standards provide a description of important elements that also apply to AIS risk management. Among the suggested principles are:

- involvement of the highest level of management in determining the scope of activities in derivatives trading
- mark to market valuation of derivatives, if possible
- performance of stress tests and forecasting cash and futures funding needs

- establishment of an independent risk management unit reporting directly to senior management

- installation of risk systems capable of measuring, reporting and managing risks in an accurate and timely manner.

In October 2000 the Investor Risk Committee (IRC) published a set of consensus guidelines for Hedge fund disclosure entitled 'What is the Right Level of Disclosure by Hedge Funds?'[4] The IRC consists of institutional investors and individuals running Hedge fund managers. One goal of the report is to establish an industry-wide standard for risk measures and calculation procedures. The report elaborates on a number of risk indicators that investors in different AIS styles could find useful: VaR, aggregate exposures to asset classes and to geographical regions, stress tests, cash to equity ratio, tracking error, measures of optionality and key spread relationships. According to the consensus, the three primary investor objectives in seeking disclosure from managers are *risk monitoring* (ensuring that managers do not take on risks beyond allowable investments and represented levels of notional exposures and leverage), *risk aggregation* (ensuring the investors' ability to aggregate risks across all their investments in order to understand portfolio level implications) and *strategy drift monitoring* (ensuring that managers are adhering to the stated investment strategy or style). The document endeavours to develop a set of disclosure rules for the AIS industry and introduces four aspects of disclosure: content (type of disclosure), granularity (the level of detail), frequency (how often disclosure is given) and time delay (how current the disclosed information is).

The IRC members state that disclosure of position information should be carried out in a way that minimizes 'the possibility that it could adversely impact the fund'. They go on to say that 'full disclosure is not the solution', expressing the concern that detailed disclosure will put manager returns in jeopardy. Finally, the IRC report indicates that the complexity of positions in an AIS portfolio may lead to 'operational difficulties associated with processing such vast quantities of data'. Monthly disclosure is suggested as sufficient disclosure frequency, but a distinction is made between large and small funds. The discussion within the IRC group is ongoing and further meetings in 2002 and later aim at elaborating on the details of recommended disclosure norms for individual strategies.[5]

The Highly Leveraged Institutions Working Group (HLIWG), a joint working group set up by the Basel Committee on Banking Supervision and the International Organization of Securities Commissions for the purpose of reviewing banks and securities firms dealing with 'highly leveraged institutions', issued a report in March 2001.[6] The report indicates that 'highly leveraged institutions' (i.e. Hedge funds and Managed Futures) have become greater in number, but generally less leveraged since 1998. It further indicates that the willingness of Hedge funds to provide financial information to investors regarding their trading activities and risk exposures has improved, but progress has been inconsistent. Many investors remain all too willing to accept a level of transparency that is insufficient to enable them to make a full assessment of a manager's soundness.

The discussion concerning transparency and the necessary disclosure for Hedge funds is ongoing, but the trend is clear. The AIS industry is confronted with stronger demand for investment transparency, especially from institutional investors with fiduciary responsibilities. AIS allocators and portfolio managers (fund of funds) focus increasingly on achieving transparency (e.g. through a managed account) in order to perform frequent positions monitoring, detailed risk analysis and continuous manager control.[7]

Multi-manager portfolios

The complexities of AIS risk management and the recognition of the importance of diversification across managers have contributed to the rapid growth in AIS multi-manager funds of funds. The emergence of funds of funds has made AIS investing accessible to investors who do not have the necessary resources to address the many challenges of AIS investment. At the same time, not all funds of funds are created equal. There is a wide variability in the level of expertise and rigour exercised by fund of funds managers and the dispersion of their returns has clearly increased in recent years, primarily on the downside.[8] One must ensure that the additional fees associated with a fund of funds are justly earned.

The AIS industry itself is not informational efficient but rather opaque. In other words, experienced fund of funds managers with a competitive advantage are able to add value through strategy and manager selection. With demand for AIS exposure growing and the number of Hedge funds increasing the selection of highest quality managers might become more difficult. The resulting imbalance between demand for Hedge fund exposure and supply of quality managers is likely to increase the added value of an experienced fund of funds manager.

In order to perform the complex tasks of strategy sector allocation, manager due diligence and investment monitoring/risk management, fund of funds managers have to be AIS specialists with an in-depth understanding of strategy sectors and particular managers' trading approaches. This includes the specific factors contributing to risk and return. They must understand how numerous macroeconomic factors influence the performance of the individual strategies. Further, one of the main benefits of a fund of funds approach, sector and manager diversification, can only be achieved if a fund of funds manager has a detailed understanding of correlations between strategy sectors and asset classes in different market environments. A diversified AIS portfolio should hold investments in strategy sectors that have low correlations to one another and a diversity of return characteristics in different market environments. Within each sector, risk that is specific to each manager must be diversified across different managers.

If properly performed, a fund of funds can provide the security created by continuous monitoring of each manager's trading activities for which the fund of funds managers should have the necessary resources and infrastructure. The relationship between the fund of funds manager and the single hedge fund he invests with must provide sufficient transparency and liquidity to allow active risk management.

In summary, there is significant added value to an investor from a fund of funds provided the fund of funds manager:

- has a complete understanding of the individual strategies and their risks
- has access to relevant information and the necessary data about AIS managers (be inside the 'information loop' of high-calibre investment talent)
- performs thorough due diligence of the managers and their respective 'edges'

- diversifies among sufficiently different strategy sectors and individual managers
- implements a system for continuous monitoring of open positions
- performs active risk management of the investment exposure.

Funds of funds provide the further advantage of better access to more managers for the investor. The minimum investment for a fund of funds is generally much lower than for an individual Hedge fund. For a single Hedge fund an investment of several million dollars is often required, making it very difficult for an individual to build a diversified portfolio. Further, while individual investors cannot invest with managers who have closed their investment program to new investors, fund of funds managers with good relationships in the industry are often able to invest in strategies even if these are technically closed to new investments.

Pooling assets in a fund of funds provides the *possibility* of a more transparent and more liquid investment platform than investing in single Hedge funds directly. However, today most funds of funds have similar transparency problems to single Hedge funds (see later). The redemption and subscription process for fund of funds is usually similar to those of mutual funds, but generally comes with significantly longer redemption periods. Monthly or quarterly periods are the norm. Some (mostly closed-end) investment vehicles try to provide for better liquidity through listings on an exchange (e.g. in Luxembourg, Ireland or Switzerland) or trading OTC in a secondary market. In this case, dealing occurs on an intra-day basis involving designated market makers. Due to the lack of a broad market, these funds are generally not traded very actively, however.

The expertise and portfolio management skills of fund of funds managers come at a price. Funds of funds carry an extra layer of fees on top of the usual manager fees. This leads to lower returns compared to the mean of the individual managers. On a risk-adjusted basis, however, reduced volatility due to diversification tends to offset the lower absolute return of (see Chapter 4). Typical fees for funds of funds include a 1–2% management fee and performance fee in the range of 10%, plus custodian and administration fees of about 0.5%.[9] Some fund of funds managers are able to mitigate the higher fees charged on the fund of funds level by obtaining fee rebates from the trading managers, taking advantage of the higher allocations they can make to single managers.

Fund of funds managers usually do not invest across all possible strategy sectors. Instead, they take a certain view on the attractiveness of individual strategies. Some AIS allocators go as far as developing their own views on the future market environment and structure their portfolio accordingly. A portfolio manager predicting rising equity markets, for example, will have a disproportionally high investment in net long equity strategies (such as Long/Short Equity). There is disagreement as to whether 'strategy timing', i.e. the systematic or discretionary switching between different strategies, is a useful investment philosophy. Investors should be aware of the inherent dangers underlying such an approach. Erroneous market forecasts or the careless assumption that performance drivers will be the same in the future as they have been in the past are among the main sources of underperformance in AIS portfolios. During the equity bull market of the late 1990s, many funds of funds were heavily invested in Long/Short Equity strategies. The strong market had enabled this strategy sector to capture impressive returns, and many AIS portfolio managers believed the bull market was going to continue. When Long/Short Equity strategies showed much weaker performance in falling equity markets during the later part of 2000 and 2001, the over-allocation to Long/Short Equity strategies caused many funds of funds to perform significantly below their expectations (see Chapter 4 for more details).

A much more robust approach to generating steady portfolio returns is diversifying systematically across those strategies that, by their nature, perform differently in various market environments (see Chapter 5 for a more detailed discussion on portfolio diversification). The consideration of 'conditional correlations' (see Figures 4.4 and 4.5) is useful for this purpose. A good portfolio is diversified across different performance and risk factors and not necessarily across different managers within one strategy sector only.

The issue of transparency in AIS

Unfortunately, most Hedge funds confront direct investors as well as AIS portfolio managers/allocators with numerous liquidity and transparency issues. The investor faces lengthy redemption periods and is often not provided with the necessary degree of disclosure regarding the Hedge fund manager's activities. This is one of the most widely perceived disadvantages of AIS investments. The resulting risks are severe and could be better controlled if regular disclosure of relevant information about risk and trading exposure were provided. Furthermore, transparency can provide the peace of mind necessary for many new investors to enter the field of AIS. The story of LTCM serves as an illustration. In September 1998 the failure of the Hedge fund Long-Term Capital Management (LTCM) is said nearly to have brought down the world financial system. The losses LCTM incurred were so large that the Federal Reserve Bank took the unprecedented step of initiating the bailout of a private investment vehicle, as the fear spread that forced liquidation would cause global financial turmoil. Something very fundamental had gone wrong.[10]

The fund had earlier made very handsome returns following its core strategy, which can be referred to as 'Convergence Arbitrage' and fell into the class of Fixed Income Arbitrage. The managers at LTCM had placed a large amount of money in trades involving the converging interest rates within the European Monetary System in the wake of the euro, the European currency unit. The most prominent example was buying Italian Government Bond (BTP) Futures and selling short German Bund contracts. The strategy was clearly defined and paid off handsomely. Other examples of LTCM trades involved US, European and Japanese yield curve and government bond swap spreads.

At the end of 1997 the fund back paid a significant amount of money to investors, about $2.7 billion, with the NAV of the fund being at around $7.5 billion. The original core strategy had clearly lost most of its edge. The yield spread between Italian and German 10-year government bonds had narrowed from about 550bp in early 1993 to only about 20bp by the end of 1997. The fund managers were looking for other opportunities and correspondingly found themselves engaged in a much wider spectrum of strategies, e.g. Merger Arbitrage, Mortgage-Backed Securities Arbitrage and Emerging Markets debt. Furthermore, in order to continue generating the attractive returns of the past, the fund increased its leverage substantially, from about 19 at the end of 1997 to about 30 in early 1998 and 42 in the summer of 1998. Neither the style drifts nor the increase in leverage had ever been communicated to investors. On September 23, 1998 (the day of the bailout), the fund had lost 92% of its asset year to date and the leverage had gone up to about 120.

LTCM clearly shifted its investment practice in the course of the months before the disaster. Investors had no knowledge of the strategy that LTCM was following at the time. The excessive leverage employed by the fund managers (partly a result of unrealised losses) remained undetected until the fund had already lost most of its capital. LTCM's investment process and the lack of disclosure to investors violated the core principles of diligent AIS investing, namely strategy understanding, knowledge about the strategic edge of the manager and continuous monitoring and risk management of the investment exposure.

Disclosure of the LTCM investment activities would quickly have made investors aware of the style drifts and 'bets' performed by LTCM's managers. It would have further allowed the investor to understand the core strategy in more detail, its requirements for earning its return and its behaviour in different market circumstances (especially the unfavourable ones). This understanding would likely have led to the detection of previously unknown (or unrecognized) risks of the investment strategy, in this case, the disappearance of the strategy's core edge. Thorough understanding of market conditions that would result in the edge of the manager disappearing would have enabled investors to exit the strategy in time. Finally, investors would likely have reacted to the excessive leverage employed by LTCM. Of course, all this would have required the investor to look beyond the returns of the past and to be proactive in assessing the strategy's future outlook.

As already discussed, fund of funds managers specialize in finding the most promising strategies and managers. Thereby, they have to diversify two main sources of AIS risk: (1) the 'market risk' of each strategy, which is the a priori known risk of potential market behaviours affecting the strategy (and its sector) adversely and (2) the specific 'credit risk' (or manager risk) of each individual Hedge fund or Managed Futures fund, which is the risk related to the specific manager experiencing a large loss. Investment transparency is necessary for the appropriate management of both, credit (manager) as well as market risk.

There are different views on how to achieve sufficient protection against *manager risk*. Some AIS allocators follow the approach of selecting 50 to 100 different managers, thus limiting the impact of a single trading advisor 'blow up' in their portfolio, and thereby achieve diversification comparable to managing a corporate bond portfolio. This results in more required manager due diligences and less time spent per manager and can quickly lead to over-diversification, which often results in mediocre performance. A well-diversified portfolio can be built with 12 to 15 managers.[11] Transparency and more detailed knowledge of the individual managers and their strategies decreases *manager risk* and thus the number of managers needed for its appropriate diversifications:

■ Access to regular information about the manager's trading activities allows style changes, undesired bets by the manager and leverage increases to be quickly recognized and addressed.

■ Transparency allows leverage to be controlled.

■ Transparency enables the investor to examine all agreements the Hedge fund is a party to such as prime brokerage agreement, fee agreements, past audit reports, corporate registration and others.

■ Transparency allows for following a strategy in 'real time' and thus leads the AIS allocator to a further understanding.

■ Transparency significantly decreases the probability of fraud.[12]

The *market risk* is best dealt with through appropriate diversification among strategy sectors. This requires precise knowledge of the various strategy sectors including their particular favourable and unfavourable market environments. An understanding of how past returns were generated is imperative to successful asset allocation (this includes an assessment of whether they were generated at all; often returns that look too good to be true *are* not true). A diversified AIS portfolio contains strategies which have their strengths and weaknesses in very different market environments (see Chapter 5). Without transparency *and* the appropriate knowledge of the strategy, diversification of a multi-manager portfolio remains largely a guessing game with the tendency to allocate most money to the 'stars of the past'. Transparency is important for performance evaluation:

■ Transparency provides the possibility of detecting previously unknown (or unrecognized) risks in the investment strategy. While one might obtain good insights from past performance behaviour, certain risk factors may have yet to be experienced.

■ Transparency provides support for the challenging task of performance measurement. Reported NAV often does not take into account the liquidity of open positions, especially when a position is large compared to daily trading volume of the asset or the asset is not actively traded at all (e.g. in Regulation D[13] and Distressed Debt strategies). In these cases, asset values remain estimates until gains or losses are realized. Knowing the nature of illiquid positions enables the investor to perform his own assessment of the manager's performance in consideration of the liquidity of open positions.

Despite growing investor awareness of the importance of transparency, there remains a surprising degree of resistance against such in the AIS industry. The 'black box' investing approach is still widespread. Direct investors in Hedge funds, AIS allocators and fund of funds investors often do not receive the appropriate amount of information or have the necessary knowledge of manager activities to make educated investment choices. The following three arguments are frequently used against transparency to the level of full position disclosure. Trading managers often bring up the first two arguments and many AIS allocators raise the third.

1 Confidential position information reaches the market place, potentially causing the strategy to: (a) lose its edge, if more players adopt the strategy; and (b) be actively traded against by other market participants.

2 Investors lack the skills necessary to evaluate the massive amount of information provided by daily positions. This could lead to overload and/or false comfort.

3 The best Hedge fund managers do not disclose their positions. The request for transparency will thus eliminate the opportunity to invest in the most promising investment strategies.

For the first argument, one must consider who actually poses a threat to AIS managers. The threat of being copied or actively being traded against comes largely from the dealer community and the investment banks' proprietary trading desks rather than from AIS allocators or direct investors. Once Hedge funds know who their investors are and what their intention with the disclosed information is, they can set up appropriate confidentiality agreements which keep the investor from proliferating any relevant information. The necessary transparency can be provided to investors, while details about the manager's trading positions remain undisclosed to the wider public.

The second argument neglects the increasing expertise and capacity of fund of funds managers. In combination with the appropriate level of strategy understanding, information about the details of the trading activities is very useful to the investor and AIS allocator. With the advent of information technology and powerful computers, the compilation of large amounts of data has become an easy undertaking for professional investors and portfolio managers. Positions and transactions can be downloaded and analyzed very efficiently and a large variety of tools and risk management software packages are today commercially available (see Chapter 6 for a more detailed discussion) to support AIS portfolio managers in the task of monitoring managers' trading behaviour and assumed risk levels.

Fund of funds managers often raise the third argument and claim that the best managers are unwilling to provide transparency or insight into their trading approach. They argue that AIS allocators that require transparency necessarily have to invest with lower performing managers. There are indeed some managers with excellent performance track records who refuse to provide transparency to investors, but it is incorrect to link attractive returns with lack of transparency. The belief that the best managers are necessarily non-transparent and that AIS portfolio managers focusing on transparency are therefore left with 'second tier' managers finds no empirical support. Many high-quality managers with excellent track records are willing to offer the desired transparency, if asked or required (for an investment) to do so. Good performance has nothing to do with a lack of transparency. Inversely, managers who refuse to provide transparency of their investment activities are not necessarily the most preferable for the investor. It should be noted that the more openly a trading manager discloses his strategy, the more likely it is that he is able to present a clear edge. The lack of a manager's willingness to provide transparency can correspond to his inability to illustrate why his approach makes money. A manager who is unwilling to explain his edge may not have one and therefore hides behind a 'black box' approach.

Many investors continue to regard AIS as an industry where returns are generated by mysterious means and judge successful managers exclusively on the basis of their stellar past returns. Examples of secretive, non-transparent and, for certain periods of time, very successful strategies are LTCM, Quantum Fund, Tiger and Niederhoffer, all of which failed spectacularly in the end. Investors failed to understand that high past returns were connected to high risks, which eventually led to failure.

The incorrect assumption that the best performing managers must operate in secret is linked to persistent misperceptions about AIS. Many investors believe that AIS returns are generated through the identification of unrecognized market 'inefficiencies'. The reality of AIS investing is that most strategies systematically earn premiums in return for assuming certain risks (see Chapter 2). Most managers follow systematic investment strategies that, not surprisingly, perform better in certain market environments than in others and that bear a range of risks. Transparency is needed to allow for an adequate assessment of risks and returns. With some effort most strategies are actually not very difficult to understand. As with all investing, past performance is an insufficient indicator of a strategy's future performance potential.

Investors must learn to look beyond past return and instead look at how and in what market environment returns have been achieved. Even the most brilliant investors of the past are not protected against losses and drawdowns and the conditions for success are constantly changing. Recent studies have shown that there is little convincing evidence that above average performance repeats itself in a way that can be exploited by investors.[14] The best way to predict future performance is to understand the investment process, the underlying strategy and the manager's real 'edge' and to assess these factors in the context of the current and possible future market environments. Strategy assessment is an ongoing process and includes the effort of following the manager's activities on a regular basis. It is not enough to wait for the monthly arrival of NAV and then begin analyzing facts and asking questions.

A note on the relationship between size and performance of a manager's trading program: A good track record leads to asset growth and the largest players in the AIS industry have shown impressive performance in the past. But many investors are not aware of the 'survivorship bias' inherent in relating size to future performance outlooks. The following (extreme) example illustrates this:

EXAMPLE

Take 10,000 different 'random' strategies (i.e. positions are taken on a completely random basis) and let them run for a few years. Good performance is rewarded with asset inflow, bad performance with asset outflow. Most of the strategies have to close their programs due to sluggish performance. But among the many strategies a few will turn out to be successful by pure coincidence. These are the ones that survive and, after a few years, they will have grown to be large.[15] This does not mean, of course, that they are more trustworthy than the majority that failed.

Recent reports have actually shown that small and young programs have the best future performance.[16] With the 'institutionalization' of the AIS industry more and more managers will be forced to disclose the details of their trading activities to investors. If one considers the monitoring of investment activities *inside* financial institutions such as banks, broker–dealers, corporate finance departments of large firms, insurance companies, endowments, pension funds and foundations, it seems difficult to imagine that external managers would be allowed to pursue completely unmonitored and largely unregulated investment activities. To make matters worse, these strategies are exposed to a much larger variety of risk factors and can be made riskier at the discretion of the manager.

There is much ongoing discussion about what the right level of disclosure to AIS investors is. The discussion centres on the question whether aggregated 'risk information' is sufficient for monitoring and risk management purposes or whether full disclosure of all positions is needed. The belief that AIS risk can be adequately monitored without obtaining the underlying positions is widespread. I strongly disagree with this view. Along with the investor there is another party that is exposed to the risk of financial losses as a consequence of a manager's trading activities. This is the prime broker as a lender of securities and provider of leverage. If sufficient risk and exposure monitoring without disclosure of positions was possible, the industry would likely see according 'best practices' by the prime brokers. The prime brokers would then monitor their exposures to Hedge funds based on 'aggregated risk information' without bothering with the tedious job of identifying single positions. But, in reality, prime brokers have full insight into positions on a continuous basis and so should the sophisticated investor. A high level of transparency provides the very foundation for effective risk management. Without it, reliable performance and risk measurement remain impossible.

The necessity for position disclosure and usefulness of full transparency varies among strategies. For some strategies, disclosure of each individual position is not always absolutely necessary for integrating exposure information into a risk management system. Neither do direct investors and allocators always need transparency on a daily basis for each strategy to manage and measure risk effectively. But in most cases and for most strategies frequent and detailed position information remains the best way to ensure that the necessary information is available to the portfolio and risk manager to fulfil his monitoring task. This information should be disclosed as regularly and frequently as appropriate to the strategy and, in many cases, daily disclosure is the appropriate frequency. It is the fund of funds manager's responsibility to define the necessary amount of position information needed.

Transparency may take a variety of forms, from regular conversations with the managers (the weakest form) to obtaining a daily download of all positions from the manager's prime broker (the strongest form). Model-based systematic strategies are easier to monitor and understand on a daily basis than discretionary Long/Short Equity, Macro and Short Selling strategies, where it is more difficult to follow the rationale of positions on a standalone basis, i.e. without further information provided by the manager. For Relative Value strategies (Fixed Income Arbitrage, Convertible Arbitrage, Equity Market Neutral) transparency is necessary, as leverage and potential style drift are important risk factors that have to be controlled. This also applies to Event Driven strategies (Merger Arbitrage, Distressed Securities, Regulation D), but here a deeper analysis of positions in light of the underlying strategy is necessary, which requires additional resources and capacities on the side of the portfolio manager. The optimal frequency of disclosure is also related to the liquidity of traded instruments. For Distressed Securities and Regulation D strategies, weekly or monthly disclosures can be sufficient, while for most Managed Futures strategies, daily transparency is most appropriate.

To summarize then, the 'transparency approach' of funds of funds is characterized by the following:

- detailed understanding of the return sources and risks of all strategies
- appropriate disclosure of positions by each manager
- continuous position monitoring and risk measurement
- high asset liquidity (note that most, but not all, AIS managers trade instruments that are traded on public exchanges offering daily liquidity)
- active risk management on a continuous basis.

Liquidity of AIS

Liquidity issues are among the most complex in AIS investing. A good understanding of liquidity is critical to the investment process and risk management for AIS portfolios and the lack thereof imposes risks that in the past have often received insufficient attention. 'Liquidity' has two different aspects: the ability to sell an investment without a price impact (instrument liquidity) and the availability of financing for leverage (funding liquidity). The AIS allocator should understand the liquidity of each of the instruments a strategy invests in and the sources and reliability of leverage financing. An important question to ask is the '90/10' question: 'How long would it take under normal market circumstances to liquidate 90% of the positions without a price impact?' Further, it is important to note that the liquidity of investments can change dramatically in times of market turbulence. Liquidity tends to evaporate when most needed, i.e. just when investors most want it, it disappears. An extreme example of previously unknown liquidity risk in a 'flight to quality' event led to the failure of LTCM described earlier.

In order to avoid any asset–liability mismatch, there must be a realistic relation-ship between the liquidity of the traded instruments and the fund's redemption provisions. This applies equally to the redemptions agreements of funds of funds with the individual managers, which have to be in line with the fund of funds' own redemption policies. Note that most redemption policies can be overridden in extreme market environments, as many managers include sections in their offering memorandums that give them the right to suspend redemptions under certain vaguely defined scenarios of market turmoil, regardless of the normal liquidity policies of their funds. Obviously, the best liquidity indicator for a strategy is the market liquidity of the traded instruments. Managed Futures, large cap Long/Short Equity, Macro, Market Timing and Risk Arbitrage strategies involve liquid exchange traded instruments, as do most Arbitrage and Relative Value strategies (with some exceptions for Convertible and Fixed Income Arbitrage strategies). Convertible bonds are usually traded OTC as are swaps and other fixed income derivatives, but the liquidity of these instruments is often sufficiently high. On the other side of the spectrum are Distressed Debt and Regulation D strategies, which are generally extremely illiquid.

An important factor that requires an allocator's attention when considering liq-uidity risk is fund size. Large funds, even those operating in very liquid markets, can easily encounter problems when shifting positions. There are excellent man-agers with smaller investment programs who are able to provide better liquidity simply because their position shifts do not impact market prices. Too often investors and funds of funds avoid these trading advisors simply as a result of their small size, despite research indicating that small and young programs tend to show superior performances (see above).

The benefits of transparency in an AIS portfolio cannot be fully realized with-out the individual managers providing sufficiently short redemption periods. If redemption periods do not correspond to the frequency of disclosure, the fund of funds manager is prevented from responding to time sensitive portfolio informa-tion with immediate action (e.g. de-leveraging).

Many strategies employ leverage and thus rely on external funding. Funding liquidity risk is largely determined by the prime brokers' 'haircut' policies, which specify the leverage and margin requirements for a particular strategy. The AIS allocator should consider the 'haircut sensitivity', i.e. the sensitivity to changes in the haircut policy of the broker, when examining a strategy's liquidity risk. Managers can become victims of leverage in situations of financial turmoil, when prime brokers refuse to continue to provide financing leverage because of the increased risk of positions held. This can lead to forced liquidation of the positions at inopportune times and thus create large investment losses. The manager's relationship with his prime broker is therefore an important element in the implementation of his trading strategy.

Managed accounts

The most effective way to address the need for both liquidity and transparency is via a 'managed account'. Managed accounts can provide the AIS allocator with full disclosure of the managers' trading activities together with daily liquidity (assuming the underlying instruments are sufficiently liquid). This creates the optimal basis for proactive risk management. Managed accounts also drastically reduce the risk of fraud. Figure 7.1 illustrates the set up of a 'fund of managed accounts'. The individual managers (in this context the word 'trading advisor' is more appropriate) have no direct access to the investor's money, which remains with the prime broker chosen by the fund of funds manager. The trading advisors have special authority to execute trades on behalf of the multi-manager fund in accounts that are specifically set up for that purpose. The fund of funds manager can download the positions of each manager from the prime broker and monitor trading activities on a daily basis. This results in maximal transparency. The fund of funds manager (or better, the 'fund of managed account manager') is in a position to reallocate investments with each manager literally on a daily basis (assuming the underlying investments are equally liquid). Ideally, he can also terminate the trading advisor's investment activities at any time. Finally, the fund of funds manager is in a position to select all involved parties and transaction counter-parties including the prime broker, custodian and auditor.

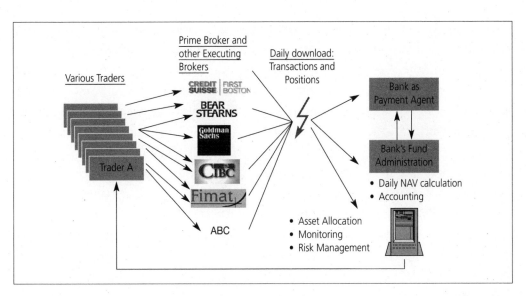

FIGURE 7.1 ■ Structure of a 'fund of managed accounts'

With the institutionalization of AIS and the fiduciary role that many funds of funds must assume the popularity of managed accounts is likely to increase in the future. However, a managed account is not always possible or practical. Not all AIS managers agree to exercise their strategy via a managed account. Some investors are constrained for tax or regulatory reasons and have to invest via the manager's funds. Managed accounts require a significant minimum investment ranging from $2 to $25 million.

Fund Redemption Policies for multi-manager investment vehicles

The redemption period of a multi-manager fund has to be in line with the liquidity offered by the individual AIS managers that the fund invests with. High liquidity on the level of a fund of funds obviously places constraints on the universe of strategies that can be included in the portfolio. Strategies whose returns are based on inefficiencies in smaller, less liquid markets and those that earn liquidity premiums (e.g. Distessed Debt, Reg D) cannot be part of a fund of funds with short redemption periods. But the AIS universe offers a large number of strategies that trade very liquid instruments.

Ultimately, it is the preference of the investor that drives the requested liquidity and return profile of a fund of funds. Some investors prefer highly liquid investments, while others are willing to invest in lower liquidity instruments in pursuit of higher returns. With the current growth rate of the AIS industry and the spectrum of investors becoming more diverse, it is likely that the request for liquid multi-manager AIS products will increase. But most Hedge fund managers – if not trading in a managed account – offer their trading strategy to investors by setting up their own fund, in which investors and AIS allocators face rather long redemption periods ranging from about one to six months. Four investment structures can be broadly distinguished for multi-manager AIS products: *open-ended funds*; *closed-end funds*; *structured notes*; and *managed accounts* (see also Chapter 5 for the details about their legal set-up). With the exception of managed accounts, all these structures confront those investors who search for high liquidity (i.e. short redemption periods) with problems.

Open-ended funds of funds are among the most common structures, with redemption periods ranging from one month to six months. The fund of funds manager invests either directly into a manager's fund or on the basis of a managed account. Besides monthly or longer redemption periods, open-ended funds often have lengthy settlement processes, increasing the time span between redemption and receipt of the money beyond the official notice period. The redemption process involves a number of tasks involving different parties: Net Asset Value calculation by the administrator, money transfer by the custodian of the fund and internal booking of the money at the investor's bank.

Closed-end vehicles, wrapped as investment companies and listed on exchanges, were established in part as an attempt to improve liquidity for the investor. The fund manager of a closed-end investment company usually invests directly into the Hedge fund manager's funds. There are neither settlement problems nor redemption periods as with an open-ended fund, because the investment, i.e. the investment company's stock, can be bought and sold daily in the open market. However, other problems render these closed-ended products unsuitable for most investors. Due to the lack of a broad market, the stocks of the investment companies are not traded very actively and large investments cannot be sold in timely fashion without a large impact on prices. This usually leads to a significantly lower market value compared to the NAV (discounts of up to 30% are frequently observed). The volatility of the discount often greatly exceeds the NAV volatility, which makes an investment in such an instrument very unattractive.

Structured notes are often designed to fulfil specific investment needs such as capital protection, regulatory specifications, legal constraints and tax protection. Structured notes usually have a defined investment period and cannot be redeemed for full value before maturity. They are generally open ended and often traded in a secondary market provided by the issuer. The issuer defines certain buyback terms, which include significant discounts to NAV. The fund manager invests either directly into a manager's fund or on a managed account basis. In cases where the issuer provides principal protection, managed accounts are used for reasons of risk control. Structured notes usually come with higher fees compared to other investment vehicles.

The fourth investment structure – based on a *managed account* – offers a solution to the liquidity limitations of other structures. The liquidity of investments through managed accounts is limited only by the nature of the underlying securities, not by managers' redemption policies or other factors. As long as there is a ready market for the investments (as is the case with most securities in AIS funds, the exceptions being mostly Distressed Debt and Regulation D), the positions can be liquidated or adjusted on a daily basis. This, in combination with daily transparency of positions and transactions, allows for real-time proactive, rather than reactive, risk management. 'Fund of managed accounts' which pass the benefits of short redemption periods and full transparency on to the investors are not yet widely offered. But this structure raises a simple question: 'Why can there not be a multi-manager AIS fund with daily liquidity based on NAV that is as easy to buy and sell as a traditional mutual stock fund?'

Leverage

Whereas leverage for companies is a function of balance sheet exposure,[17] for AIS investments, leverage describes the financing required to achieve a desired (gross) exposure level that is in excess of net asset value (NAV). Many strategies achieve leverage through external funding. For Futures strategies, leverage can be achieved without additional financing, as only a fraction of the exposure has to be placed as margin. Note that US (SEC regulated) funds are limited in the amount of leverage they can carry by Regulation T (maximum leverage 2:1).

Leverage is not always undesirable and, in certain instances, can be very helpful for achieving the desired risk–return profile of a strategy. Leverage on a stand-alone basis is not a very useful measure of risk and a high leverage factor does not necessarily imply unacceptably high risk. It is important to understand the implications of leverage (rather than stick to rigid policies such as investing in strategies with little or no leverage only), because of its impact on other risks such as market, credit and liquidity risk.

In order to understand a single manager's risk level as well as the risk in an AIS portfolio, leverage has to be assessed diligently. One should distinguish between gross and net leverage. Gross leverage is defined by (long positions + absolute value of short positions)/(portfolio equity) and net leverage is (long positions − absolute value of short positions)/(portfolio equity). The level of acceptable leverage depends strongly on the strategy. Gross and net leverage provide some insight into hedge exposure when comparing similar strategies, but it is difficult to compare leverage levels across strategies. For Fixed Income Arbitrage strategies, leverage factors of higher than ten are not unusual, while Distressed Securities or Regulation D strategies usually do not employ leverage at all. Defining a maximum accepted level of net and gross leverage for each strategy and monitoring these limits closely is an important element of portfolio risk management. If a manager exceeds predefined leverage limits, this should raise a red flag.

Leverage increases volatility by the employed leverage factor. But leverage also bears further risks linked to liquidity and funding risk and it is important to analyze instrument liquidity as well as financing risk for each leveraged strategy. Asset liquidity, leverage and financing risk are interrelated and cannot be seen in isolation. When instrument liquidity evaporates (e.g. in market stress situations), counter-parties, mostly prime brokers as providers of leverage financing, can quickly withdraw funding. Prime brokers have policies as to how much a certain type of strategy can borrow and the margins that have to be provided to each strategy. These policies can be subject to sudden change. The manager's relationship with prime brokers is therefore very important. It is essential to know loan and collateral requirements, margin policies, the intricacies of the stock loan market (e.g. how often a manager is subject to stock loan recalls) and how prime brokers and other counter-parties behave in times of market stress.

Fee structure and other key administrative considerations

The fee scheme and other administrative aspects of the set-up of an investment structure have a significant impact on its ability to meet performance goals. The investment and allocation strategy should be supplemented with an efficient and cost-sensitive administrative structure. Well-run AIS portfolios can suffer mediocre performance when the costs of the investment activities are too high. Funds can face problems that could have been avoided had fund set-up and the selection of counter-parties been approached more carefully. The choices of the prime broker, fund's jurisdiction, legal counsel, administrator, auditor and accountant have to be undertaken diligently by the fund of funds manager.

Fees

The fee structure should be chosen such that it balances fair compensation to the investment managers (fund of funds as well as AIS managers) with the interests of the investor. Fees that are too high can cause the net performance to the investor to be below expectations. Fund of funds fees usually range between 1 and 2% fixed fee and about 10% performance fee (fixed management fees above 3% can be observed in some rare cases, which clearly exceed the range of a reasonable fee structure). Besides the compensation structure for fund of funds managers (AIS allocators), other fees borne by the fund include administration fees, auditing fees, fees for fund set-up and possible sales fees. The AIS allocator should be sensitive to the level of fees charged by each AIS manager and should actively negotiate these fees, the spectrum of which is wide, ranging from 0 to 3% fixed and 10 to 30% performance fee.

Prime broker

Prime brokerage describes the function of providing custodian services, clearing, brokerage, financing (providing leverage), reporting and stock lending to AIS managers. These are essential services to any AIS fund (single and multi-manager) and the chosen prime broker should have solid experience and sufficient competence in the core areas of the business. Technical competence is equally important, as the internet has become one of the most important communication tools between prime brokers and their clients. Hedge funds and Managed Futures have become an important client segment for investment banks and brokers, and prime brokers work often in close relationship with the AIS managers as providers of a broader range of services. Examples are economic research and risk analysis tools for complex multi-instrument strategies. Furthermore, prime brokers are increasingly active as providers of Hedge fund start-up assistance, distributors of the latest industry news and supporters of managers' marketing efforts. Many investors fail to realize that the selection of a prime broker is one of the most important choices for the AIS manager. This applies to the single Hedge fund as well as to the multi-manager fund[18] (for the latter a solid prime broker relationship is especially important, if managed accounts are employed). Important considerations besides the prime broker's ability to deliver high-quality services in these areas are the global firm's commitment to its brokerage unit (i.e. its willingness to invest in technology and people), the way the firm handles conflicts of interest with other parts of the firm, especially the proprietary trading units (set-up of 'Chinese walls'), its connections in the AIS industry and its flexibility in accommodating the individual fund's structuring and support needs. Finally, AIS investors and allocators should be aware of the fees charged by prime brokers for their services. The costs of prime brokerage services are often hidden in different layers of execution, clearing and service fees, which can, in most cases, be negotiated.

Administrator

Most AIS funds are registered offshore and thus work with offshore fund administrators. An efficient administrator is critical, because he represents the investment fund to the investors. He is responsible for independent preparation of the fund's books and records and carries out other important back-office operations such as

NAV calculation, determination of fee attributions and maintenance of capital account balances. Bad fund administration is more than just a headache, as mistakes and significant time delays in NAV calculations or incorrect accounting can be very harmful to the fund. The administrator should be experienced in the duty of administrating a Hedge fund or fund of funds, use appropriate technology and be globally connected to provide the necessary services. He should be responsive to the fund's and investors' needs, accurate in his calculations and accommodating to the chosen investment structure. Further, he should have systems in places that are sophisticated enough to deal with the pricing of exotic investments and the calculation of complex performance fee structures. Important issues for the selection of the administrator are the experience of the staff, the IT and telecommunication structure, global presence and the fee structure. Administrators' fees are usually in the range of 0.1 to 0.2% of assets under management, often with a minimum base fee.

The investment and risk management process for AIS multi-manager portfolios

The performance characteristics of AIS are extremely diverse. While some strategies are driven by similar factors as traditional bonds and stock performance, such as corporate earnings, yield curves, credit spreads (they are often referred to as 'return enhancers'), others are little affected by these factors and depend on other market parameters (these are regarded as 'diversifiers').

The goal of investing in AIS is to earn an appropriate return for being exposed to certain known and accepted risks. The different steps towards this goal include the selection of the right strategy sectors and managers and the implementation of thorough post-investment monitoring and risk management. In the remainder of this chapter, I will discuss the core elements of the investment and risk management process for AIS multi-manager portfolios. As described in Chapters 2, 3 and 5, Hedge fund and Managed Futures strategies generally display more complex risk profiles than traditional investments. Figure 7.2 summarizes these various risks of AIS.

Generally, AIS risk management should: (a) be integrated into the strategy and manager allocation process prior to investment; and (b) include continuous monitoring post investment. Effective AIS risk management is proactive rather than reactive and

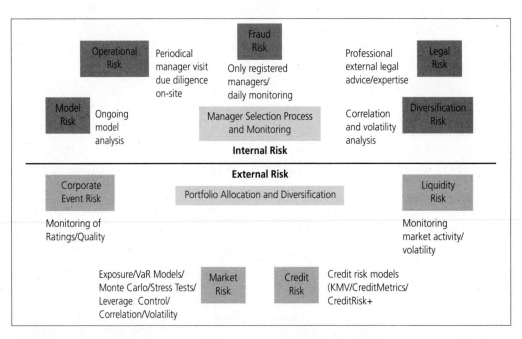

FIGURE 7.2 ■ The different sources of risk and how they can be approached

entails quantitative and qualitative analysis as well as a good amount of common sense. Figure 7.2 distinguishes between 'internal risks' (or 'manager risks'), which mainly need to be addressed during the manager due diligence process and 'external risks' (market risks), which have to be diversified through appropriate (pre-investment) strategy sector selection and then monitored regularly after investment initiation.

The most important features of both the investment and risk management process for AIS multi-manager portfolios are illustrated in Figure 7.3 and can be summarized by three core elements.

1 *Strategy sector selection and allocation*: Identification and selection of appropriate AIS sectors.

2 *Manager evaluation*: Thorough analysis and due diligence for individual trading managers.

3 *Investment monitoring and control*: Continuous supervision of the trading managers' activities, leverage and risk levels, taking corrective action when necessary.

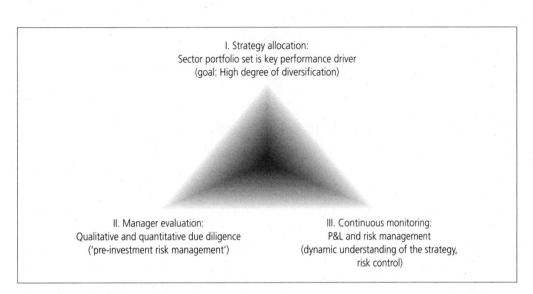

FIGURE 7.3 ■ The three key dimensions of AIS investing

Top down strategy sector analysis and bottom up manager evaluation, although principally pre-investment activities, must be periodically reassessed after the investment initiation. As is the case for equity investments, sector allocation is the most important determinant of performance in an AIS portfolio and should precede the selection of individual managers.[19]

'Post-investment risk management' is a frequently neglected part of the AIS investment process and requires particular emphasis. Monitoring and risk measurement are prerequisites for effective risk management. Armed with a quantitative analysis of risk, the risk manager should: (a) continuously assess whether the general risk level in the portfolio is too high or the losses under certain scenarios potentially too great; and (b) evaluate whether single managers are operating outside their predefined parameters (which can, for example, be due to style drifts, excess leverage or lack of diversification). The risk manager must take appropriate steps to separate risks that are accepted as a consequence of the trading approach, from those that are not related to the strategy or accepted by the investment profile. Appropriate actions range from discussing problems with managers by telephone to reducing allocations or terminating the relationship with a manager altogether. It is important to note that investment monitoring and active risk control do not mean interfering with the managers' core strategy, but rather monitoring the investment relative to the agreed investment principles and risk parameters and taking corrective action, if deemed necessary.

Strategy sector selection (top down approach)

The risk and return properties of AIS portfolios are very sensitive to sector allocation and the right selection of strategies is the key performance driver for a multi-manager AIS portfolio. The goal of the sector allocation is to select those risk factors and levels that match the investor's risk profile and to reach effective diversification among them. Diversification is the fundamental building block for portfolio sector allocation and risk management. Effective diversification means that the targeted performance can be reached in a variety of different market environments. Important determinants of diversification are asset and strategy correlations[20] (see Chapter 5 for a discussion of AIS portfolio diversification) across the different sources of return. Style-pure sub-indices of Hedge fund returns often provide more accurate estimates of strategy performance characteristics and correlations than broad composite indices.

Portfolio allocation should take into account the changing dynamics of risk. A statistical asset allocation can result in widely fluctuating portfolio risk. The AIS allocator has to find a balance between a predefined and fixed strategy sector allocation and an opportunistic switching between strategies. In the past few years the concept of 'risk budgeting' (or 'risk bucketing') has gained considerable attention.[21] Risk budgeting is the process of allocating an acceptable level of measurable risk to certain investment strategies, assessing frequently whether the risk limits are exceeded and taking corrective measures, if deemed necessary. Hereby, performance is always measured on a risk-adjusted basis. Usually, the risk budgeting approach requires the statistical characterization of each strategy based on past returns, which has some pitfalls, as discussed in the following.

Determining the appropriate sector allocation for an AIS portfolio is a complex undertaking. Unfortunately, for the purpose of AIS sector allocation, quantitative analysis based on past performance and correlation data is of limited value. While such tools can be quite useful in analyzing the general scope for efficiency enhancement from adding AIS to a global traditional balanced portfolio (equity and bonds), they show their limitations when it comes to sector allocation in an AIS portfolio itself. Statistical analysis and Markowitz-type portfolio optimizations are very sensitive to the return and risk input used for the calculation. The statistical significance and the predictive power of performance and correlation data for individual strategies based on historical data are generally insufficient for that purpose:

■ Return and risk properties and the correlation characteristics of individual strategies vary substantially over time as well as in different market environments (see Figure 4.3 for an illustration of unstable correlation patterns). The performance variability of managers within one strategy sector is not reflected in the average performance numbers for the sector as given by data providers. This dispersion of returns of AIS managers is much higher than the dispersion in performance of traditional asset managers (measured by the 'tracking error') or the variability of different stocks in one industry sector.

■ The amount of available data is generally low. Performance data is usually only provided on a monthly basis and does not go back far into the past. It is also biased due to the exceptional equity bull market in the 1990s.

■ One of the main assumptions of the standard portfolio optimization process is that investment risk can be completely described by the second moment (variance) of returns. But the variance of returns (or its square root, the standard deviation), does not describe the risk for AIS completely and is therefore not very well suited for AIS portfolio optimization. As discussed in different parts of this book, skewed and leptokurtic (i.e. fat-tailed) return distributions are very general characteristics of many strategies. Differences in historical returns as provided by different index data providers may lead to large deviations in the obtained results for an optimized portfolio.

■ Hedge fund indices have some generic problems: (1) Not all AIS managers disclose their performance to databases; (2) indices potentially suffer from the 'survivorship bias', which is due to managers terminating their (mostly poorly performing) program and, as a consequence, disappearing from the index completely; (3) the choice of a weighting scheme, i.e. whether managers are weighted equally or asset based, has a significant impact on the AIS indices (see discussion about strategy performance in Chapter 4).[22]

- Some strategies include illiquid instruments, which cannot be reliably priced on a regular basis. Performance tends to appear less volatile and correlations lower for these strategies, as manager provided estimates leave space for performance smoothing ('stale price bias'). The less liquid the instruments traded, the more knowledgeable and wary the investor has to be about the particular strategy.

- Given the rapid and dynamic change within the industry and the heterogeneity of Hedge fund investment strategies, optimization-based past performances are not sufficiently representative.

Estimating correlations that are useful for the application of quantitative optimization techniques thus requires more than collecting past return data. In his seminal article 'Portfolio Selection', Markowitz notes the difficulty in determining the correct inputs for portfolio optimization:

[We] must have procedures for finding reasonable [means] and [variances]. These procedures, I believe, should combine statistical techniques and the judgement of practical men. My feeling is that the statistical computations should be used to arrive at a tentative set of [means] and [variances]. Judgement should then be used in increasing or decreasing some of these [means] and [variances] not taken into account by the formal computation.[23]

The detection of strategy performance drivers and the analysis of factor models for AIS returns have been subject to much discussion and research in the academic as well as the financial community in the past few years. But the statistical significance of AIS factors models has, to date, been rather low. The heterogeneous nature of AIS strategies requires more detailed examinations, including other than quantitative factors, to render an understanding of their specific return generation possible.[24]

Two points require particular attention: First, certain strategies contain significant 'short option'-type exposure, i.e. their risk reward structure is similar to selling options. The investor receives a fixed premium for being exposed to the possibility of large losses in some rare cases (which I refer to as the strategy's 'stress events'). This helps to create impressive Sharpe ratios in 'normal periods' with no event of loss, but can ultimately lead to large losses (or 'blow ups') following a 'stress event'. For most of these strategies, quoted risk-adjusted returns tend to be overestimated if only historical data is considered and quantitative mean variance-based portfolio optimization tends to recommend inappropriately large allocations to these strategies. The risk inherent in these strategies has usually not yet manifested itself during a manager's brief performance history. A second matter of concern should be that the reported performance and risk numbers of many strategies do not include certain risk factors such as low liquidity and event risk. The use of historical data for the purpose of strategy and manager selection in combination with conventional portfolio optimization techniques usually results in portfolios with inappropriately high non-systematic risks and low liquidity (e.g. large allocations to Regulation D and Distressed Debt securities).[25]

The preceding discussion makes it clear that the set-up of an AIS portfolio requires more than just 'number crunching'. The allocation process is less a quantitative science than an art based on the allocator's experience. Due to the limitations of quantitative tools for portfolio allocation, qualitative understanding of AIS strategies' performance characteristics and good judgement are essential.[26] Empirical performance and correlation studies should serve as a general guideline for the AIS allocator, but he should equally consider 'semi-quantitative' and qualitative elements such as an assessment of economic sources of return and risk, distinction between premium-based and skill-based returns and the determination of particularly hostile market environments (which might not yet have tested the strategy). An AIS allocator must understand the performance drivers as well as the weaknesses of strategy sectors in order to choose the appropriate combination of strategies in a portfolio.

A significant part of the qualitative understanding required for AIS portfolio allocation is the assessment of the (economic) sources of return and correlation features. In Chapters 2 and 3, I discussed the underlying economic functions of the individual strategies. Many strategies earn a return by capturing a (risk) premium, which provides an inherent and permanent positive expected return. The underlying return potential of 'premium strategies' does not disappear if other investors spot its existence. The AIS allocator should generally invest in strategies with an economic risk premium that he understands. Other AIS strategies benefit from temporary mispricings and market inefficiencies. These usually disappear quickly when spotted by other investors. The returns of these 'pure skill' strategies depend primarily on the existence of such market inefficiencies and the manager's skill and research resources in detecting and quickly acting on them.

The following constitutes a summary of the key elements for successful sector allocation within the AIS portfolio:

1 *Analysis of general attractiveness of each strategy sector*: The risk–return profiles of the sectors should be examined and the performance drivers and underlying general economic rationales assessed. Each chosen sector should have a reason for being included in the portfolio. Selected sectors should display attractive returns with appropriate risks (considering risks that do not directly show in historical performance numbers). Understanding the relationship (correlations) between different sectors is important.

2 *Assessment of market environment*: It is important for the AIS allocator to understand the strategies' behaviour in different market environments. He should determine the specific favourable and unfavourable market conditions for each sector, continuously follow the developments of financial markets and monitor key economic and financial variables that drive returns. This is similar to what an equity portfolio manager does with respect to different stock sectors, but extends over a much wider universe of financial instruments (equities, foreign exchange, fixed income, commodities). A helpful tool for the analysis of sensitivities to specific market environments is the analysis of conditional correlations, which show the behaviours of AIS in particular market environments (see Figures 4.4 and 4.5). The pitfalls of quantitative analysis must be kept in mind, however. Common sense and solid economic reasoning should back statistics.

3 *Assessment of risk factors*: The particular risk factors (and risk premiums) of the strategies should be understood. The portfolio/risk manager should try to measure and quantify these risks and determine measures and procedures for controlling them. Managers in the same strategy sector can have different focuses (e.g. sector, country, credit quality) and therefore different exposure to particular risk factors. The number of individual trading managers needed to reach sufficient diversification within a strategy sector is an important consideration.

4 *Analysis of past and anticipation of future correlations*: Correlations are the key determinant of diversification and the optimal risk–return ratio within a portfolio. The correlations between strategies as well as each strategy's correlation to other, traditional, asset classes (i.e. bonds and stocks) should be analyzed and understood (see also the discussion in Chapter 5). Strategies that behave in complementary ways in particular market environments are especially interesting from the viewpoint of portfolio diversification.

It should be noted that the sector allocation process does not end with the initial investment, but requires ongoing market monitoring and portfolio reassessment. Changes in the economic environment may make portfolio modifications necessary. Furthermore, the attractiveness of particular strategies can change or even vanish over time, due to increased market efficiency, regulatory constraints, limited capacity or other reasons. This might require a sector reallocation within the AIS portfolio. Finally, portfolio considerations have to take into account the (possibly changing) liquidity requirements of the client, legal constraints (concerning e.g. shorting stocks, instrument constraints), home currency and tax status.

Manager evaluation (bottom up approach)

Each investment involves certain 'manager risks' specific to trading styles and employed investment techniques such as leverage, investment instruments and Short Selling. Manager-specific risks also include operational risks, legal risk, key person risk, model risk and fraud risk. Two measures are essential in minimizing these risks: proper due diligence and manager diversification. Thorough due diligence should, *without exception*, be a requirement for an investment with a particular AIS manager and should lead to a detailed understanding of the investment strategy. Managers within the same strategy sector can differ with regards to strategy implementation, instrument diversification, hedging, use of derivatives, short selling and the degree of leverage.

There are qualitative and quantitative aspects to the process of AIS manager due diligence. Quantitative analysis consists mostly of 'number crunching' and should include the analysis of past returns, volatility, drawdowns, Sharpe ratio and other performance measures,[27] as well as correlation studies, benchmark comparisons and peer group analysis. It should be noted that quantitative performance evaluation is easier to perform for 'premium-based' strategies, as benchmarks are more uniform and peer group comparison more informative. In comparison, it is more difficult to evaluate the performance of 'pure skill' strategy managers. There is usually no clear benchmark to compare the single managers to and it is more difficult to distinguish past performance as a result of skill from pure luck. Thus, due diligence of the particular approach and the manager becomes even more important.

Unfortunately, many investors still rely too much on past performance when selecting managers, without thorough qualitative analysis. Qualitative aspects of the due diligence involve knowing the manager's 'edge for returns', the investment style and attitude of the manager, details of the investment decision-making processes, the organization and structure of the manager's operations, the trading facilities and the character, quality and background of key people.

The precise process of manager selection varies among AIS allocators, but there are some due diligence rules that one should keep in mind.

Concerning the track record

■ A good track record is a necessary but certainly not a sufficient condition for a high-quality trading strategy. Poor strategies can come with good records obtained in a favourable market environment (e.g. equity bull market) or simply because of luck. Database analysis often defines the starting point of manager selection, but the AIS allocator cannot rely on quantitative analysis alone for manager selection. Understanding the strategy and its sources of returns and the strategy's weaknesses and risks is crucial. Strategies can be vulnerable to certain types of market stress, which might not be apparent from historical return numbers ('short option' type of strategies).

About meeting the manager

- It is important to meet many managers and build up experience. Managers have different focuses and comparisons between managers in one peer group can be helpful in understanding important nuances.

- The AIS allocator should prepare a due diligence questionnaire which should be filled out by the manager at the beginning of the due diligence process. The questionnaire should be designed thoroughly, as it can be one of the most important sources of information for desk research.

- Manager due diligence has a strong subjective component. It is useful to visit and evaluate managers in a team, as several people observe more than one person by himself. References are a good starting point for a due diligence and a good industry network can be helpful for discussing and evaluating managers.

- It is important to talk to the key people (trader, fund manager, CEO) directly instead of the marketing staff. Generally, the latter do not know the strategy in sufficient detail. Onsite visits are an important element of the due diligence.

Necessary background checks

- Valuable information can be obtained from the marketing and legal material (offering memorandum, past letters to investors, audited track record, annual reports and any marketing material). This rather broadly composed material is usually of limited value in respect of the details of the investment process, but contains important information about fees, NAV calculation, biographies of key people, legal set-up, redemption periods, restrictions on leverage, counterparties and disclosure policies.

- Independent checks of the background of key personnel are a necessity. Many cases of fraud could have been detected early on had investors performed sufficient background checks.[28] Sources of information are ex-employers, auditors, administrators, prime brokers, other investors and government agencies.

The steps of the due diligence process are illustrated in Figure 7.4. Due diligence usually progresses through the following stages: initial screening; first contact; quantitative analysis; desk research; onsite meetings; final evaluation. The outcome of the due diligence process is a decision as to whether or not to invest with the manager. Initial screening usually requires database analysis to reduce the global manager universe to a manageable size. Other sources of information include personal references, conferences, manager sales visit, prime brokers and industry hearsay. One of the edges of a fund of funds manager is to be inside the 'information loop' of high-calibre managers. The next step is quantitative analysis, which includes numerical analysis of performance (return, volatility, drawdowns, Sharpe ratio etc.) and correlations to other managers in the peer group/strategy sector and in the AIS portfolio as well as to other asset classes. The following desk research is the beginning of the qualitative analysis and includes reviewing legal documents, the fee structure, assets under management, investment capacity, auditor statements, reference checks and, possibly, a completed due diligence questionnaire. An onsite visit to the manager completes the qualitative due diligence process and should include the following: a discussion with key personnel about the investment approach, strategy implementation and details of risk management techniques; a review of operations and trade executions; an examination of back-office structures; an assessment of the firm's working atmosphere.

Some AIS allocators try to formalize the due diligence process by creating a 'point system', where the manager is given points for each area of investigation according to a predefined system. Whether one prefers a point system or another approach, the allocator should cover the following key issues during his due diligence.

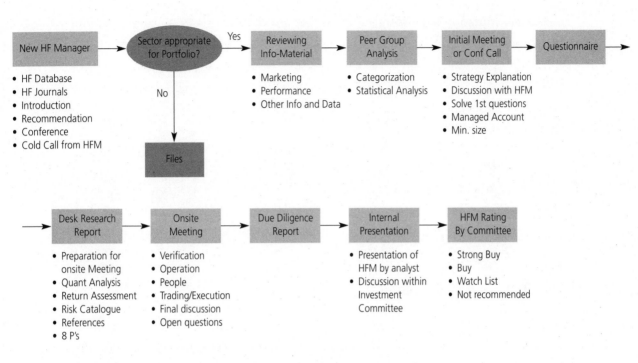

FIGURE 7.4 ■ The process of Hedge fund manager (HFM) due diligence

Manager due diligence: The 'eight P analysis'

PEOPLE

The allocator should examine the background, experience, integrity, attitude and lifestyle of key people in the manager's firm. Information sources include prior employers, other investors, auditors, administrators and prime brokers. He should also check whether any key person or director has been subject to an investigation by a government regulatory agency. It is advisable to invest only with managers that are registered and regulated by regulatory authorities (e.g. with CFTC, NFA, SEC, SFA etc.).

PRODUCT

The manager's investment strategy (his 'product') is defined by certain characteristics such as target return and risk (e.g. volatility, drawdowns); investment instruments; level of diversification; position entry and exit criteria; hedging tools; time horizon; asset liquidity; leverage; use of derivatives; short selling. The investor should familiarize himself with the details of these characteristics. Additionally, he should assess the manager's fee structure and obtain information about targeted investors and existing investor base.

PROCESS

A key element of the due diligence is to evaluate how investment decisions are made. The allocator should know the key steps and people involved in making and executing decisions. Where investment decisions are based on a model, the model developer is an important person to talk to. The allocator should familiarize himself with the details of the model development and testing and assess the potential danger of model over-optimization/curve fitting. Performance reports should distinguish between in-sample and out-of-sample testing (in-sample testing refers to the optimization of the model's parameters on historical data, while out-of-sample testing means examining model performance on historical data that was not used during the optimization process).

PERFORMANCE

Quantitative analysis of the track record is an important part of the performance evaluation process. The AIS allocator should request audited performance numbers of all relevant trading accounts of the manager. Performance presentation standards can vary among different managers. The calculation assumptions and methods used by each manager should be clear.[29] Performance analysis should include the examination of returns, risk and correlations. Returns should be measured on a risk-adjusted basis. Measures for risk are standard deviation, maximal drawdown, downside deviation, semi-variance and leverage factors. Risk-adjusted performance measures are Sharpe ratios, Sortino ratios, Information ratios, Park ratios, Treynor's measure, Risk-Adjusted Return On Capital (RAROC), 'effective return' and others.[30]

As emphasized throughout this book, besides examining the manager's historical returns, the allocator should ask about the sources of the manager's returns. He should understand the economic reasons for the strategy's returns and risk and familiarize himself with the trading manager's 'edge'. Trading discipline and solid risk management are important edges for 'premium-based' strategies. For strategies based primarily on forecasting skills ('pure skill strategies'), edges can be of a different nature. Informational edges can be better or faster access to relevant information, superior research capabilities or simply better knowledge about particular sectors/countries and the relevance of information or the behaviour patterns of investors. Statistical edges are based on recognizing market features such as trends, price patterns, seasonal price developments or conditional (auto-) correlations.[31] It must be emphasized that statistical and informational edges can disappear over time, e.g. when other market participants copy and adopt a proven strategy.

The intricate trade secrets and details about models are, for the most part, not too important for the AIS allocator. Non-confidential information is generally much more informative than the details the manager is unwilling to disclose. Relevant information can be obtained by discussing the general approach, philosophy and economic edge of the strategy, which the manager should be more than comfortable discussing.

PARTNERSHIP

The AIS allocator has to know the firm's legal and ownership structure. Incentive and compensation schemes within the firm can give important hints as to the commitment of its employees, especially the dedication of key people. The geographic location of the firm matters for attracting investment talent. The allocator should make an assessment of the firm's business risk. Hedge funds sometimes fail for pure business reasons such as employee turnover, partner disputes, poor accounting or others. Finally, he should know whether the manager is investing his own money into the strategy and assess the principle's personal commitment to, and belief in, the strategy.

PORTFOLIO

Diversification and portfolio management are important considerations for the allocator. Systematic model-based trading should occur over a broad universe of different instruments and possibly asset classes, while discretionary approaches are more likely to be successful in a limited range of instruments. Limits on positions in certain instruments and asset classes, if any, provide a good idea about possible concentration risk.

PEERS

The allocator should examine the uniqueness of the strategy and its return correlations with peer strategies. One should differentiate between the inherent return of the strategy sector (see Chapter 3) and the edge of a particular manager, i.e. his 'alpha'. Earning a general risk premium does not necessarily constitute an edge. The manager should be able to distinguish himself clearly from other managers within the sector.

POTENTIAL

Most managers have capacity limits, i.e. their strategies are constrained in the amount of assets they can manage without diluting performance. The indicated dollar capacity should be compared to what can reasonably be expected for the strategy. Managers sometimes accept more money than they can efficiently invest. It is also important to follow up on this issue, as managers often change their view on capacity once the initially indicated limit is reached. This should raise a warning flag. Often managers who have reached maximal capacity for their core strategy offer other investment programs in order to benefit from their positive reputation in the market and further increase their assets under management. The allocator should be careful about being persuaded to invest in another program, when the original program of his choice is closed for further investments.

The manager's risk control

There are important risk management procedures on the single strategy level (see Chapter 5). The allocator should pay particular attention to the following points:

1 He should know the details of the manager's internal risk management procedures such as stop-loss limits, maximal allocations to particular instruments and asset classes, portfolio diversification, hedging tools, risk monitoring, risk budgeting etc.

2 He should ask the manager how large he expects a maximal drawdown to be. Further, he should assess at what point the manager would lose confidence in his approach and stop trading. It is also interesting to know what level of positive performance would significantly exceed the manager's expectations. Outstanding

performance during a certain period can be a sign of increased risk and can quickly turn into severe losses when market conditions change.

3 He should address the manager's possible past mistakes and discuss the lessons learnt from these mistakes. Often internal risk management procedures are the result of those past mistakes. A good manager has nothing to hide and should openly discuss this issue.

4 The details about the strategy's risk factors should be listed in a risk catalogue.

Market environment analysis

The performance of each strategy strongly depends on the market environment. Each strategy has particular weaknesses and strengths, which show at different moments. It is the AIS allocator's responsibility to structure a well-diversified portfolio, where the weaknesses and strengths that single strategies display in different market environments balance out to yield consistent and smooth overall portfolio returns. For this purpose, he should consider three issues during the manager due diligences:

1 He should assess the favourable and unfavourable market environments for each manager. Again, this requires more than evaluating historical returns. The allocator should be aware of the inherent 'survivorship bias' of AIS performance numbers. Managers have often never experienced a particularly painful period and therefore looking at past returns does not reveal all possible weaknesses of their trading strategy. The first occurrence of a 'stress period' can easily lead to the end of a trading program, such that survivors tend to be 'untested' managers. Common sense might yield a better understanding of critical market environments for a strategy than pure number crunching.

2 The AIS allocator should know the key performance drivers (and risk factors) for the trading strategies included in the portfolio. These can be equity market direction (e.g. for most Long/Short Equity, Short Selling and Equity Market Timing strategies), the volatility of equity markets (most Risk Arbitrage and Convertible Arbitrage strategies), yield curve configurations (e.g. Fixed Income Arbitrage), the volatility of commodity markets (Managed Futures strategies)

and others. A significant part of this assessment should take place on the level of sector allocation, but the market environment analysis has to consider specific manager characteristics.

3   Hedge funds and Managed Futures are 'absolute return' investments. Their goal is not to beat a particular index, but to yield absolute returns independent of the broad equity and bond markets. Nevertheless, certain manager benchmarks can be helpful for the purpose of performance evaluation. This applies in particular to 'premium strategies', i.e. strategies based on capturing specific (risk) premiums. There are a number of sector indices offered by various data providers (see appendix to Chapter 4), most of which come with conceptual problems. Commonly used AIS benchmarks are the returns of the median (or mean) manager in a certain pool of managers. It should be noted that benchmarks defined in this way can be flawed.[32]

Final questions of the due diligence process should centre on 'soft issues' such as fee agreements with brokers,[33] the manager's personal trading and investments in the fund and elsewhere, fee rebates and special fee arrangements for other investors, business targets and other possible concerns.

Investment monitoring: 'Post-investment' risk management

Diligent pre-investment analysis is essential for making successful AIS investments. But the job of an AIS allocator is far from complete after strategy and manager allocation. The allocator and AIS portfolio manager should by no means neglect the importance of 'post-investment risk management', i.e. ongoing investment monitoring and active risk control after investment with the chosen managers. While one might learn a great deal during due diligence, it is almost certain that risk factors not encountered before will emerge. In dealing with the current and future risks in the portfolio, risk management should thus be proactive rather than solely reactive to reported performance. Manager monitoring and risk control is at least as time consuming and challenging as sector selection and manager due diligence.

A key element of managing AIS risk is continuous and independent monitoring of positions, P&L and risk levels. This can be seen as an ongoing post-investment manager due diligence. Investment monitoring in combination with good strategy knowledge enables the allocator to obtain a 'dynamic understanding' of the strategy and the manager's behaviour in various market circumstances, detect previously unknown (or unrecognized) strategy risks, quickly recognize style changes, undesired 'bets' and increases of leverage employed by the manager, perform independent performance evaluation and decrease the probability of fraud risk. Continuous monitoring is a prerequisite for controlling the risks of the managers' trading activities, performing active risk management (e.g. de-leverage) and reallocating investments within the portfolio when circumstances change.

At a minimum, post-investment risk management should involve reading the monthly reports of managers with great care and speaking with each of them on a regular basis in order to receive first-hand information about the market situation, the background of performance numbers and changes in the strategy such as modifications in the investment decision process, adjustments to the manager's operating facilities and possible staff turnover. The AIS allocator should further observe the relevant financial markets and with his understanding of key performance drivers develop his own views on the current market environment and the performance of his managers. For strategies that involve credit risk (e.g. Regulation D or Distressed Securities) he should monitor the credit markets and the ratings of the relevant companies and possibly perform independent research on default and loss probabilities. Periodically, he should check volatility patterns and correlation features in order to assess whether the manager has changed anything relative to his original approach. Changing performance and correlation behaviour can be an indication of long-term style drifts. Information about the size of assets under management, the nature of new investors and possible redemptions should be obtained on a regular basis.

Ideally, post-investment risk management should involve frequent – in best cases daily – monitoring and risk analysis as discussed in the following.

Independent pricing and performance analysis and performance attribution

Considering the numerous instruments and asset classes traded by AIS, pricing, NAV calculation and performance measurement is a non-trivial task. Assigned prices may fail to recognize position size, low market liquidity, instrument complexity (e.g. derivatives), flaws in the valuation model and possible circular reference to 'independent' price sources. The portfolio and risk manager must be critical of the integrity of the pricing or mark to market valuations provided by the manager and obtain market prices from independent sources, preferably directly from prime brokers and market makers. Prices should be discounted in the case of low liquidity.

The analysis of performance attribution (possibly by asset class, sector and instrument) can be very helpful for a further understanding of the trading strategy and an evaluation whether the manager followed his indicated investment strategy (examination of possible style drifts). Performance attribution is twofold:

1 Breakdown of performance to individual asset classes and sectors.

2 Analysis of performance with respect to different investment styles.

The latter is an important part of traditional asset management (e.g. 'value vs. growth') and often requires an underlying factor model.

Exposure analysis

Besides aggregating exposure on the level of the global portfolio, the analysis should include a breakdown of gross exposure into different aggregation levels such as asset class, sector and instrument type. Without this 'drilldown' the risk manager might miss possible exposure concentrations in the portfolio. A seemingly small net equity position on the level of the total portfolio, for example, can still result in large gross exposures to certain sectors. Figure 7.5 shows an example for the analysis of equity exposure in an AIS portfolio. If a manager tends to take large positions in single sectors or instruments, these should be monitored with special care and checked for possible violations of pre-defined maximum position sizes. An important part of the exposure analysis is the monitoring of leverage. Leverage analysis should be considered on a gross and net basis.

Correlation and volatility analysis

The AIS allocator and risk manager should observe volatilities and correlations between strategies and with stock and bond markets and analyze those on the level of the global portfolio as well as the individual managers. Short-term shifts as well as persistent changes of volatility and correlation patterns can be indications of possible problems of a strategy or of manager style drifts.

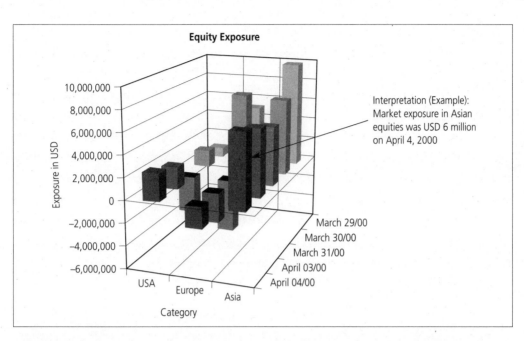

FIGURE 7.5 ▪ Example for the equity exposure analysis in an AIS portfolio. The development of exposure is displayed over one week

Value-at-Risk (VaR)

VaR is a volatility-based portfolio risk measure that describes the maximal loss in a portfolio or sub-portfolio for a specified confidence level (e.g. 95% or 99%) over a certain trading horizon (e.g. 1 day or 5 day). It provides a measure that enables the risk manager to quantify and compare portfolio risk across different instrument and asset classes uniformly. One drawback of VaR is that it does not explicitly consider the extreme part of the return distribution (see discussion in Chapter 6). It is also often criticized that the measurement of volatility (and VaR) includes upside deviations, i.e. volatility caused by excessive gains. But the prudent risk manager is actually well advised to include upside deviations in his risk measurement. Often excessive gains are due to higher risk and upside deviation can quickly turn into downside deviation, when markets turn against a strategy. Not all managers are skilled at reducing position sizes just at the right time to avoid the downward move when market conditions change.

The selection of time horizon and confidence intervals depends on the objective of the analysis. For daily monitoring, a one-day time horizon is most appropriate. A 95 or 99% confidence interval is usually chosen. The risk manager also has to make a choice concerning the employed calculation method (see Chapter 6). Because of the non-linear and complex derivative positions present in most AIS portfolios, the variance-based method can be quite misleading and should not be used exclusively. Historical simulations are attractive, because they make no distributional assumptions, but the results depend strongly on the historical period chosen for the analysis. The most reliable is the Monte Carlo method, but it is computationally also the most intensive. Further, as long as normally distributed draws are used, the Monte Carlo VaR does not address the issue of non-normally distributed asset returns (for more details, the reader is referred to Chapter 6).

VaR can be analyzed along two different dimensions:

1 'VaR tracking' is the measurement of risk as a function of time. This provides an indication of how high current risk is compared to risk levels experienced in the past. Analyzing VaR over time can provide valuable insights for the assessment of how often single managers push their risk level to certain limits and whether over time risks are in line with expectations. Tracking VaR is another tool for the diagnosis of 'style drifts'.

2 'Risk drilldown' is the analysis of risk at different aggregation levels. Risk drilldown helps the risk manager to break down risk with respect to different sectors or trading managers. This answers the question about where the overall portfolio risk originates.

Figure 7.6 shows an example of AIS portfolio risk analysis with VaR tracking and drilldown of VaR.

A concept related to VaR is Expected Shortfall (also called 'Conditional VaR'; see Chapter 6), which describes the mean portfolio value conditional on the portfolio loss exceeding a certain threshold (which is usually chosen to be the 95 or 99% confidence limit VaR). Expected Shortfall supplements VaR by providing more insight into the tail of the return distribution.

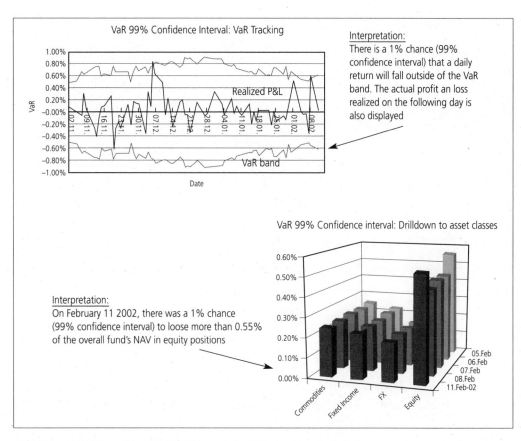

FIGURE 7.6 ■ VaR tracking and 'Drilldown' of VaR in an AIS portfolio

Marginal and incremental VaR analysis

Marginal VaR expresses the amount by which a portfolio's VaR is changed on inclusion of a particular position or sub-portfolio. This measure can be used to evaluate how much an individual trading manager or position affects the risk structure of the entire portfolio. An asset or a particular trading strategy with a negative correlation to the rest of the portfolio gives a favourable contribution to the portfolio VaR, i.e. it decreases the total risk in the portfolio if included.

Stress tests and scenario analysis

Stress tests provide the risk manager with insights about the portfolio behaviour under extreme, but plausible market conditions. They can be performed by considering corresponding scenarios, e.g. a 5+ standard deviation move of single risk factors (such as an 8% drop in the S&P500), a correlation 'breakdown' (i.e. the scenario of certain assets displaying a correlation close to one) or longer liquidation periods (i.e. applying longer time horizon VaR calculations). Scenario analysis consists of applying the predetermined changes, the so-called 'what-if' scenarios, to the risk factors and calculating the resulting effect on the portfolio value. This analysis can be applied independently to each risk factor (which affects only those instruments that directly depend on it) or in consideration of the correlation structure between all risk factors. A scenario analysis can also be performed with respect to external factors such as policy changes, election outcomes or weather conditions. The effects on security values must then be 'guesstimated'. An example of a stress test report is presented in Figure 7.7.

Liquidity analysis

The risk manager should examine the liquidity of individual positions in the portfolio by assessing how quickly and at what price they could be liquidated. This is especially important in times of financial distress. Important indicators for instrument liquidity are trading volume, bid–ask spreads and market capitalization (in relation to position size).

Computational technology plays a more and more important role in the analysis and measurement of risk. AIS investors and portfolio allocators can today choose from many different off-the-shelf risk analysis tools which are based on increasingly sophisticated software running on faster, comparably cheaper computers. Today's computers can handle highly complex calculations and simulations (e.g. Monte Carlo simulation, stress tests) in a very short time frame and at high frequency (e.g. every day or even intra-day). Prime brokers offering risk analysis as a value-added service to clients are often at the frontier of technical development for the calculation and reporting of risk. With the use of modern information technology, risk managers are in a position to gather all relevant positions and transactions, extract the relevant information and perform the necessary risk analytics (VaR, scenario analysis, stress tests etc.) without any significant time delay. While not having to develop risk analysis systems themselves, risk managers must be equipped with the skill base and experience necessary to apply the tools, interpret their outcome and act when necessary.

Simulated Scenario	−10%	−5%	5%	10%
S&P 500	−1.94%	−0.80%	1.98%	5.91%
Euro-Stoxx-50	−0.98%	−0.39%	1.01%	3.04%
Nikkei 225	−0.31%	0.02%	0.91%	2.87%
	80 bp down	40 bp down	40 bp up	80 bp up
US government curve	2.16%	0.65%	−1.34%	−3.14%
	30 bp down	15 bp down	15 bp up	30 bp up
Corporate single A yield spread	2.01%	1.01%	−2.02%	−1.04%
	−8%	−4%	−4%	8%
EUR-USD	2.38%	1.19%	−1.04%	−2.01%
USD-JPY	−1.62%	−0.34%	0.56%	1.98%
	−10%	−5%	5%	10%
GS Commodity Index	3.13%	1.11%	−0.71%	−3.01%
Historical Scenario				
Stock market crash 1987	−4.91%			
Bond market crash 1994	−4.22%			
Russian default / LTCM crisis 1998	−5.48%			
Brasil crisis 1999	−1.01%			
Sept 11, 2001	−2.79%			

FIGURE 7.7 ■ Stress tests risk report

Evidently, each strategy has particular features and appropriate risk monitoring requires different tools for different strategies. The quantification of risk is generally more difficult for Merger Arbitrage, Distressed Securities, Regulation D, Convertible Arbitrage and many Long/Short Equity strategies. VaR analysis based on historical volatilities and correlations is not very insightful for Event Driven strategies in most cases, while it provides a useful tool for the analysis of risk for most opportunistic Hedge fund and Managed Futures strategies. Nevertheless, continuous exposure and leverage analysis, monitoring of large positions and checking whether the manager is adhering to the predefined guidelines and focuses of his strategy remain very important elements of risk management for all strategies. A Merger Arbitrage or Long/Short Equity manager who defines his edge in the banking industry should not have large concentrations in utility or chemical stocks and a Convertible Arbitrage manager focusing on in-the-money convertibles should not have positions in convertibles priced near their bond value. What the monitoring process boils down to is checking whether the manager's activities correspond to what the allocator expects.

Finally, risk management requires appropriate risk reporting schemes. Investment decision makers (i.e. the AIS allocators) and risk managers should work closely together and communicate efficiently. The most important information in risk reports is often buried in a vast amount of data. It is important to select and report the right measures of risk to enable decision makers to identify quickly the necessary actions to take. Reports should aggregate risk on the appropriate level highlighting the critical exposures, so that decision makers can focus their attention directly on key issues. The illustration and visualization of risk through diagrams and charts can be very helpful in the communication of risk to parties who are not directly involved in the analysis process.[34]

Active risk management

As mentioned throughout the book, risk management is both an art and a science. While the latter refers to the more quantitative elements of risk measurement, the 'art' of risk management corresponds to the wisdom and good judgement that the risk manager develops over time. The financial industry has seen an astonishing proliferation of risk analysis tools in recent years. Most of these tools provide the risk manager with the ability properly to measure and analyze risk. *Risk measurement* is indeed an important element of risk management, but in itself it remains a passive activity. In contrast, *risk management* requires action and goes beyond the pure measuring of risk. Often, quantitative reports provide necessary data, but not sufficient information. While risk measurement aims at providing an objective assessment of how much risk is present in the portfolio, risk management can be based on a variety of other (sometimes rather subjectively determined) factors, which, among other determinants, depend on the investor's risk profile. Active risk management, (a pleonasm, as 'risk management' should always be 'active'), entails the dynamic and optimal allocation of risk among different assets and   managers. It consists of defining and enforcing risk limits, performing dynamic portfolio allocation according to – possibly changing – risk parameters and accepting certain risk factors, but eliminating others that are deemed unacceptable.

As discussed throughout this book, the performance drivers in AIS are risk premiums and the investment skills of single managers. The very fact that AIS managers take risks is surely not undesirable. However, risk that is unintended, misunderstood, mismanaged or mispriced should not be accepted and it should be the risk manager's goal to avoid these risks. The individual AIS manager is responsible for executing his particular trading strategy. If he executes his strategy along the investment guidelines and the AIS allocator accepts the known underlying risks, there should be no reason for concern on the part of the risk manager. The less the manager's activity has to be interfered with the better. Ideally, the manager follows his strategy and shows performance as expected in given market conditions.

But the risk manager needs to able to take proactive steps, once this ideal does not apply any longer, in order to remedy critical situations quickly. He should be concerned when, in given market environments, strategies deviate from their performance expectations. Deviations from expected performance are indications for strategy style shifts, which are among the main reasons for sudden unexpected losses. Performance deviations can be mediocre performance in favourable market conditions as well as better than expected performance in unfavourable market environments. When a crisis has arrived, it may be too late to make adjustments. Within a framework of active AIS risk management there are various ways to manage risk and exercise control over trading managers:

■ *Regular conversations.* The AIS allocator should frequently talk with managers about the current and potential future risks of their trading strategy. He should know how the individual manager judges his strategy's current risk profile and, based on his understanding of the strategy, develop his own view about its vulnerability in the prevailing market conditions. The allocator should identify changes in a strategy's risk structure at the earliest possible stage, if possible before they occur.

- *Risk or exposure limits.* The risk manager should distinguish between risk levels and sources which are acceptable and those which are not. He can define certain 'risk budgets' on the level of the global portfolio, single asset class or strategy sector. These are ceilings on the amount of acceptable risk as indicated by measures such as VaR, notional exposure or possible stress test losses. The definition of specific values for these limits is critical and depends on the investor's investment objectives and risk tolerances. They should be dynamic rather than fixed.[35] Once predefined limits are exceeded, the risk manager must undertake action such as re-allocation or de-leveraging.

- *Imposing leverage controls and margin requirements.* Each manager should be restricted as to how much leverage he is allowed to employ at any time. The maximal leverage should be set in agreement with the manager before trading starts. A violation of the allowed leverage limits should trigger immediate action ranging from information requests to closure of positions or complete exclusion of the strategy from the portfolio.

- *Definition of stop-loss limits.* The portfolio manager can set limits on each manager's maximal drawdown. The definition of such a limit should depend on the strategy and should be made in consultation with the manager before investment. Once a drawdown exceeds the maximal loss limit, the corresponding manager should be excluded from the portfolio.

- *Request for explanations about unusual positions.* Unexpected and unexplained high exposures to certain securities or asset classes or unusual leverage factors should be immediately addressed. They are warning signs for upcoming problems. If the manager does not provide a convincing explanation for such exposures, the allocator should force him to close the positions and consider excluding him from the portfolio.

- *Firing of managers with 'issues'.* Managers who have breached certain agreements, are convicted of illegal or unethical behaviour by regulatory authorities or take excessive single bets that do not correspond to defined trading strategies should be quickly excluded from the portfolio.

It has to be noted that risk management does not, by itself, lead to positive performance neither does it prevent losses under all circumstances. But it may help to decrease the severity of losses. Risk monitoring and active risk management help to detect managers who are deviating from their strategies and thus prevent accidents and investment disasters from happening. Performance generation is a matter of sector and manager allocation. For each strategy there exist hostile market environments that will lead to the strategy showing weak performance or losses. In a well-diversified AIS portfolio, lacklustre performance of single strategies should be balanced by above average performance of others for which prevailing market conditions are more favourable.

Finally, a word about the tragic events of September 11, 2001. It is clear that Hedge funds, like all other financial institutions, are exposed to operational risks of different severity. Some of these risks might be perceived as 'acts of God and other things you cannot plan for'. While banks and large financial firms have offsite operations centres and back-up facilities, smaller firms cannot afford the 'luxury' of thorough contingency planning. While the direct impact of the attack on the World Trade Center on Hedge fund and Futures managers was very limited, AIS firms might nonetheless have to revisit operational and other risk management policies in light of the events on September 11 and put corresponding emergency measures in place. But the key principles discussed throughout the book remain applicable even in the most extreme of circumstances. Managers should stick to the risk management basics by remaining diversified and understanding their exposures.

Notes

1. Caxton Corporation, Kingdom Capital Management, Moore Capital Management, Soros Fund Management LLC, Tudor Investment Corporation.

2. 'Sound Practices for Hedge Fund Managers', report issued by the group of five Hedge fund managers, February 2000.

3. Group of Thirty, 'Derivatives, Practices and Principles for Dealers and End Users', New York; the report is available on the IFCI web page http://risk.ifci.ch, maintained by the International Finance and Commodities Institute (IFCI), a non-profit Swiss organization.

4. Investor Risk Committee (IRC), 'Hedge Fund Disclosure for Institutional Investors', available on the IAFE web page http://www.iafe.org or on http://www.cmra.com. The report was amended in July 2001. The discussion within the IRC is ongoing. I am referring to the document published on July 27, 2001.

5. See discussion in 'Hedge Funds to Clear the Information Hurdle' in *Risk Management*, October 2001, p.8.

6. See http://www.bis.org/publ/bcbs79.htm for more details.

7. See also the results of a survey by the firm Capital Market Risk Advisors (CMRA) in early 2002, available on http://www.cmra.com.

8. For a detailed discussion of the value added of fund of funds and some interesting statistics on their performance, see the contribution by A. Ineichen, 'The Search for Alpha Continues – Do Fund of Hedge Fund Managers Add Value?'.

9. See A. Ineichen in *The Search for Alpha Continues – Do Fund of Hedge Fund Managers Add Value?* for more details about the fee structure of funds of funds.

10. For a detailed discussion of the LTCM bankruptcy see Ph. Jorion, 'Risk Management Lessons from Long-Term Capital Management', downloadable from http://www.gsm.uci.edu/~jorion/research.htm; also 'Hedge Funds, Leverage, and the Lessons of Long-Term Capital Management', report of the President's Working Group on Financial Markets, April 1999, on http://risk.ifci.ch/146530.htm.

11. Interesting studies about how many managers are needed to reach sufficient 'manager diversification' in an AIS portfolio can be found in 'Fund of Fund Diversification: How Much is Enough?' by J. Park and J. Strum.

12. The other side of the coin of the Hedge fund boom is a boom in Hedge fund fraud. A good article about Hedge fund fraud cases is presented by D. Kramer in the article 'Hedge Fund Disasters: Avoiding the Next Catastrophe' in the *Alternative Investment Quarterly*, October 2001; see also an interesting article by T. Fedorek, 'Is Fraud Flourishing At Your Hedge Fund?', *Pension & Investments*, March 19, 2001, p.14.

13. Regulation D managers have been among those with the highest risk-adjusted performance in recent years, as measured e.g. by the Sharpe ratio. As the underlying investments are very illiquid and cannot be accurately priced, reported volatility is usually much lower than the real risk of the investment.

14.   See the following articles: M. Peskin et al., 'Why Hedge Funds make Sense', *Quantitative Strategies,* Morgan Stanley Dean Witter, November 2000; V. Agarwal and Y. Narayan, 'Multi-Period Performance Persistence Analysis of Hedge Funds'; F. Edwards and M. Caglayan, 'Hedge Fund Performance and Manager Skill'.

15.   N. Taleb illustrates this example in the chapter 'Monkeys on Typewriters' in his book *Fooled by Randomness: The Hidden Role of Chance in the Markets and in Life.*

16.   See the following articles: M. Peskin et al., 'Why Hedge Funds make Sense', *Quantitative Strategies,* Morgan Stanley Dean Witter, November 2000; Crossborder Capital, 'The Young Ones', *Absolute Return Fund Research,* April 2001; and M. Howell in 'Fund Age and Performance', *Journal of Alternative Investment,* fall 2001. A more general audience is addressed in the following article: 'The Big, the Bold, and the Nimble', *The Economist,* February 24 2001, p.87. See also the discussion in T. Schneeweiss in 'Understanding Hedge Fund Performance: Research Results and Rules of Thumb for the Institutional Investor', *Lehman Brothers Publications,* December 2001. Here, evidence is given that smaller funds tend to overperform larger funds but also have higher risk. Results differ among the various substrategies, though.

17.   In corporate finance, leverage describes the ratio of assets to equity and accounts for the difference between return on equity (ROE) and return on assets (ROA). ROA is the return on all assets of a company including debt, while ROE describes the company's profit regardless of debt levels.

18.   See the article 'Prime Brokers can make and break Hedge Funds', *Pension & Investments,* September 3, 2001. This article refers to the importance of the prime brokerage relationship, particularly in crisis situations.

19.   See also the study by T. Schneeweiss et al., 'Understanding Hedge Fund Performance: Research Results and Rules of Thumb for the Institutional Investor', *Lehman Brothers Publications,* December 2001.

20.   For a discussion of diversification within a multi-strategy portfolio, see J. Park and J. Strum, 'Fund of Fund Diversification: How Much is Enough?', *The Journal of Alternative Investments,* Winter 1999. See also R. McFall Lamm, 'Portfolios of Alternative Assets: Why not 100% Hedge Funds?', *The Journal of Investing,* Winter 1999, pp.87–97.

21.   For a coverage of the different aspects of 'risk budgeting', see the collection of articles edited by L. Rahl, *Risk Budgeting: A New Approach to Investing,* 2000.

22. See also the article 'The Benchmark Bane' in *The Economist* from August 31, 2001.

23. H. Markowitz, 'Portfolio Selection', *Journal of Finance*, March 1952, p.91.

24. See the following articles for a further discussion: T. Schneeweiss et al., 'Understanding Hedge Fund Performance: Research Results and Rules of Thumb for the Institutional Investor', *Lehman Brothers Publications*, December 2001; T. Schneeweiss and G. Spurgin, 'Multifactor Analysis of Hedge Funds, Managed Futures, and Mutual Fund Returns and Risk Characteristics', *Journal of Alternative Investments*, Fall 1998; B. Liang, 'On the Performance of Hedge Funds', *Financial Analysts Journal*, July 1999; S. Fung and D. Hsieh, 'Empirical Characteristics of Dynamic Trading Strategies: The Case of Hedge Funds', *The Review of Financial Studies*, 1997, 10, 2.

25. An interesting discussion of the optimization problem, some illustrations of the pitfalls of relying on historical data only and the introduction of an alternative method for Hedge fund performance and risk evaluation is provided by A. Weismann and J. Abernathy in the article 'The Dangers of Historical Hedge Fund Data', in *Risk Budgeting: A New Approach to Investing*, 2000.

26. H. Kazemi and T. Schneeweiss discuss the effects of non-normality in Hedge fund returns for the quantitative portfolio allocation process in their paper 'Traditional Asset and Alternative Asset Allocation'. They show some possibilities to deal with the problem through various constraints.

27. See also Chapter 27 in *Investment Analysis and Portfolio Management* by F. Reilly and K. Brown for a discussion of performance measures in traditional portfolios.

28. See the article, 'Hedge Fund Disasters: Avoiding the Next Catastrophe' by D. Kramer in *The Alternative Investment Quarterly*, October 2001.

29. The Association for Investment Management and Research (AIMR) defined the AIMR-PPS standards aiming to define a well-accepted industry standard for performance presentation of money managers; see also http://www.aimr.org/standards/pps.

30. See the paper by M. Dacorogna et al., 'Effective Return, Risk Aversion and Drawdowns' for a discussion of risk-adjusted performance measures. See also Chapter 27 in *Investment Analysis and Portfolio Management* by F. Reilly and K. Brown.

31. The presence of any of these 'edges' contradicts the well-known efficient market hypothesis (EMH). An abnormal (risk-adjusted) return based on superior information is a violation of the semi-strong form of EMH, while a statistical edge contradicts the 'weak form of EMH'. For more information on market efficiency theoriews, see the seminal papers by Eugen F. Fama, 'Efficient Capital Markets: A Review of Theory and Empirical Work', 1970 and 'Efficient Capital Markets: II', 1991.

32. See the discussion by J. Bailey, 'Are Manager Universes Acceptable Performance Benchmarks?'.

33. An example is 'soft dollar', which refers to an agreement between manager and broker to pay higher brokerage fees in exchange for added value service to the manger, such as access to research or risk management tools.

34. A number of risk firms have developed visualization tools recently; see the article by G. Polyn, 'Getting a Better Risk Picture', *Risk Management*, August 2001.

35. For a detailed discussion of risk budgeting, see *Risk Budgeting: A New Approach to Investing* by L. Rahl (ed.).

CHAPTER 8

Conclusion and Outlook

The AIS investment process, risk management, transparency and liquidity

AIS have had excellent performance records on a standalone basis in recent years. The case for AIS becomes even more compelling when considered in the context of a global portfolio, where their low correlations to traditional investments result in significantly more attractive risk–return properties for the overall investment portfolio. At the same time AIS have been subject to extensive criticism and investor concern after several widely publicized investment disasters. More and more investors recognize that evaluating the 'risk dimension' is critical for achieving the benefits of AIS.

> **More and more investors recognize that evaluating the 'risk dimension' is critical for achieving the benefits of AIS**

With the institutionalization of the AIS industry that followed the 1998 Hedge fund crisis has come a heated debate over the appropriate approach to transparency, manager control and risk management. The different views range from managing risk through extremely broad diversification, such that a limited number of unavoidable 'blow ups' have a minimal effect on the portfolio, to a fully transparent, risk-controlled investment approach including detailed understanding of strategies and managers' trading edges, continuous independent monitoring of manager investment activities, and active risk management. This book has focused on the merits of the second approach, which I referred to as 'the transparency paradigm'. The integration of transparency and risk control into the investment process through the three-pillar framework of strategy sector allocation, manager due diligence and continuous post-investment monitoring was outlined. These three elements of an integrated investment and risk management approach are effective means for preventing investment 'accidents'.

With detailed knowledge of the various AIS sectors and a good understanding of individual managers' trading edges, combined with the appropriate portfolio risk management investment in AIS allows for the 'fine tuning of risk'. The skilled investor can choose from a universe of risk factors and can select those he is willing to accept and avoid others he does not want to be exposed to. The task of an AIS allocator and portfolio manager is to ensure that the right types and levels of risk are taken and continuously monitored. Expected returns should be in line with the risk levels.

Risk management starts with strategy assessment. Investment strategies typically fulfil various economic functions, which are in particular capital formation, risk transfer, creation of efficient markets and liquidity generation. The prudent AIS investor should invest in strategies with sources of return and economic rationales (risk premiums) he understands, avoid strategies with strong elements of specula-tion and monitor risk regularly. It is useful to distinguish two sources of AIS returns: risk premiums and manager skill. The returns of many managers are the result of premiums for taking particular risks. Other strategies rely more strongly on the manager's ability to identify mispricings and forecast future price develop-ments. The goal of the AIS asset allocation is to be in the right sector during the right time and avoid too high exposure to the individual sectors' cycles.

It should be clear that active risk management does not necessarily mean positive investment performance. Each strategy is exposed to risks and possible hostile market environments. That is why they earn positive expected returns; return comes with risk. The essence of risk management is distinguishing 'good' from 'bad' risks, controlling the amount of risk and achieving an appropriate level of diversification.

The active risk management approach outlined in this book has an important prerequisite: transparency. Considering the additional types of risk an AIS investor is exposed to as compared to traditional equity and bond investments, the 'black box approach', i.e. investing in non-transparent and illiquid funds, has to be truly questioned. A surprising degree of resistance towards transparency remains in the AIS industry, but the trend in investors' attitude from accepting ('trust me') to requesting ('show me') is clearly observable. Transparency provides the path along which efficient monitoring and risk management can be implemented. Without transparency, risk analysis has to be performed as guesswork in an information vacuum. I disagree with the belief that sufficient transparency can be provided without disclosing underlying positions. Prime brokers seem to share this view in that they require full position disclosure from their AIS clients (i.e. Hedge funds and Managed Futures clients).

Further, transparency is not nearly as useful without the appropriate level of liquidity. Ideally, if investments are of sufficient size, the AIS allocator (fund of funds manager) should strive to have managers operate on a managed account basis. Investing via a managed account is the best route to transparency and provides maximal liquidity. This enables the allocator to exercise control, perform continuous monitoring and risk analysis and act in timely fashion once problems are identified. This liquidity can be passed on to the final investor, which creates the opportunity to structure multi-manager AIS investment products that are as easy to buy and sell as mutual stock funds (even on a daily basis).

It is sometimes argued that fund of funds managers asking for a high level of transparency are left with 'second tier' managers, as, it is argued, the best performing managers are unwilling to provide full position disclosure. The reality is that many of the top AIS managers offer managed accounts to investors if the investment size is sufficiently large. The incorrect belief that non-transparent funds are the most attractive is the result of persistent misperceptions about AIS. Many investors regard AIS as an industry where returns are generated by mysterious means. In fact, most Hedge fund strategies are no mystery and can be understood very well if studied sufficiently.

Past performance is far from being a sufficient indicator for future performance. The best way to predict future performance is by understanding the source of generated returns of the underlying strategy, the strategy's risks and the environments that are most favourable and unfavourable for the strategy.

■■■■■■■■■■■

Past performance is far from being a sufficient indicator of future performance

■■■■■■■■■■

The subject of AIS risk is complex, as is AIS risk management. Some risk factors in AIS bear no similarity to risks in traditional bond and equity investment. Proper risk management requires extensive experience in the field of AIS and a proper appreciation and accounting for the complexity of their risks. Generally, risk cannot be quantified into a single number (e.g. VaR) and, for some risk types, it is questionable whether they can be quantified at all. AIS risk management has quantitative and qualitative aspects. It does not stop with the sole measurement of risk. Active risk management consists of numerous guidelines and actions designed to distinguish desired risks from unwanted risks and to prevent accidents and unacceptable losses. It is both an art and a science. While the 'scientific' aspects refer to the quantitative elements of risk measurement, the 'art' of risk management lies in the understanding of the complexity of AIS risk and the experience and good judgement necessary to recognize when corrective actions are necessary.

Both the AIS industry and the standards for the measurement and management of risk in the financial community are subject to rapid change. Investors in AIS as well as financial risk managers are confronted with new developments every year. The combination of these two dynamic fields makes AIS risk management particularly challenging. Keeping up with the latest developments in both AIS and financial risk methods is key to mastering this challenge.

Many institutional investors have to date remained reluctant to invest more extensively in AIS instruments, as low levels of transparency and liquidity caused them a great amount of concern. With the fiduciary role that many current and potential future investors in AIS take, I predict a general development towards transparency and active risk management which will enable the industry to continue its rapid growth of recent years. Institutional and private investors are likely to invest more in AIS once they are convinced that the risks can be systematically addressed.

Regulating AIS?

An important note concerns the issue of regulation. There are increasing calls for the establishment of a Hedge fund regulation scheme that would be enforced by international monetary agencies. My argument for transparency is not a request for AIS regulation. Rather, better transparency and disclosure to investors might actually diminish the push for regulation. An efficient risk management and control structure established by the industry itself is surely preferable to a rigid set of regulations imposed by national or international regulatory authorities as a result of a political struggle.

The Hedge fund bubble?

The strong growth of the AIS industry has also led to other criticisms. Besides the lack of transparency, many investors raise concerns about the industry's capacity. Many AIS strategies are indeed limited in the amount of money they can manage without deteriorating returns. This applies in particular to Relative Value (Convertible Arbitrage, Statistical Arbitrage, Fixed Income Arbitrage) and Merger Arbitrage strategies, where investors earn specific (risk) premiums, the size of which depends on the number of other people searching for the same return. But capacity is also limited for other strategies. Sceptical market participants and investors compare the recent development of Hedge funds with the technology bubble in the late 1990s that eventually burst in 2000/2001,[1] and they predict that the current AIS euphoria will similarly end in tears.

Individual AIS sectors could indeed face comparable problems, as AIS investors are not free from herding behaviour. Many investors focus particularly on those strategies which have shown good returns in the very recent past (Chapter 4 discussed some empirical evidence of that). A 'boom and bust' cycle was experienced by Fixed Income Arbitrage strategies in the period from 1995–98, which ended with the collapse of LTCM. Another example is the huge allocations to Long/Short Equity strategies during the equity bull market in the late 1990s. In the 19 months from March 2000 to September 2001 Long/Short Equity strategies returned –13% according to the CSFB/Tremont index (–6% for the HFR index). As a third example, Convertible Arbitrage and Merger Arbitrage strategies, among the top performing strategies in the period from 1999–2000, saw huge asset increases in the same period. Concerns about capacity problems were justified when the merger market dried up in the wake of a US recession in 2001 and convertible issues began being priced more aggressively in early 2001. Merger Arbitrage strategies had performance of around zero from March to September 2001 (about –1% according to the HFR index, +4% for the Tremont ('Event Driven') Index, with September accounting for most of the losses). Convertible Arbitrage strategies yielded lower returns than before, but continued to have positive performance (around 6% according to Tremont and 7% according to HFR from March to September 2001).

For the AIS industry as a whole there is not much ground for predicting the phenomenon of a bubble.[2] The industry in its entirety is sufficiently well diversified to deal with extreme market circumstances. The AIS industry currently accounts for about 1% of the capitalization of global financial markets (equities and bonds are estimated at around $50 trillion), so its overall size is still comparably small. A bubble builds up when expectations skyrocket, valuations shift away from fundamentals and everyone does the same thing at the same time (homogeneity of expectations and behaviour). It is important to realize that opportunities and challenges in AIS differ strongly across strategies. The industry per se is

■■■■■■■■■■■■

A bubble builds up when expectations skyrocket, valuations shift away from fundamentals and everyone does the same thing at the same time

■■■■■■■■■■■■

extremely heterogeneous; strategies cover a very broad range of asset classes; favourable and unfavourable market environments deviate strongly across sectors. Many Hedge fund strategies are cyclical in their performance. Economic developments, political events and changes in the market environment create and destroy profit opportunities and some strategies do well in exactly those markets where others perform poorly.

The downturn of Fixed Income Arbitrage in 1998 was followed by the rise of other strategies (Long/Short Equity, Convertible Arbitrage, Risk Arbitrage) and the problems of Macro managers in the late 1990s occurred simultaneously to Fixed Income Arbitrage strategies showing impressive performance. The industry as a whole survived the 'Nasdaq crash' well and enjoyed massive inflows during this period (it did, however, show below average return in 2000 and 2001 as compared to historical performance). Some strategies, in particular the generation of big Global Macro players, suffered declines and scaled down, but a new generation of successful and highly skilled Hedge fund managers emerged in the first years of the new millennium.

Finally, investors in diversified AIS fund of funds products were well protected against large losses in the market turmoil following the tragic events of September 11, 2001, which were a strong stress test for global financial markets in general and the AIS industry in particular. The S&P500 lost –8.17%, the MSCI World –8.92% in the month of September 2001. The HFR fund of funds index (net of fees to fund of fund managers) and CSFB/Tremont Hedge Fund index (gross of fees to fund of fund managers) displayed performances of –1.61% and –0.83% respectively. While there were certainly managers on both ends of the spectrum with sharp gains as well as steep losses, most were able to keep portfolios relatively stable during the highly volatile month of September 2001. Long/Short Equity strategies lost the most with –3.45% (–1.57%) according to HFR (CSFB/Tremont), while Futures strategies gained 3.40% (2.39%) according to CSFB/Tremont (Zurich/MAR).

The opposite view of the 'bubble-bursting scenario' for Hedge funds is the view that Hedge funds have introduced a new paradigm in asset management. The main underlying argument for this view is that AIS have strong absolute returns and low correlations to traditional asset classes. But perhaps these benefits are being oversold, creating unrealistic expectations. A few years ago investing in emerging markets was proposed as a new way to decrease overall portfolio risk.[3] Experiences in the 1990s have aligned hype with reality. The diversification benefits of AIS are perhaps also being overestimated, as the AIS industry as a whole has a long equity bias and it is debatable whether the AIS industry can develop independently from global equity trends. Further, given the strong inflows into Hedge funds one has to seriously ask whether return expectations are decoupling from reality. The lower absolute Hedge fund performance achieved in 2000 and 2001 may help gradually to align expectations with reality. I believe that AIS investing will increasingly require strong skill on the side of the allocator (fund of funds manager, direct investor) to unravel the benefits of Hedge funds and Managed Futures while avoiding excess risk.

Outlook for AIS

Quo vadis, AIS? The 'bursting of the bubble' is an unlikely scenario for the AIS industry. A more realistic, but nevertheless unfavourable, development would be that investors simply lose interest in AIS if (absolute) returns flatten out. The downturn of the equity market in 2000/2001 coincided with a period of Hedge fund underperformance (compared to their historical returns; compared to global equity markets AIS showed very strong outperformance in 2000/2001). The Tremont Composite index showed performance of only 1.14% for the period from March 2000 to October 2001

■■■■■■■■■■■■

Quo vadis, AIS?

■■■■■■■■■■■■

and the HFR Composite index actually displayed negative performance (–0.75%) in this period. Considering these numbers the 'no correlation to equities' argument has to be critically reassessed. Again, returns varied widely among the individual sectors; Relative Value and Futures strategies proved to be good 'hedges' in the 2000/2001 equity bear market, while most Long/Short Equity strategies showed performance significantly below average in this period. Investors should generally realize that long-term return expectations exceeding 15% per annum (net of all fees) for a diversified AIS portfolio are unrealistic. Periods of low performance are part of AIS investing as for any other investment.

AIS investing is one of the most dynamic and fastest growing areas in modern finance. It is interesting to observe that some universities are now incorporating Hedge funds into their educational programs. Hedge funds are gaining acceptance

■ ■ ■ ■ ■ ■ ■ ■ ■ ■ ■

Steady growth is much more likely than a 'boom and bust' scenario

■ ■ ■ ■ ■ ■ ■ ■ ■ ■ ■

as legitimate investments by academics. One example is the London Business School, which is now running a Hedge fund research institute. Change is so rapid that it is extremely difficult to predict what the field will look like in just a few years. However, for a number of reasons steady growth is much more likely than a 'boom and bust' scenario.

First, the investor base has changed. The AIS industry has developed and will continue to develop towards satisfying the needs of institutional investors (private and public pension funds, endowments, family offices, university trusts etc.) which have started to realize how well AIS fit into their portfolios.

Along with this has come a change in the industry's attitude about transparency and investment liquidity as more investors will question the perception that Hedge funds must, by nature, be non-transparent and secretive. Better investor understanding and a higher degree of transparency will add to the credibility of AIS.

Third, the spectrum of AIS has expanded dramatically. New strategies have joined the most prominent strategies of the past, Global Macro and Long/Short Equity. The heterogeneity of AIS provides internal diversification and protection for the industry from a fallout due to sudden and unforeseen events. The downturn of equity markets in the early 1970s led to the end of the first 'Golden Hedge fund' era, while in sharp contrast during the 2000/2001 equity crisis, which is comparable in magnitude, investors' interest in AIS investments increased remarkably.

Fourth, increased interest on the part of (comparably risk averse) institutional investors together with some well-publicized 'investment accidents' has led to the recognition that AIS risks have to be more systematically addressed. As a result, risk management techniques have become much more sophisticated. The old 'cowboy mentality' of Hedge funds has given way to new investment managers who are better and more professional risk managers and thus more credible in the eyes of the investor.

The greatest hurdle for AIS strategies' further growth is image. The well-documented problems of LTCM as well as the events surrounding the Manhattan Investment Fund, where investors were defrauded of $350 million, prompted genuine concern about unregulated and uncontrolled Hedge funds potentially putting the global financial system at risk and causing investors to lose their entire investments. A further focus on increased liquidity, higher transparency and more sophisticated risk management will surely help to improve investor perception about AIS investing and prevent further investment disasters that might undermine the future of AIS. Effective risk management is essential to continued rapid growth in AIS and to their unambiguous recognition as a legitimate investment class.

> *Effective risk management is essential to continued rapid growth in AIS and to their unambiguous recognition as a legitimate investment class*

Notes

1.   See, for example, 'Hedge Funds – The Latest Bubble?', *The Economist*, September 1, 2001; 'The $500 billion Hedge Fund Folly', *Forbes Magazine*, August 6, 2001; 'The Hedge Fund Bubble', *Financial Times*, July 9, 2001. These articles express a great deal of scepticism towards hedge funds. Unfortunately, their focus is mainly on polemics rather than discussing the risks and merits of Hedge funds adequately. It is quite unfortunate that it is mostly non-AIS experts who lead the discussion about a possible 'Hedge fund bubble' and who refuse to account for some of the basic characteristics of AIS.

2.   See L. Jaeger, 'Is There a Speculative Bubble in Hedge Funds?', *Risk & Reward*, April 2002.

3.   For an interesting (unfortunately pre-1997) study on emerging markets, see the report by C. Barry, J. Peavy, and M. Rodriguez, 'Emerging Stock Market: Risk, Return, and Performance'.

Glossary

Active Discretionary Futures The manager's approach is primarily fundamental in nature. In this regard, trading decisions are based largely on the study of external factors that affect the supply and demand of a market (commodities in particular). By monitoring relevant supply and demand factors, a state of dis-equilibrium of conditions may be identified that has yet to be reflected in the price of the commodity. Such factors may include weather, the economics of a particular commodity, government policies, domestic and foreign political and economic events and changing trade product.

AIS Alternative Investment Strategy, i.e. Hedge funds and Managed Futures.

AIS manager The individual or the firm operating a Hedge fund or Managed Futures strategy.

alpha Difference between a manager's return and the return appropriate for the given level of risk (as measured by a 'benchmark portfolio').

Arbitrage Profiting from differences in price when the same or a similar security, currency or commodity is traded on two or more markets.

backwardation Pricing structure in commodities in which deliveries at present or in the near future have a higher price than those made later on. The inverted situation is called *contango*.

broker Agent who effects securities transactions on behalf of and for the account of the trust or the manager (securities dealer).

Capital Asset Pricing Model (CAPM) Asset pricing model developed by W. Sharpe relating the return of individual securities to the return of the broad market. According to CAPM, each security's value depends on a return linked to the systematic market risk (determined by the security's specific 'beta') and an unsystematic (idiosyncratic) risk term (which can be diversified away in a portfolio).

carry   Charge for carrying the actual commodity instead of a futures contract, including interest, storage, and insurance costs.

CFTC   Commodity Futures Trading Commission of the United States.

contango   Pricing situation in which Futures prices are progressively higher as maturities get longer. The increase reflects financing, storage (carrying), insurance and other costs. The inverted situation is called *backwardation*.

convenience yield   A certain portion of the difference between the spot price and the Futures price of a commodity that cannot be explained by interest rates or storage costs. The convenience yield is simply the price of having a certain commodity available now instead of later (can also be negative).

Convertible Arbitrage   An effort to capitalize on relative pricing inefficiencies, by purchasing long positions in convertible securities, generally convertible bonds, convertible preferred stock or warrants and hedging a portion of the equity risk by selling short the underlying common stock.

correlation   A (linear) measure of comovement of different assets.

CTA (Commodity Trading Advisor)   Trading advisor of Managed Futures strategies, regulated with the CFTC.

Distressed Security Strategy   Involves investing in debt, equity or trade claims of companies in financial distress.

drawdown   Peak to bottom loss in the performance curve of an investment.

due diligence   Thorough analysis procedure including assessment, evaluation, selection of managers for inclusion in an asset allocation.

Equity Market Neutral   Involves investing in securities both long and short, attempting on average to have a very low net market exposure. Generally attempts to select long positions that are undervalued and short positions that are overvalued.

Equity Market Timing   Involves allocating assets among investments by switching into investments that appear to be beginning an up trend and switching out of investments that appear to be starting a downtrend. This primarily consists of switching between mutual funds and money markets.

Event Driven Strategy   Invests in companies with 'special situations', e.g. mergers, restructuring, distress.

Extreme Value Approach   An approach to risk measurement based on the use of the statistical field of Extreme Value Theory (EVT).

fat tails   Extreme areas of the return probability distribution that are larger than those of the normal distribution.

Fixed Income Arbitrage A market neutral hedging strategy that seeks to profit by exploiting mispricings in fixed income instruments utilizing a variety of strategies, including cash vs cash, butterflies, basis trading, Treasury vs Eurodollar (TED) spreads, cash vs Futures. A different type of Fixed Income Arbitrage is forecasting the change of the shape of the yield curve (duration trade) or profiting from yield differential of issuers with a different quality (credit quality).

fund of funds A multi-manager fund which invests in other (AIS) funds.

Futures Derivative taking the form of a standardized forward exchange contract based on currencies, financials, commodities etc.

Global Macro A strategy that employs an opportunistic, 'top down' approach, following major changes in global economies and expecting to profit from significant shifts in the global economy.

haircut A reduction from market value in computing the value of assets deposited as collateral or margin.

Hedge fund A fund (often not regulated) that engages in non-conventional investment techniques and strategies, making use of derivatives, selling short positions and borrowing and thereby achieving a leverage effect. Because Hedge funds are private limited partnerships the SEC limits Hedge funds to sophisticated accredited investors.

high watermark (also called 'loss carryforward') Method of calculation of the performance fee whereby the manager, having incurred a loss for the investor, is only entitled to further profit sharing by way of the performance fee once this loss has been recuperated.

Incremental VaR The change in VaR resulting from the inclusion of a particular investment instrument or sub-portfolio.

Jones model The method of investing originally used by Alfred W. Jones in 1949. His method was to invest in US stocks, both long and short, to reduce exposure to the broad market and focus on stock selection.

leverage Effect achieved when assets of the investor are pledged in order to increase investment exposure. Use of derivatives may create the same effect.

long position Ownership of securities, which are not hedged in any way.

Long/Short Equity Combines core long holdings of equities with short sales of stock or stock index options. The portfolio may be anywhere from net long to net short depending on market conditions. The manager generally increases net long exposure in bull markets and decreases net long exposure or is even net short in bear markets. Generally, the short exposure is intended to generate an ongoing positive return in addition to acting as a hedge against a general stock market decline. Stock index put options are also often used as a hedge against market risk. Profits are made when long positions appreciate and stocks sold short depreciate. Conversely, losses are incurred when long positions depreciate and/or the value of stocks sold short appreciates. Long/Short Equity managers' source of return is similar to that of traditional stock pickers on the upside, but they use short selling and hedging in an attempt to limit the risk on the downside.

managed account Trading account held with a broker and wholly owned by the fund of funds or directly by the investor. The managers employ their strategies through executing in the trading account on behalf of the investor.

Managed Futures An investment strategy mainly involving trading on derivatives and forward markets. This primarily comprises Futures, as well as other derivatives in the equity, fixed income currency or commodity sectors.

manager *see* 'AIS manager'

Margin to Equity The ratio between the margin required to be deposited with the broker to overall exposure.

Master feeder fund Involves a master trading vehicle domiciled offshore with two investors: another offshore fund and a US (usually Delaware) Limited Partnership (feeder funds). A typical structure for a Hedge fund.

Mean Variance Approach An approach to portfolio analysis based on the premise that the determination of the optimal portfolio is possible using only information about means, variances and co-variances of returns (i.e. no information about higher moments of the return distribution).

Modern Portfolio Theory (MPT) Theory of investment decision making that permits investors to classify, estimate and control both the kind and amount of expected risk and return. The core of MPT is the assumption that investors must be compensated appropriately for taking risks. MPT departs from traditional security analysis as it describes risk in the context of the investor's entire portfolio rather than on the level of the individual security. In MPT, the correlations between the different instruments in the portfolio are the key components of portfolio risk.

net asset value (NAV) The net asset value is the aggregate value of all of a fund's investments determined on a middle market basis less the aggregate amount of its liabilities and accrued expenses.

NFA   National Futures Association of the United States.

Opportunistic   Description for a trading strategy that acts mostly according to presented opportunities. Opportunistic strategies are usually quite aggressive in nature.

option   Derivative embodying the right to buy (in the case of a call option) or sell (in the case of a put option) a fixed number of a particular underlying asset within a specified period and at a predetermined price.

OTC transaction   Financial transaction that does not take place in a regulated market ('over the counter').

over-fitting ('curve fitting')   The systematic optimization of a model on historical data and the subsequent failure of the model to perform on untested data.

performance fee (also called 'incentive fee') Fee paid to the manager for achieving a certain investment result.

portable alpha   The alpha of a manager is transported to a target index, e.g. swapping total returns of an equity index with the risk free rate.

prime broker   Institution that provides the global settlement, clearing and execution of the trades done by an AIS manager. It furthermore provides credit lines for leverage and short selling.

Regulation D   An Event Driven strategy where investment usually takes place in the form of a convertible debenture with an exercise price that floats or is subject to a look-back provision. Investment occurs according the Regulation D US Securities Act 1933.

Relative Value strategies   Seek to generate profits by investing simultaneously in related instruments that are, in the eye of the manager, mispriced. The goal is to capture the difference between the current market price and the fair value.

Risk Arbitrage   Also known as Merger Arbitrage; involves investing in securities of companies that are subject to some form of extraordinary corporate transaction, including acquisition or merger proposals, exchange offers, cash tender offers and leveraged buyouts. These transactions will generally involve the exchange of securities for cash, other securities or a combination of cash and other securities. Typically, a manager purchases the stock of a company being acquired or merging with another company and sells short the stock of the acquiring company. A manager engaged in Merger Arbitrage transactions will derive profit (or loss) by realizing the price differential between the price of the securities purchased and the value ultimately realized when the deal is consummated. The success of this strategy is usually dependent on the proposed merger, tender offer or exchange offer being actually consummated.

Scenario Analysis A form of stress testing focusing on the impact of only one or a few specified scenarios.

SEC Security Exchange Commission of the United States.

SFA The Securities and Futures Authority (United Kingdom). The SFA is the regulatory organization established under the Financial Services Act 1986 with responsibility for regulating members of the organized City investment markets.

Sharpe ratio A risk-adjusted performance measure originally introduced by W. Sharpe consisting of the ratio of return minus risk free rate and the standard deviation of returns. A related measure is the Sortino ratio, which uses the downside deviation in the denominator and a minimum required return in the numerator (the 'Minimal Accepted Return', MAR), which is subtracted from the return (instead of the risk free interest).

short position Sale of securities, which the seller does not own.

short rebate The portion of the interest on the cash proceed from selling short a stock that the short seller earns.

Statistical Arbitrage Strategy that tries to capture momentary pricing aberrations in the stock market, often by employing quantitative statistical models.

Stress Testing The process of determining the vulnerability of the portfolio to an extreme hypothetical event (scenario).

survivorship bias Performance bias in a data sample as a result of disappearing managers dropping out of the data set.

Systematic Futures – Passive Commercial hedging strategies mirroring the inherent returns in the commercial futures markets by systematically assuming the opposite position to commercial hedgers. These indices take long or short positions in different markets depending on the supply and demand balance between producers (e.g. oil company) and consumers (e.g. airline). They capture these inherent returns in the commodity, foreign exchange and interest rate futures markets by assuming the price risk commercial hedgers seek to transfer.

Systematic Futures – Technical Model-based trading in Futures markets at any time horizon (short, medium, or long term). For long-term models (longer than one month), trend following is typically the main strategy. For managers with a short-term time frame, various statistical tools including momentum and countertrend techniques are used.

trading advisor/manager Trading organization that trades and invests on behalf of the investor via a fund or a managed account.

Value-at-Risk (VaR) The maximum likely loss over some specified holding period at a particular confidence level. VaR depends on a specific calculation procedure. One distinguishes between the variance/co-variance method, the Monte Carlo method, and the Historical method.

volatility Statistical measure for the degree of price fluctuations (usually expressed by standard deviation of the returns).

Bibliography

Ackermann, C., McEnally, D. and Ravenscraft, R., 'The Performance of Hedge Funds: Risk, Return and Incentives', *Journal of Finance*, 2 (1999)

Agarwal, V. and Naik, N., 'Multi-Period Performance Persistence Analysis of Hedge Funds', *Journal of Financial and Quantitative Analysis*, 35, 2 (2000)

Agarwal, V. and Naik, N., 'Performance Evaluation of Hedge Funds with Option-based and Buy-and-Hold Strategies', Working Paper (September 2000)

Alexander, C., *Risk Management and Analysis: Measuring and Modelling Financial Risk*, John Wiley & Sons (1999)

Alexander, C. (ed.) *The Handbook of Risk Management and Analysis*, John Wiley & Sons (1996)

Alexander, G., 'Efficient Sets, Short-selling, and Estimation Risk', *Journal of Portfolio Management* (winter 1995)

Amin, G. and Kat, H., 'Hedge Fund Performance: 1990–2000: Do the Money Machines Really Add Value?', ISMA Centre Working Paper 2001–5 (January 2001)[download able from www.ssrn.com]

Amin, G. and Kat, H. 'Welcome to the Dark Side: Hedge Fund Attrition and Survivorship Bias over the Period 1994–2001', ISMA Centre Working Paper (December 2001)

Arnott, R. and Pham, T., 'Tactical Currency Allocation', *Financial Analysts Journal*, p.47 (May 1993)

Artzner, P., Delbaen, F., Eber, J. and Heath, D., 'Coherent Risk Measures', *Mathematical Finance*, 9, 3, p.203 (1999)

Asness, C., Krail, R. and Liew, J., 'Do Hedge Funds Hedge?', forthcoming in the *US Journal of Portfolio Management* [downloadable from www.aqrcapital.com]

Bank for International Settlement, 'Overview of the New Basel Capital Accord' (January 2001)

Bank of England, 'Report of the Board of Banking Supervision Inquiry into the Circumstances of the Collapse of Baring', HMSO (1995) [downloadable from http://risk.ifci.ch]

Barry, C., Peavy, J., and Rodriguez, M., 'Emerging Stock Market: Risk, Return, and Performance', The Research Foundation of The Institute of Chartered Financial Analysts (1997)

Basel Committee on Banking Supervision, 'Credit Risk Modelling: Current Practices and Applications', Basel Committee Publications (1999) [downloadable from www.bis.org]

Basel Committee on Banking Supervision, 'Review of Issues relating to Highly Leveraged Institutions', Basel Committee Publications No. 79 (March 2001) [downloadable from www.bis.org/publ/bcbs79.htm]

Bernardo, J. and Smith, A., *Bayesian Theory*, John Wiley & Sons (2001)

Best, P., *Implementing Value at Risk*, John Wiley & Sons (1998)

Bohn, J., *A Survey of Contingent Claim Approaches to Risky Debt Valuation*, Haas School of Business (1999)

Bohn, J., *Empirical Assessment of a Simple Contingent-Claims Model for the Valuation of Risky Debt,* Haas School of Business (1999)

Bollerslev, T., Chou, R. and Kroner, K., 'Arch Modelling in Finance', *Journal of Econometrics*, 52, pp.5–59 (1992)

Brock, W., Lakonishok, J. and LeBaron, B., 'Simple Technical Trading Rules and the Stochastic Properties of Stock Returns', *Journal of Finance*, 5 (December 1992)

Butler, C., *Mastering Value at Risk: A Step-by-Step Guide to Understanding and Applying VaR*, Financial Times Prentice Hall (1999)

Caglayan, M. and Edwards, F., 'Hedge Fund and Commodity Fund Investment Styles in Bull and Bear Markets', *Journal of Portfolio Management*, 27, 4, p.97 (summer 2001)

Capital Market Risk Advisors, 'NAV/Fair Value Practices Survey Results' (July 2001) [downloadable from www.cmra.com]

Cass, D., 'Hedge Funds to Clear the Information Hurdle', *Risk Magazine*, p.8 (October 2001)

Caxton Corporation, Kingdom Capital Management, Moore Capital Management, Soros Fund Management LLC and Tudor Investment Corporation, 'Sound Practices for Hedge Fund Managers', report issued by a group of five Hedge fund managers (February 2000)

Chalmers, J., Edelen, R. and Kadlec, G., *The Wildcard Option in Transacting Mutual-Fund Shares*, Wharton School of Finance (2000)

Clair, C., 'Hedge Funds Suffer without a Benchmark', *Pension & Investments*, p.1 (June 11, 2001)

Clair, C., 'Prime Brokers can Make and Break Hedge Funds', *Pension & Investments*, p.3 (September 2001)

Connolly, K., *Pricing Convertible Bonds*, John Wiley & Sons (2000)

Cosandy, D., 'Adjusting Value-at-Risk for Market Liquidity', *Risk Magazine*, p.115 (October 2001)

Cottier, P., *Hedge Funds and Managed Futures*, Verlag Paul Haupt, Bern (1997) [down loadable from www.aima.org/aimasite/indexfrm.htm]

Counterparty Risk Management Policy Group, 'Improving Counterparty Risk Management Practices', CRMPG (1999)

Credit Suisse Financial Products, 'CreditRisk+' (1997)

Crossborder Capital, 'TSS(II)-Tactical Style Selection: Integrating Hedge Funds into the Asset Allocation Framework', Hedge Fund Research (August 2000)

Crossborder Capital, 'The Young Ones', Absolute Return Fund Research (April 2001)

Crouhy, M., Galai, D. and Mark, R., 'A Comparative Analysis of Current Credit Risk Models', *Journal of Banking and Finance*, 24, pp.59–117 (2000)

Crowder, G. and Hennessee, L., 'Hedge Fund Indices', *Journal of Alternative Investments* (summer 2001)

Cruz, M., 'Modelling and Measuring Operational Risk', *Journal of Risk*, 1, 1 (1998)

Dacorogna M., Gencay, R., Müller, U. and Pictet O., 'Effective Return, Risk Aversion and Drawdowns', *Physica A*, 289, pp.229–48 (January 2001)

Danielsson, D. and de Vries, C., 'Value at Risk and Extreme Returns', Tinbergen Institute Discussion Paper, TI 98-017/2 (1998) [downloadable from www.fee.uva.nl/BIEB/TIDPs/TIDP98nr.htm]

Davidson, C., 'Shopping in the E-market', *Risk Magazine* (August 2000)

Davidson, C., 'Software Survey 2001', *Risk Magazine* (January 2001)

Dowd, K., *Beyond Value at Risk,* Wiley Frontiers in Finance (1998)

Duffie, D. and Singleton, K., 'Modelling the Term Structure of Defaultable Bonds', Stanford University Paper (1998)

Dunbar, N., 'French Fight over Hedge Fund Products', *Risk Magazine* (February 2001)

The Economist, 'The Big, the Bold, and the Nimble', p.87 (February 24, 2001)

The Economist, 'The Benchmarking Bane', p.67 (September 1, 2001)

The Economist, 'The Latest Bubble', p.59 (September 1, 2001)

Edwards, F. and Caglayan, M., 'Hedge Fund Performance and Manager Skill', Working Paper (May 2001)

Eichengreen, B. and Mathieson, D., 'Hedge Funds and Financial Markets Dynamics', International Monetary Fund Occasional Paper (1998)

Embrechts, P., Klüppelberg, C. and Mikosch, T., *Modelling Extremal Events for Insurance and Finance*, Springer (1997)

Embrechts, P., McNeil, A. and Straumann, D., 'Correlation and Dependence in Risk Management: Properties and Pitfalls', *Risk Management: Value at Risk and Beyond*, Dempster, M. (ed.) Cambridge University Press, (2002) pp.176–223 [download able from www.math.ethz.ch/~mcneil/pub_list.html]

Embrechts, P. (ed.) *Extremes and Integrated Risk Management*, Risk Books (2001)

Fabozzi, F., *Fixed Income Analysis*, Frank J. Fabozzi Associates, New Hope, Pennsylvania (2000)

Fama, E., 'Efficient Capital Markets: A Review of Theory and Empirical Work', *Journal of Finance*, 25, 2, p.383 (May 1970)

Fama, E., 'Efficient Capital Markets: II', *Journal of Finance*, 46, 5, p.1575 (December 1991)

Fama, E. and French, K., 'The Cross Section of Expected Stock Returns', *Journal of Finance*, 47, 2, p.427 (June 1992)

Fama, E. and French, K., 'Size and Book-To-Market Factors in Earnings and Returns', *Journal of Finance*, 50, 1, p.131 (March 1995)

Fama, E. and French, K., 'Multifactor explanations of Asset Pricing Anomalies', *Journal of Finance*, 51, p.55 (1996)

Favell, A., 'To ASP or not to ASP', *Risk Technology*, p.14 (October 2001)

Fedorek, T., 'Is Fraud Flourishing At Your Hedge Fund?', *Pension & Investments*, p.14 (March 2001)

Fender, I. and Gibson, M., 'The BIS census on stress tests', *Risk Magazine*, p.50 (May 2001)

Financial Times, 'The Hedge Fund Bubble' (July 9, 2001)

Forbes Magazine, 'The $500 Billion Hedge Fund Folly' (August 6, 2001)

Frees, E. and Valdez, E., 'Understanding Relationships Using Copulas', *North American Actuarial Journal*, 2,1, p.1 (1998)

Frey, R., McNeill, A. and Nyfeler, M., 'Copulas and Credit Models', *Risk Magazine*, p.111 (October 2001)

Fung, W. and Hsieh, D., 'Empirical Characteristics of Dynamic Trading Strategies: The Case of Hedge Funds', *Review of Financial Studies*, 10, 2 (1997)

Fung, W. and Hsieh, D., 'A Primer on Hedge Funds', *Journal of Empirical Finance*, p.309 (1999)

Fung, W. and Hsieh, D., 'Measuring the Market Impact of Hedge Funds', *Journal of Empirical Finance*, 7, pp.1–36 (2000) [downloadable from www.faculty.fuqua.duke.edu/~dah7/vitae.htm]

Fung, W. and Hsieh, D., 'Performance Characteristics of Hedge Funds and Commodity Funds: Natural versus Spurious Biases', *Journal of Financial and Quantitative Analysis* (2000)

Fung, W. and Hsieh, D., 'The Risk in Hedge Fund Strategies: Theory and Evidence from Trend-Followers', *Review of Financial Studies*, 14, 2, p.313 (summer 2001)

Fung, W. and Hsieh, D., 'Benchmarks of Hedge Fund Performance: Information Content and Measurement Biases', *Financial Analyst Journal* (2001)

Glassermann, P., Heidelberger, P. and Shahabuddin, P., 'Portfolio Value at Risk with Heavy Tailed Risk Factors', Working Paper, Columbia Business School and Paine Webber (2000) [downloadable from www.columbia.edu/cu/business/wp]

Goldmann, Sachs & Co. and Financial Risk Management Ltd., 'The Hedge Fund "Industry" and Absolute Return Funds', *Journal of Alternative Investments* (1999)

Golin/Harris Ludgate, 'The Future Role of Hedge Funds in European Institutional Asset Management 2001', Golin/Harris Ludgate (2001)

Gordy, M., 'A Comparative Anatomy of Credit Risk Models', *Journal of Banking and Finance*, 24, pp.119–49 (2000)

Group of Thirty, 'Derivatives: Practices and Principles', New York (1993) [downloadable from http://risk.ifci.ch]

Hauksson, H., Dacorogna, M., Domenig, T., Müller, U. and Samorodnitsky, G., 'Multivariate Extremes, Aggregation, and Risk Estimation', *Quantitative Finance*, 1, p.79 (2001)

Hayt, G., 'How to Price Credit Risk', *Risk Magazine* (January 2000)

Hedge Fund Research, 'Market Neutral and Hedged Strategies' (August 2000)

Hendricks, D., 'Evaluating Value at Risk Models using Historical Data', Federal Reserve Bank of New York, Economic Policy Review (April 1996)

Hull, J., *Options, Futures, and Other Derivatives* (4th edn) Prentice Hall (1999)

Ineichen, A., 'In Search of Alpha – Investing in Hedge Funds', UBS Warburg, London (October 2000)

Ineichen, A., 'The Search for Alpha Continues – Do Fund of Hedge Fund Managers Add Value?', UBS Warburg, London (September 2001)

Investor Risk Committee (IRC), 'Hedge Fund Disclosure for Institutional Investors', [downloadable from www.iafe.org or from www.cmra.com]

ISI Publications, 'Starting a Hedge Fund – A European Perspective' (2001)

ISI Publications, 'Starting a Hedge Fund – A US Perspective' (2001)

ISI Publications, 'The Capital Guide to Alternative Investments' (2001)

Jaeger, L., 'Risk Management for Multi-Manager Portfolios of Alternative Investment Strategies', *AIMA Newsletter* (April 2001)

Jaeger, L., 'The Benefits of Alternative Investment Strategies in the Institutional Portfolio', saisGroup (Partners Group) Research Publication (November 2001) [available on http://www.saisgroup.com]

Jaeger, L., 'Risk Management for Multi-Manager portfolios of Alternative Investment Strategies – Part I & II', ISI Publications, *Alternative Investment Quarterly* (October 2001, January 2002)

Jaeger, L., 'Hedge Funds in Marktturbulenze', *Neue Zürcher Zeitung* (8 January 2002)

Jaegar, L., 'Is There a Speculative Bubble in Hedge Funds?', *Risk & Reward* (April 2002).

Jaeger, L., Jacquemai, M. and Cittadini, P., 'The saisGroup Futures Index (sGFI) – A New Passive Futures Investment Strategy', saisGroup Research Paper 2000, forthcoming in the *Journal of Alternative Investments* [downloadable from www.saisgroup.com]

Jorion, P., 'Risk Management Lessons from Long-Term Capital Management', *European Financial Management*, 6, p.277 (2000) [downloadable from www.gsm.uci.edu/~jorion/research.htm]

Jorion, P., *The FRM Handbook 2001/2002*, John Wiley & Sons, The GARP Risk Management Library (2001)

Kazemi, H. and Schneeweiss, T., 'Traditional Asset and Alternative Asset Allocation', CISDM/SOM Working Paper, University of Massachusetts (2001)

Keynes, J. M., *A Treatise on Money* Volume II, Macmillan & Co. (1930)

Kim, J. and Finger, C., 'A Stress Test to Incorporate Correlation Breakdown', *RiskMetrics Journal* (May 2000)

King, J., *Operational Risk: Measurement and Modelling*, John Wiley & Sons (2001)

Koyluoglu, U. and Hickmann, A. 'Reconcilable Differences', *Risk Magazine* (October 1998)

Kramer, D., 'Hedge Fund Disasters: Avoiding the Next Catastrophe', ISI Publication, *Alternative Investment Quarterly*, p.5 (October 2001)

Krokhmal. P., Palmquist, J. and Uryasev, S., 'Portfolio Optimization with Conditional Value-At-Risk Objective and Constraints', *Journal of Risk*, 4, 2 (2002)

Lake, R., *Evaluating and Implementing Hedge Fund Strategies*, Euromoney Books (1996)

LeBaron, B., 'Forecast Improvements using a Volatility Index', *Journal of Applied Econometrics*, 7, p.137 (1992)

LeBaron, B., 'Some Relation between Volatility and Serial Correlations in Stock Market Returns', *Journal of Business*, 65, 2, p.199 (1992)

Lederman, J. and Klein, R. *Hedge Funds: Investment and Portfolio Strategies for the Institutional Investor*, Irwin Professional Publishing (1995)

Lefevre, E., *Reminiscences of a Stock Operator*, John Wiley & Sons (1994; first published 1923)

Liang, B., 'Hedge Funds: On the Performance of Hedge Funds', *Financial Analysts Journal* (July 1999)

Longstaff, F. and Schwartz, F., 'A Simple Approach to Valuing Risky Fixed and Floating Rate Debt', *Journal of Finance*, 50, pp. 449–70 (1998)

Loomis, C., 'The Jones Nobody Keeps up With', *Fortune*, p.237 (April 1966)

Lore, M. and Borodovsky, L. (eds) *The Professional's Handbook of Financial Risk Management*, General Association of Risk Professionals (GARP), Butterworth-Heinemann (2000)

McFall Lamm Jr., R., 'Portfolios of Alternative Assets: Why not 100% Hedge Funds?', *Journal of Investing* (Winter 1998)

McNeil, A. 'Extreme Value for Risk Managers', in *Internal Modelling and CAD II*, Risk Books, pp.93–113 (1999) [downloadable from www.math.ethz.ch/~mcneil/pub_list.html]

Malz, A., 'DataMetrics Technical Document', RiskMetrics Group Publications (2001)

Markowitz, H., 'Portfolio Selection', *Journal of Finance*, 7, 1, p.77 (March 1952)

Markowitz, H., *Portfolio Selection – Efficient Diversification of Investment*, John Wiley & Sons (1959)

Merton, R., 'On the Price of Corporate Debt: The Risk Structure of Interest Rates', *Journal of Finance*, 29, pp.440–70 (June 1974)

Moore, K.M., *Risk Arbitrage: An Investor's Guide*, John Wiley & Sons (1999)

Neftci, S., 'Value at Risk Calculations, Extreme Events, and Tail Estimation', *Journal of Derivatives*, p.23 (spring 2000)

Nelson, R., *An Introduction to Copulas*, Springer (1999)

Park. J. and Strum, J., 'Fund of Fund Diversification: How Much is Enough?', *Journal of Alternative Investments* (winter 1999)

Parker, V. R. (ed.) *Managing Hedge Fund Risk*, Risk Books (2001)

Patel, N., 'Courting the Hedge Funds', *Risk Magazine*, p.31 (November 2001)

Peskin, M., Urias, M., Anjilvel, S. and Boudreau, B., 'Why Hedge Funds make Sense', *Quantitative Strategies*, Morgan Stanley Dean Witter (November 2000)

Pictet, O., Dacorogna, M., Müller, U., Olsen, R. and Ward, R., 'Real-time Trading Models for Foreign Exchange Rates', *Neural Networks World*, 26, p.713 (1992)

Pitaro, R., *Deals, Deals, and More Deals*, Gabelli University Press (1999)

Polyn, G., 'Value-at-Risk for Merger Arbs', *Risk Magazine*, p.6 (April 2001)

Polyn, G., 'Hedge Funds placed under the Microscope', *Risk Magazine*, p.12 (August 2001)

Polyn, P., 'Getting a Better Risk Picture', *Risk Magazine*, p.12 (August 2001)

President's Working Group on Financial Markets, 'Hedge Funds, Leverage, and the Lessons of Long-Term Capital Management', Report of the President's Working Group on Financial Markets (April 1999) [downloadable from http://risk.ifci.ch/146530.htm]

PricewaterhouseCooper, 'European Private Banking/Wealth Management Survey 2000/2001', presented at the GAIM Conference, Geneva (June 2001)

Rahl, L. (ed.) *Risk Budgeting: A New Approach to Investing*, Risk Books (2000)

Reilly, F. and Brown, K., *Investment Analysis and Portfolio Management*, Dryden Press (1997)

Riley, B., 'Hedge Funds come in from the Cold', *Financial Times* (June 12, 2000)

Risk Magazine, 'Hedge Funds look to Cultivate Technology Roots', *Risk Magazine*, p.S24 (August 2001)

RiskMetrics, 'RiskMetrics – Technical Document', (1996) [downloadable from www.riskmetrics.com]

RiskMetrics, 'CreditMetrics – Technical Document', (1997) [downloadable from www.riskmetrics.com]

RiskMetrics, 'Return To RiskMetrics – The Evolution of a Standard', (2001) [downloadable from www.riskmetrics.com]

Rohrer, J., 'The Red Hot World of Julian Robertson', *Institutional Investors* p.86 (May 1986)

Rosenberg, B., Reid, K. and French, K, 'Persuasive Evidence on Market Inefficiencies', *Journal of Portfolio Management*, 11, 3, p.9 (Spring 1985)

Ross, S., 'The Arbitrage Theory of Capital Asset Pricing', *Journal of Economic Theory*, 13, 2, p.341 (December 1976)

Saunder, A., *Credit Risk Measurement*, Wiley Frontiers in Finance (1999)

Schenk, C., 'Convertible Arb Funds turn to Default Swaps', *Risk Magazine*, p.14 (July 2001)

Schneeweiss Partners, 'A Review of Alternative Hedge Fund Indices' (2001)

Schneeweiss, T. and Kazemi, H., 'The Creation of Alternative Tracking Portfolios for Hedge Fund Strategies', CISDM/SOM Working Paper, University of Massachusetts (2001)

Schneeweiss, T. and Martin, G., *The Benefits of Hedge Funds*, Lehman Brothers Publications (August 2000)

Schneeweiss, T. and Pescatore, J., 'Alternative Asset Returns; Theoretical Bases and Empirical Evidence', *Handbook of Alternative Investment Strategies*, Institutional Investors Inc., New York (1999)

Schneeweiss, T. and Spurgin, R., 'Multifactor Analysis of Hedge Funds, Managed Futures, and Mutual Fund Returns and Risk Characteristics', *Journal of Alternative Investments* (1998)

Schneeweiss, T. and Spurgin, R., 'Trading Factors and Location Factors in Hedge Fund Return Estimation', CISDM/SOM, University of Massachusetts (2001)

Schneeweiss, T., Kazemi, H. and Martin, G., *Understanding Hedge Fund Performance: Research Results and Rules of Thumb for the Institutional Investor*, Lehman Brothers Publications (December 2001)

Schwartz, R. and Smith, C. (eds) *Derivatives Handbook*, John Wiley & Sons (1997)

Sharpe, W., 'Capital Asset Prices: A Theory of Market Equilibrium Under Conditions of Risk', *Journal of Finance*, 19, 3, p.425 (September 1964)

Sharpe, W., 'Asset Allocation: Management Style and Performance Measurement', *Journal of Portfolio Management*, 18, 2 (winter 1999)

Shefren, H., *Beyond Greed and Fear: Understanding Behavioural Finance*, Harvard Press, Boston (1999)

Shiller, R., 'Human Behavior and the Efficiency of the Financial System', in *Handbook of Macroeconomics*, Taylor, J. and Woodford, M. (eds), North-Holland (1999)

Stratman, M., 'Behavioural Finance: Past Battles and Future Engagements', *Financial Analysts Journal* (1996)

Taleb, N., *Fooled by Randomness: The Hidden Role of Chance in the Markets and in Life*, Texere (2001)

Tavakoli, J., *Credit Derivatives: A Guide to Instruments and Applications*, 2nd edn, Wiley & Sons (2001)

Till, H., 'Life at Sharpe's End', *Risk and Reward*, p.39 (September 2001)

Till, H., 'Measure for Measure', *Risk and Reward*, p.33 (October 2001)

Tremont, Partners Inc. and TASS Investment Research Inc., 'The Case for Hedge Funds' (1999)

Uryasev, S. and Rockafellar, T., 'Optimization of Conditional Value-At-Risk', *Journal of Risk*, 2, 3, pp.21–41 (2000) [downloadable from www.ise.ufl.edu/uryasev/roc.pdf]

Watson Wyatt Partners, 'Alternative Investment Review relating to the Continental European (the United States, the United Kingdom) Marketplace', (fall 2000)

Watterson, P., 'Offering Private Investment Funds in the Capital Markets', *Alternative Investment Quarterly*, p.43 (October 2001)

Weismann, A. and Abernathy, J., 'The Dangers of Historical Hedge Fund Data' in *Risk Budgeting: A New Approach to Investing*, Rahl, L. (ed.) Risk Books (2000)

Index